BEYOND THE *SEWOL*

HAWAIʻI STUDIES ON KOREA

Beyond the *Sewol*

Activist Theatre and Performance in South Korea and the Diaspora

AREUM JEONG

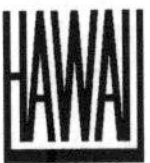

University of Hawaiʻi Press, Honolulu
and
Center for Korean Studies, University of Hawaiʻi

Printed in the United States of America

First printed, 2025

Library of Congress Cataloging-in-Publication Data

Names: Jeong, Areum, author.
Title: Beyond the Sewol : activist theatre and performance in South Korea and the diaspora / Areum Jeong.
Description: Honolulu : University of Hawai'i Press : Center for Korean Studies, University of Hawai'i, [2025] | Series: Hawai'i studies on Korea | Includes bibliographical references and index.
Identifiers: LCCN 2024059332 (print) | LCCN 2024059333 (ebook) | ISBN 9798880701766 (hardcover) | ISBN 9798880701773 (trade paperback) | ISBN 9798880701797 (epub) | ISBN 9798880701803 (kindle edition) | ISBN 9798880701780 (pdf)
Subjects: LCSH: Disasters in art. | Sewŏrho (Ferry) | Ferryboat disasters—Korea (South) | Art and social action—Korea (South) —History—21st century. | Political art—Korea (South)
Classification: LCC NX650.D57 J46 2025 (print) | LCC NX650.D57 (ebook) | DDC 700/.4556—dc23/eng/20250318
LC record available at https://lccn.loc.gov/2024059332
LC ebook record available at https://lccn.loc.gov/2024059333

Cover art: Yellow ribbon installation at Danwon High School (top image). Commemorative classroom (bottom image). Both photographs courtesy of Areum Jeong.

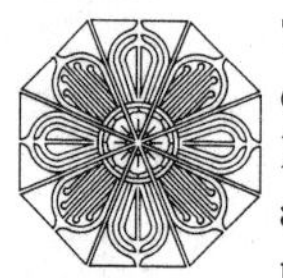

The Center for Korean Studies was established in 1972 to coordinate and develop resources for the study of Korea at the University of Hawai'i. Reflecting the diversity of the academic disciplines represented by affiliated members of the university faculty, the Center seeks especially to promote interdisciplinary and intercultural studies. Hawai'i Studies on Korea, published jointly by the Center and the University of Hawai'i Press, offers a forum for research in the social sciences and humanities pertaining to Korea and its people.

University of Hawai'i Press books are printed on acid-free paper and meet the guidelines for permanence and durability of the Council on Library Resources.

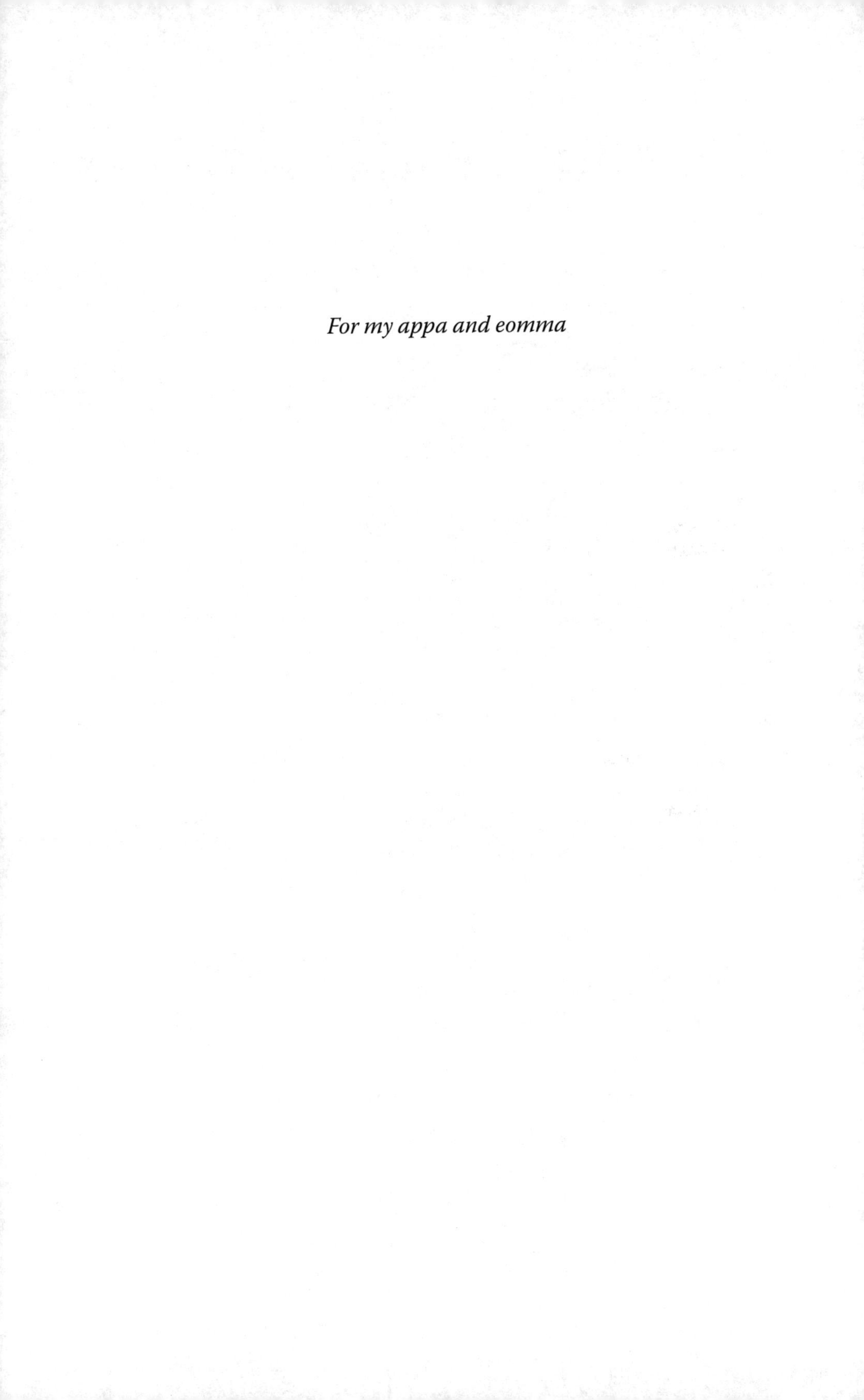

For my appa and eomma

CONTENTS

ACKNOWLEDGMENTS

First and foremost, this book is for the *Sewol* families, supporters, activists, and artists who inspired this project. I am especially indebted to the mothers of Yellow Ribbon—Gim Myeong-im, Yi Mi-gyeong, Choe Ji-yeong, Gim Do-hyeon, Bak Yu-sin, Bak Hye-yeong, and Gim Sun-deok—and director Gim Tae-hyeon, Yi Ji-seong and the staff of the 4.16 Institute of Democratic Citizenship Education, Black Jaguar, the organizers of Camino de Ansan, Jang Geun-hui, Jayoung Chung, Bak Sang-hyeon, Diane Na Yeon Kim, and the Sesamo communities: Gu Bo-gyeong (Bokyoung Koo) of Houston's Hambi; Gwon O-dal (Odal Kwon), Gim Yeong-geun (Young Kim), Gim Tae-hyeong (Taehyoung Kim), Yi Jong-guk (Chong-kuk Lee), Mel Lee, and Suna Lee of Philadelphia Sesamo; and Gim Nak-gyeong (Shawn Nak Kyung Kim) and Gim Mi-suk (Misuk Nam) of San Francisco's One Heart for Justice. Thank you for trying to make the world a better place.

I am grateful to the scholars who have offered comments and feedback on earlier drafts of the research at conferences and meetings that took place at the American Comparative Literature Association, the American Society for Theatre Research, the Association for Asian Performance, the Association for Asian Studies, the Association for Theatre in Higher Education, the Critical Global Studies Institute at Sogang University, the Disaster Haggyo at the Korea Advanced Institute of Science and Technology, the International Association for the Study of Popular Music, the International Federation for Theatre Research Asian Theatre Working Group Colloquium, the Korean Humanities Conference of the James Joo-Jin Kim Center for Korean Studies at the University of Pennsylvania, the Memory Studies Association, and Performance Studies International. I have learned so much from our discussions.

The 4.16 Foundation, the Academy of Korean Studies, and the American Society for Theatre Research supported this project, helping me to travel and conduct research.

Cambridge University Press, Johns Hopkins University Press, and Taylor and Francis allowed me to use portions of writings I published in earlier versions: "Beyond the *Sewol*: Performing Acts of Activism in South Korea," *Performance Research: A Journal of the Performing Arts* 24, no. 5 (2019): 33–43; "Representing the Unrepresentable in South Korean Activist Performances," *New Theatre Quarterly* 36, no. 4 (2020): 292–305; "Performing Memory and Testimony after a National Disaster: The *Sewol* Mothers in *Talking about Her* (2016), *VEGA* (2016), and *His and Her Closet* (2016)," *Studies in Theatre and Performance* (2023); and "From Witnessing to Redress: Objects, Remnants, and Wreckage After the *Sewol*," *Theatre Journal* 75, no. 2 (2023): 167–186.

I would also like to express my gratitude to the anonymous reviewers as well as to the journal editors whose hard work helped strengthen my writing: Gianna Bouchard, Patrick Duggan, Maria Shevtsova, Tom Six, Laura Edmondson, and Sean Metzger.

Robert Morris University provided time and space to complete the manuscript. I will always cherish my time at the Rooney House, and I would like to thank Sushil Acharya, Jennifer Creamer, and Anthony Moretti for their warm hospitality and support.

I am grateful for my wonderful colleagues and students at Arizona State University, especially Dean Jeffrey Cohen, Director Michael Tueller, and my mentors Sookja Cho, Markus Cruse, Ana Hedberg Olenina, Robert Tuck, and Daniel Gilfillan. Thank you for your strong leadership and support.

Special thanks to Jena Gaines and Shanon Fitzpatrick, who read every word of this project, and to Laura Portwood-Stacer, who demystified the book proposal writing process. I could not have done this without your thorough editing and feedback. I would also like to express my gratitude to Cheehyung Harrison Kim and Masako Ikeda at the University of Hawaiʻi Press for believing in and supporting this project.

This project began after I finished my doctoral dissertation, and I am grateful to the friends and mentors who cheered me from the early stages of research: Ga Young Chung, Jongyeon Joy Ee, Jang Wook Huh, Minwoo Jung, Hieyoon Kim, Namhee Lee, So-Rim Lee, and Soo Ryon Yoon. Thank you for your encouragement and friendship.

Last but not least, to my biggest supporters, Dongyoul Jeong and Hosoon Kim, who have loved me unconditionally and guided me into who I am today: *appa* and *eomma,* I love you.

NOTE TO READERS

This book uses the Revised Romanization of Korean to transliterate Korean names and words. For Korean names, I use the original convention of placing the surname before the given name with the exception of figures who are well-known by the reverse order. Unless otherwise stated, all translations from Korean to English are my own.

Introduction

On the evening of April 15, 2014, the *Sewol* ferry set sail on its overnight journey from Incheon, in northwestern South Korea, to Jeju Island, 240 miles to the south. There were 476 people on board: 443 passengers, including 325 students and teachers from Danwon High School, plus the ship's captain and crew. On the morning of April 16, near Jindo Island, the ferry for some unknown reason made a sharp turn. At 8:52 a.m., the first distress call came not from the crew but from a male student who dialed the national emergency number. "Save us! We're on a ship and I think it's sinking," the boy told the fire officer. Three minutes later, the crew called Jeju Harbor Affairs for help.

From 8:55 a.m. to 9:37 a.m., Harbor Affairs at Jeju and at Jindo Island both urged the crew to prepare the passengers for evacuation. Instead, however, the crew instructed the passengers to stay where they were and wait for help. Survivors reported receiving repeated instructions over the loudspeaker to remain in their cabins. Most of the passengers heeded the instructions and died waiting for rescue. Mobile phone footage retrieved from the victims shows terrified students in life vests discussing whether to obey the crew's instructions or try to escape. As the ferry tilted sideways, water seeped in and objects aboard toppled over, injuring people and blocking the exits. At 9:30 a.m., coast guard boats and helicopters began to arrive. By then, the ferry was tilted sixty degrees. The captain and crew were the first to abandon the ferry. Over the next two hours, 172 passengers were rescued, but many more were trapped inside as the ferry sank. In total, 304 people perished, including 250 of the students.

The day of the incident, I was in Los Angeles. I first learned of the news in the late evening via social media. I was alarmed but, like many others, saw an incorrect news broadcast stating that all passengers had been rescued, and I breathed a sigh of relief. When I got up the next morning, however, I found very different news headlines on my social media timeline. I could not believe that the news I had viewed several hours earlier was so incorrect. And I was horrified by the footage of the sinking ferry. Like millions of other Koreans, I felt utterly helpless.

The feelings of helplessness that many South Koreans and others felt at the sinking of the *Sewol* were sharpened by the ways the government mishandled the disaster, which has become the most galvanizing event in contemporary South Korean history. After the ferry capsized, then-President Park Geun-hye said that she and the government had done everything they could to rescue the passengers, and she promised to reveal the truth about the *Sewol*. However, prosecutors found out that Park learned about the ferry sinking after the "golden time"—the short window after an accident when there is the highest likelihood that rescue will prevent casualties—had elapsed. From 8:52 a.m., when the first emergency call was made, to 10:17 a.m., when the ferry was tilted 108 degrees and no longer in a position from which its passengers could be rescued, Park was completely unaware of the incident. Fearing the public's castigation of its ineffectual handling of the disaster, the Park administration refused to cooperate with the victims' families and thwarted the efforts of the *Sewol* Ferry Disaster Special Investigation Commission (SIC).[1] The National Intelligence Service (NIS) even surveilled and compiled personal information on the victims' families and supporters, including their political allegiances. In addition, the Blue House public relations office requested that the South Korean media reduce coverage on the *Sewol* ferry disaster.

Many Koreans, already shocked and horrified by the disaster, were enraged to learn that Park's government had interfered with the SIC's activities and had tried to use institutional and legal systems to undermine the SIC's efforts. The public's anger continued to grow with revelations about the Park administration's rampant corruption and incompetence. Protests against the administration's corruption that started at Ewha Womans [*sic*] University soon captured nationwide attention and spread as anger over the *Sewol* combined with other complaints to produce a national conflagration.[2] Park was impeached and removed from office in March 2017.

At first many Koreans rejoiced. It seemed as if the dark times had ended and Korea was ushering in a bright new era of democracy and greater transparency. The presidential election, which took place immediately after the impeachment, resulted in a victory for the liberal party and the election of Moon Jae-in. The Moon administration, which called itself the "Candlelight Government" in honor of the luminous protests that had brought it into power, vowed to reveal the truth about the *Sewol*.[3] Moon had participated in *Sewol* protests before being elected president, stating that "the truth about the *Sewol* can only be revealed when there is a change in the government."[4] After he was elected president, Moon invited the victims' families and supporters to the Blue House and promised to support the establishment of the second *Sewol* SIC to thoroughly investigate the disaster. I attended workshops and performances organized by the *Sewol* families and remember how much faith they had placed in the Moon administration. They had fought tirelessly against the Park administration since 2014, and it finally seemed that their efforts would be rewarded. However, as of this writing (April 2024), these hopes have been dashed. Park's mishandling of the disaster had given rise to the people's movement, Park's impeachment, and an electoral defeat of the ruling party. Some might say that the Moon administration benefited greatly from the disaster, or even exploited it for its own political ends. Yet the Moon administration, despite its promises, failed to conduct a thorough investigation. Whatever the political complications are behind closed doors, the Moon administration's broken promise has further harmed the victims' families and undermined national trust in the government.

Throughout this roller coaster of national trauma, public outrage, hope for change, and broken promises, an activist movement has taken shape among artists working through the medium of performance to process the disaster, commemorate its victims, and advocate for public change. *Beyond the* Sewol is the first book to spotlight this creative fluorescence of performative work, which spans the genres of theatre productions, exhibitions, interactive memorial events, site-specific public performances, street protests, and even commercial K-pop music videos. This diverse corpus of performance, I argue, has emerged as a central mode through which Koreans artists, often working in collaboration with *Sewol* survivors and families, have created a public memory archive countering official versions of the event. Furthermore, as I show, theatre and performance have provided an arena through which the project of commemorating the *Sewol* has been linked by activists to broader demands for changes in politics and society, especially around issues of government accountability, redress for victims, and public empathy for survivors. By identifying and analyzing a multimedia collection of performative works commemorating the *Sewol,* this book reveals the ways activists and artists mobilizing performative strategies have labored to transform the meaning of *Sewol* from an unresolved national trauma into a catalyst for creating a safer, fairer, and more caring society.

There are long traditions of both activism and suppression of dissent in South Korea. From protests against Syngman Rhee's authoritarianism in the 1960s and Park Chung-hee and Chun Doo-hwan's declaration of martial law in the 1970s and 1980s, to when the Korean people took to the streets from late 2016 to early 2017, activists have routinely mobilized to enact change at the highest levels of power.

During the Japanese colonial period (1910–1945), the Korean independence movement was widely active in Korea. Although the March 1st movement succeeded in changing Japanese imperial policy toward Korea, it failed to achieve Koreans' independence. Various forms of cultural struggle and resistance against the Japanese were manifested. Local and international movements based on art and literature rose against the colonial regime. After liberation from colonial rule, Korea was divided into two different ideologies: communism and capitalism. Syngman Rhee, who became the first South Korean president, suppressed antigovernment activities under the pretense of warding off North Korea. Students were the main figures who led protests against Rhee's authoritarian regime.

In the 1980s, students led the *minjung* movement against Chun Doohwan's dictatorship. In her seminal book, Namhee Lee explains how the student movement, through the "nexus of senior and junior students; the circulation of texts; circles and study groups; and reading lists," motivated many students to participate in other larger movements, "such as those associated with labor, the urban poor, women, and farmers, and white-collar movements that developed in the late 1980s."[5]

After the military dictatorships, South Korea transitioned into democracy in the 1990s. In the 2000s, candlelight protests that commemorated the death of two schoolgirls who were killed by a US military car revealed new protest strategies that made use of the internet. Online strategies of circulating the "commemorative messages, parodies of the verdicts, and the photographs of the girls' bodies" were effective in sharing emotions and motivating other internet users to attend candlelight vigils.[6] Thousands gathered in Gwanghwamun Square to commemorate the victims. The candlelight vigil was picked up by activist groups and turned into a symbol of the movement against the perceived injustice. Ever since 2002, mass demonstrations in South Korea have taken the form of candlelight protests.

Jin-Wook Shin identifies two distinct characteristics of the changing patterns of South Korean social movements from the 1960s to the 2010s.[7] First, candlelight vigils of the 2000s showed how networked individuals gradually began to play a bigger role than movement organizations. These individuals were diverse in age, sex, and occupation, and there was an increase in the participation of young Koreans and housewives. Second, Shin sees vast changes in the structure of the field of social movements from the 1970s to the 2000s, moving from

> the simple coexistence of a limited number of weakly organized actors until the 1970s; through a centralized system of organizations and inter-organizational ties in the 1980s; to a set of loose networks of diverse organizations and inter-organizational networks in the 1990s; and, finally, to a highly decentralized field within which a huge number of social networks, communities and individuals communicate and interact. Until the 1970s, progressive religious groups, student movements, democratic dissidents and the labour movements were still poorly organized and the connection between the groups was not solid. After the military massacre of 1980, the democratization movements considerably reinforced their organizational capacity and a nationwide structure of solidarity. After the end of dictatorship, the field of social movements has become diversified in terms of ideology, goals, and issues. From the early 2000s, individual citizens, nonmovement communities and social networks gained great importance in the rise, spread and success of contentious actions. These recent changes drastically increased the complexity of the movement ecology and reduced the predictability and strategic manageability of the progress of mobilization.[8]

The *Sewol* activism tapped into existing activist networks and protest repertoires. When the Park administration ushered in a neo-authoritarian regime that attempted to censor Koreans and prevent demonstrations, Koreans responded with creativity and defiance, using digital media to avoid government censorship and organizing massive collective actions. Increasing political polarization made the *Sewol* a sensitive issue, one that was impossible to discuss without expressing a political opinion and perhaps starting an argument.

When the Korean people marched the streets to criticize the government's refusal to accept responsibility for the disaster, Park's administration had the police suppress the protests by force, even arresting the grieving families. Public outrage over the administration's behavior caused the popularity of Park's ruling conservative party to plunge and that of the liberal party to rise. When millions of Koreans braved frigid weather to join street protests against the Park administration, it became a turning point in South Korean history as the public voiced unprecedented levels of opposition to institutions that had previously had their support. Some even questioned the very legitimacy of South Korea's government, laws, education system, and community norms—debates that continue today.

The combination of accelerating political polarization, official repression of protest, and widespread demands for accountability and change in the wake of the *Sewol* sparked a wave of artist activism. With a sense of great urgency, and taking cues from the victims' families and supporters, a wide range of Korean artists turned to mourning the victims and expressing their concerns about the government through film, literature, music, theatre, and visual art. These forms of protest became more available and attractive given the way the government was suppressing and surveilling other forms of opposition. Even as the Park administration censored and blacklisted artists who signed petitions to reveal the truth about the *Sewol*, Korean artists continued to create works commemorating the disaster and critiquing the government.

Among the wider culture of activism and protest in the arts, performance emerged as an especially prominent mode of commemoration and critique. There is a deeply rooted dissident culture in Korean theatre. In the 1970s and 1980s, *madanggeuk*, folk dramas, theatre companies like Yeonwu mudae and Arirang, and underground theatres in the Sinchon area were full of enthusiastic students. According to theatre scholar Gim

Bang-ok, there was a communal interest in relieving political oppression through culture, and this fervor was so strong that if one in the theatre industry did not perform a play that advocated for "the people" or "the nation," or against "the West" or dictatorship, one would be considered a decadent aesthete or an object of contempt as a "brainless person."[9] The urgency to document and represent sociocultural issues in Korea through performance genres was rekindled with the *Sewol* because after the disaster, the people could no longer trust the dominant narrative delivered by the Park administration.[10] Nor were the people satisfied with ongoing official attempts to mourn and commemorate the sinking. In refusing to "stay still" and accept the status quo, Korean performance artists have merged art and activism to underscore the ineptitude of the initial rescue operation, critique the Park administration's investigation of the sinking, and show how successive government responses to the sinking have harmed victims' families and failed to address underlying issues of accountability and public safety.

In the immediate aftermath of the disaster, the South Korean government's futile rescue operation generated criticism and debate. The Korean Coast Guard, Ministry of Oceans and Fisheries, and Ministry of Security and Public Administration failed to coordinate an effective rescue mission, which could have saved the lives of the passengers waiting in their cabins. The head of the coast guard also lied, saying that divers were recovering bodies when there were only eight divers.[11] The divers were retrieving the bodies one at a time and placing them in body bags.

After the debacles of the rescue operation, Park promised that she and her government would conduct a thorough investigation. The South Korean National Assembly passed the Special Act on Investigating the Truth of the April 16 *Sewol* Ferry Disaster and Building a Safe Society ("Special Act") on November 7, 2014. It was promulgated on November 19, 2014, and went into effect on January 1, 2015. Essential to bringing the Special Act into effect was a nationwide petition circulated by the Korean people that amassed 3.5 million signatures.[12]

Instead of trying to identify the cause of the incident and why the students and others had not been rescued, however, Park's administration refused to cooperate with the survivors and victims' families and thwarted the efforts of the *Sewol* Ferry Disaster SIC, which Park accused of being leftists. In addition, Park's administration blamed the victims' families for polarizing public opinion and therefore hurting the nation.[13] For instance, right after the disaster occurred, South Korea's Defense Security Command (DSC) characterized the victims' families as *jongbuk* (i.e., people who sympathize with North Korean ideology).[14] Moreover, on April 21, 2014, six days after the accident, the DSC wrote a report titled "Espionage Prevention Plan." The report stated that the DSC would confirm whether there were *jongbuk* movements promoting antigovernment activities among the victims' families, and it vowed to block any such activities. According to the DSC's May 29, 2014, report, the Committee for the *Sewol* Victims, an organization that supported the *Sewol* families, was listed as a *jongbuk* force. Thus, from the outset the DSC viewed the *Sewol* families and their supporters as North Korean sympathizers and thereby positioned them not as deserving citizens but, rather, as enemies of the state. This move was clearly meant to deflect criticism of the government's ineffectual handling of the disaster articulated by the *Sewol* families and their supporters.

During the eleven-month investigation period, Park's government and the ruling conservative party made it as difficult as possible for the SIC to do its job.[15] First, the government curtailed the SIC's authority via the Special Act Enforcement Decree. Announced by the Ministry of Oceans and Fisheries on March 27, 2015, without any explanation, if the Enforcement Decree were put into effect, the dispatched government officials would take full control of the SIC and reduce the authority of commission members.[16] The SIC demanded that the ministry rescind the Enforcement Decree, arguing that it violated the purpose of the Special Act's legislation, interfered with the SIC's investigation, and even undermined the SIC's independence.[17] However, on May 11, 2015, the government took up a slightly revised version of the Enforcement Decree.[18] Further limiting what the SIC could do was its insufficient budget. On August 4, 2015, the Ministry of Economy and Finance allocated 8.9 billion won instead of the 16 billion won initially requested to support activities such as digital forensics and scientific research. With such a reduced budget, it would be difficult to conduct a comprehensive scientific investigation into the *Sewol* ferry disaster.[19]

Meanwhile, the government refusals to cooperate with SIC's information gathering stymied the investigation. The Blue House and the National Intelligence Service did not submit any data on Park's activities on the day of the incident. Nor did the court, the prosecution, or the Board of Audit and Inspection send any data to the SIC.[20] And although the SIC discovered 1 million coast guard frequency communication recordings, only 7,100 were handed over.[21] The Ministry of Oceans and Fisheries was very reluctant to provide data on the salvage of the ferry and in the end provided less than half of the data the SIC had requested.[22]

Thus, although the SIC was created by law and had the legal authority to investigate, it was unable to exercise that authority because the government interfered with its activities. Then, under the pretense of passing the Special Act to help the families of victims, Park's government continued using institutional and legal systems to hinder the SIC's efforts to uncover the truth.

When the Korean people marched in protest, Park's administration had the police suppress the crowd and even arrest the grieving families. When Korean artists created works to commemorate the disaster and hold the government accountable, Park's administration denied them grants and funding. In October 2014, when the Busan International Film Festival screened the documentary *The Truth Shall Not Sink with* Sewol (2014), festival director Yi Yong-gwan was asked to resign. Jo Yun-seon, former minister of the Ministry of Culture, Sports and Tourism, asked the ruling conservative party to denounce the documentary.[23] Jo also ordered that all the tickets be bought up before the screening and that negative reviews of the documentary be posted on the internet.

Suspicions about government surveillance and censoring of the arts and culture came to the fore when theatre critic Gim Mi-do reported that Bak Geun-hyeong's play *All Soldiers Are Unfortunate* was initially selected for funding by Arts Council Korea but that members of the council had reconvened the jury members and demanded that the funds be rescinded.[24] In addition, in October 2015, Arts Council Korea interrupted a performance at the Seoul Performing Arts Festival because it contained references to a school trip and to a clothing brand worn by many students that evoked the *Sewol* ferry disaster. In October 2016, it was revealed that Park's administration had censored prominent artists and blacklisted 9,473 of them, including those who had signed petitions to reveal the truth about the *Sewol* ferry disaster. According to the list, 594 artists who signed the petition to abolish the *Sewol* Special Act Enforcement Decree and 754 who participated in the Declaration of the Korean State of Affairs were blacklisted.[25]

The lack of transparency and accountability, forms of obstruction and repression, and general animosity toward critics did not end with the Park administration. In the wake of regime change, numerous Koreans, including the victims' families, have expressed their anger, disappointment, and sense of betrayal on social media. Yu Gyeong-geun, the father of student victim Yu Ye-eun, posted on Facebook in December 2020, "After waiting three years and seven months for President Moon Jae-in and his administration to keep their promise, the mothers and fathers are now in a place where it feels more difficult than when we were fighting against Park Geun-hye's government. Please consider the graveness of this situation."[26] This is from a statement that the families sent to the Congress, pleading with the Moon administration to act by extending the SIC's activities until June 2022. On December 8, 2021, the 4.16 Foundation, a nonprofit organization that supports the *Sewol* survivors and victims' families, evaluated how the Moon administration handled the investigations of the *Sewol* ferry disaster during the past five years. Despite Moon's promises, nobody was held accountable, and there were no clear findings from the investigations. The foundation gave the Moon administration an evaluation score of D or F. In many ways, the public health crisis of the COVID-19 pandemic overshadowed the *Sewol,* even though the families have staged protests in front of the Blue House and tried to meet with citizens to discuss the investigation throughout the pandemic.[27]

Complicating matters, since 2014 the Korean people have increasingly come to disagree about the *Sewol.* While some remain sympathetic to the victims' families, others are tired of hearing about it and want the protests to end. Since the disaster, media coverage and right-wing politicians have contributed to spewing hate speech and misinformation about the disaster and victims' families. For instance, during local elections, right-wing politicians have spread misleading information on the soon-to-be-constructed 4.16 Life Safety Park, a memorial for the victims. Referring to the park as an "ossuary" and claiming that the memorial will take up the entire Hwarang Amusement Park in Ansan, when it in fact will take up only a small portion of it; they worked to undermine a project that is profoundly important to bereaved families and many others.[28] When such politicians defamed the victims' families and spread misinformation and even hate speech, Korean media outlets responded with provocative headlines designed to garner clicks and views. For example, on two days alone (April 22 and 23, 2014), there were 190 news articles that contained hate speech toward the victims' families, calling them "pro–North Korean" or "red commies."[29] From April 16 to 17, 2019, coinciding with the time that right-wing politicians stated that they were sick and tired of the disaster, there were more than 160 articles that referred to the *Sewol* ferry disaster as "tiring."

The *Sewol* is not an incident that has been concluded. Although more than ten years have passed, the *Sewol* ferry disaster is still regarded as a traumatizing incident for bereaved families, of course, but also for the many who helplessly watched the sinking in person or through the media. It has even been called a national trauma. Whether a new investigation will move forward and reveal the truth about the *Sewol* is beyond the scope of this book, but it remains clear that many questions have yet to be answered, and the *Sewol* families' struggle to conduct a thorough investigation and achieve legal redress continues to this day. Moreover, despite significant repression, activist performances of art and protest continue to represent the families and supporters' fight for justice, revive public interest in the truth about the *Sewol*, and shape the lessons and legacies of the disaster for the nation and the future.

My book discusses the real-world stakes of the *Sewol* ferry disaster and the activism that followed, with an emphasis on performance created in response to the tragedy and its impacts on viewers and the broader Korean society. To do this, it brings together a wide variety of case studies of performances that have been staged by activists and artists in response to the *Sewol*. In the face of considerable repression, works of protest and performance, many of them representing collaborations between artists and bereaved families, staged (and restaged) the disaster, remembered and mourned the victims, and stood in solidarity with the victims' families, including against government suppression and political attacks. As many of these works were temporary or ephemeral, documenting and analyzing them together here helps bring into focus and preserve what might be seen as a movement of *Sewol* art and activism.

Performance, as scholars have shown, is a "vital act of transfer" that transmits social knowledge, cultural memory, and identities.[30] Performances are not merely enactments of past times and places but a medium through which the unwritten past is reproduced, reexamined, and renegotiated.[31] Just as performances invent and re-create the past through ritual, they similarly influence communities by forging their identities in the present and imagining their futures. The interactions and relationships that performances create are central to these processes, as performances "exist only as actions, interactions and relationships."[32] By examining how several specific performances address or represent the *Sewol* ferry disaster, we can see the role performance has played in creating alternative spaces for the Korean people to mourn and remember, enact solidarity with victims and their families, and in so doing, shape broader transformations in politics, society, and culture.

Through a close examination of the case studies, this research looks at how performances documented the *Sewol* disaster and the *Sewol* families' narratives in ways that often differed markedly from official accounts and representations. In particular, it identifies the strategic use of speech acts and objects by performance artists and their collaborators to convey messages and elicit emotions. Through the use of these and other strategies, I show how performances archive and document the disaster in ways that raise awareness of injustice and the need for social change.

Speech acts and objects are what performances use to engage auditory and visual senses and bring attention to the survivors and the victims. Speech acts do not merely pass on information; they can be "performative" and become a performance in themselves.[33] Due to the experiences of not only losing their children but also being attacked by the right-wing political parties, the speech acts of the *Sewol* parents manifest vulnerability as they discuss the incident and its aftermath. Through such speech acts, vulnerability is "not exactly overcome by resistance, but becomes a potentially effective mobilizing force in political mobilizations."[34] In addition, vulnerability can "characterize a relation to a field of objects, forces, and passions that impinge on or affect us in some way."[35] Objects, I contend, can be just as powerful as speech in creating moving experiences during performances, because our relationships with particular objects can produce and perform affect.[36] This focus on speech acts and objects, and accompanying theories about how these performance strategies produce meanings and impacts, provides a framework for analyzing a range of works in which the families' speech acts and victims' remnants reveal and focus public attention on emotional wreckage. In contrast to the ocean-swallowed physical remains of the *Sewol* as a contained past disaster, emotional wreckage centers the ongoing impacts of personal and national trauma while also underscoring the need for certain as-yet-unmet forms of care and redress.

When examining in these performances how objects document the *Sewol* and how they become witnesses to the aftermath, it is necessary to consider how certain objects can perform affect based on personal experiences of them, which can include experiences of national tragedy. Marita Sturken uses the term "cultural memory" to denote "memory that is shared outside the avenues of formal historical discourse yet is entangled with cultural products and imbued with cultural meaning."[37] Cultural memory, in other words, is inseparable from history. Examining how a "range of cultural products" have generated the cultural memory of tragic events, Sturken argues that these cultural products are "technologies of memory, not vessels of memory in which memory passively resides so much as objects through which memories are shared, produced, and given meaning."[38] Because memory is articulated through processes of representation, these objects are "technologies of memory in that they embody and generate memory and are thus implicated in the power dynamics of memory's production."[39] Applied to the *Sewol* performances discussed in this book, Sturken's ideas help elucidate how objects not only represent the *Sewol* but also hold cultural history and personal memory and are given meaning through the forms and modes of loss processing that they encourage.[40]

Susan Stewart's theorization of how objects work to narrativize experiences is also important here, especially when combined with scholarship on time.[41] As my analysis shows, in activist and artistic representations of the *Sewol,* objects hold multiple temporalities—of the original owner, of the families who cherish them, of the artist who uses them in performances, and of the audience member who tries to make sense of the disaster. The victims' families, especially, struggle to make sense of the disaster by obsessively investigating, studying, and revising the timeline of April 16, 2014, and this is an ongoing theme in the works I highlight, which show that the time of the victims' families operates differently from that of other normative families. J. Halberstam theorizes that "queer uses of time and space" develop according to other logics of location, movement, and identification.[42] Halberstam writes that queerness is "an outcome of strange temporalities, imaginative life schedules, and eccentric economic practices," allowing one to imagine alternative relations to time that move away from normative temporalities.[43] Imagining the time—or, rather, the defamiliarization of time—of the victims' families in relation to Halberstam's idea of queer temporalities allows for an examination of the *Sewol* objects' multiple temporalities and of the families' imaginings of alternative relations to time.

Dori Laub's work has also been particularly useful in framing my own research on how the *Sewol* performances, and particularly their speech acts, represent the *Sewol* victims and how the audience receives them. Laub discusses how the listener may "partially experience trauma" when listening to testimonies of traumatic events.[44] The *Sewol* performances I discuss are not firsthand testimonies from the survivors or victims. Rather, they are adaptations of testimonies by the family members of victims and survivors. In other words, audience members bear witness to the tragedy, and in doing so they are able to reflect on the tragedy and the families' struggles in these moments and try to make sense of what it means, and maybe also what should happen next. Caroline Wake has argued that there are two concepts of witnessing at work within theatre and performance studies. One is associated with performance, which positions the spectator at the scene of trauma; the other, associated with documentary and verbatim theatre practices, positions the spectator at the scene of the testimony or the account.[45] Each person attending the *Sewol* performances belongs to the latter as "a witness to an account of the accident rather than to the accident itself; a witness to testimony."[46] Testimony helps performance represent the unrepresentable and turns viewers into witnesses to the traumatic past.

When discussing how art can memorialize traumatic histories, Dominick LaCapra argues that literature that remembers war or the Holocaust can provide a "safe haven in which to explore post-traumatic effects."[47] In doing so, he stresses that it is important to avoid redemptive narratives and simple conclusions in works that remember traumatic narratives because the process of listening to, reading, or witnessing someone else's suffering involves ethical responsibilities to the event itself and the people involved.[48] The *Sewol* performances examined in this book align with LaCapra's interests, as they do not merely represent and memorialize the tragic incident but also endeavor to challenge the status quo. Augusto Boal used the term "spect-actor" to describe the process by which one becomes both spectator and actor in performance.[49] Boal advocated for the need to enable the audience member to become an active performer, moving away from the preexisting notions of the viewer as a passive being. Marcela A. Fuentes takes such discussions further by looking at how performance not only represents but also engages in discourses on social change. Fuentes defines "artivism" as "productions by artists who use their craft to mobilize concrete action in response to social issues. The term 'artivism' characterizes a drive toward action in the making of an artistic intervention. In artivist projects, the main goal is to trigger responses and not merely represent a state of affairs."[50] Fuentes's idea of "artivism" is useful when examining how performance and political activism come together and complicate each other. This notion also enables us to question the ways that transnational performances—that is, performances that take place across national borders or bring together performers from different places—"redefine the terms of interaction between bodies and state power at different geographical scales."[51]

In recent years, there has been a renewed academic interest in how South Korean activist performance contributes to social change. At the grassroots level, Chungmoo Choi and Namhee Lee have examined how *madanggeuk,* a Korean theatre genre that involves mask-dance and satire, played a significant role in engaging audiences in political issues and popular protest.[52] More recently, Jiyeon Kang has analyzed the ways Koreans organized nationwide protests in 2002 and 2008 via online communities.[53] Elizabeth W. Son's work documents past and present histories of "comfort women"—women forced into sexual slavery by the Imperial Japanese Army during World War II—and examines how the history of comfort women activism has changed in both South Korean and diasporic communities.[54] I find Son's work particularly useful in framing my own research on how the *Sewol* performances document, remember, and engage in activism. Son explains that the framework "focuses more on the process of redress" and that "collective participation and involvement in the process bring about possibilities for redress."[55] The narrative of her work is not only about the survivors but also about the people who continue to fight with them. It becomes a documentation of "communities of remembrance," which Son describes as "the involvement of nonstate actors in activism, theater, and memorial building" that are "connected by the actions of remembrance in the pursuit of justice."[56] Thus, each piece of performance becomes an act of documenting and letting the activists, survivors, and supporters know that they are not alone in their struggles. Not only does Son's work fill the gap in the literature of comfort women activism by focusing on performative strategies used by activists, survivors, and supporters; her book also performs in its own way, serving as a stage for their stories. Building from Son's framework, this book aims to examine how the *Sewol* performances document and memorialize the tragic incident and engage in discourse on social change and, through doing so, to provide another platform for these performances to be documented and shared.

Son examines how memorials invite "performances of care," embodied acts that materialize concern and interest by providing for the needs of or looking after what one is caring for.[57] My work illustrates examples of how activists and artists use the materiality of *Sewol* objects, as well as speech acts that make audiences witness to testimony, to elicit embodied engagements and performances of care that are otherwise not being elicited in official discourse.[58] While there has been much academic interest in the psychological symptoms of the *Sewol* survivors and bereaved families, what has been less examined, with only a few exceptions, is how performative works represent the *Sewol* and shape responses to it that seek to engage care in and through arenas of policies, politics, and projects rather than only through personal feelings and relations.[59]

Combining scholarship in performance studies, memory studies, and trauma studies with ethnographic methodologies provides additional insights into *Sewol* performances and their impacts. During my fieldwork from 2017 to 2022 in Korea, I conducted research as a participant-observer and as a "coperformer witness" whenever I could participate. According to Dwight Conquergood and D. Soyini Madison, coperformer witnessing is a way of accessing the cultural knowledge stored in the body.[60] Since the disaster, I have joined online and offline events organized by the families and supporters of the victims. I have attended protests and seminars that discuss the disaster with the victims' families, including the *Sewol* Academy seminar series organized by 4.16 Act and the People's Commission for the Truth of the *Sewol* Ferry Sinking (September 13–22, 2017); the "Plaza Democracy, Art Action, and Public Nature of Culture and Arts Policy" forum organized by Seoul Foundation for Arts and Culture (September 15, 2017); and the Ansan Mental Health Trauma Center's Beyond Trauma Symposium (December 3, 2018). From 2017 to 2022, I have viewed all of theatre troupe Yellow Ribbon's performances multiple times and all performances organized by Hyehwadong ilbeonji—an annual theatre festival showcasing works that represent the *Sewol*. I have visited the commemorative classrooms in Ansan in 2019 and 2022, and in May 2019 I participated in the Ansan pilgrimage performance that was organized by *Sewol* families and supporters. In the summer of 2022, I attended Yellow Ribbon's weekly play-reading workshops. During these events, I met with several *Sewol* mothers and Yellow Ribbon director Gim Tae-hyeon. I reflect on my own experiences and observations to explain the operative process of how performative works that represent the *Sewol* affect viewers. My participation in *Sewol* performances and protests helped me understand the vital moments in these case studies and is key to my interpretation of them.

Each chapter of this book explores a different arena in and through which Korean artists document and remember the *Sewol*, and in doing so the text performs a kind of collaborative public counter-memory that pushes back against dominant narratives about the disaster and contributes to a form of activism through commemoration. Similarly, this book itself, as a repository of key performances that also archives my own affective responses as a witness-participant, seeks to join this project of activist documentation, memory making, and commemoration.

The book begins by focusing on performative works that are closest and most immediate to the victims, including one that is performed by the victims' mothers. Next it moves to works that require more effort from the local community—such as in Ansan, the victims' hometown. It then expands to the larger culture scene in Korean theatre, performance, and popular music, and the diaspora.

Chapter 1, "Redressive Theatre: The *Sewol* Mothers on the Stage," examines theatrical works that adapt the mothers' testimonies and are also performed by the mothers themselves. Through a close reading of Creative VaQi's *Talking About Her* (2016) and Black Jaguar's *VEGA* (2016), the chapter shows how both the performers and audience members become listeners to the mothers' testimonies, bearing witness to their trauma. Next, the chapter focuses on theatrical works by Yellow Ribbon, which was founded in 2016 after the victims' mothers had participated in therapeutic workshops that included play readings. Through a close reading of *His and Her Closet* (2016), *Living and Dying Next Door* (2017), *Talent Show* (2019), *Memory Trip* (2021), and *Continuing, Drama* (2023), the chapter analyzes how Yellow Ribbon gives the mothers a space to tell their stories, connect with the local community, and transform their grief into political activism. Although the mothers' activities can be said to reflect conventional gender roles, I argue that by expressing positive energy as active resistance through craft workshops and theatrical performances, the mothers extend and even reconceptualize motherhood activism in Korea.

Chapter 2, "Memorializing Through Performance: Site-Specific Performances with Objects in Ansan and Paengmok Port," examines the commemorative performances that took place in the student victims' hometown and the disaster site. Through a close reading of several of these works—*The Children's Room,* a photography exhibit that documents the victims' remnants; the commemorative classrooms at Danwon High School; *Camino de Ansan,* an annual pilgrimage project at Ansan; and *The Blanket Project,* a series of performances that took place at Paengmok Port—it shows how performances embody the image of victims, or rather their absence, in the public imagination. The site-specific performances at Ansan and Paengmok Port invite the participants to remember the victims while choreographing and documenting the space through embodied performance, ultimately imbuing the space with experiences and stories that materialize ongoing loss and link this loss to persisting structures of government malfeasance and unaccountability.

Chapter 3, "Reimagining Justice: The *Sewol* in Korean Theatre and Performance," examines multimedia and theatrical works created by local Korean activists and artists. Through a close reading of performances staged in public at Gwanghwamun Square and in national performance venues, including Jayoung Chung's *Empathy* (2017) and Bak Sang-hyeon's *From Pluto* (2019), the chapter analyzes how such works not only created spaces for memory and mourning but also resisted government censorship and surveillance, thereby reimagining justice. While the language of law is lacking, I argue that embodied performance can transcend language and constitute interventions in public discourse that contribute to social change.

Chapter 4, "Singing for a Spring Day: The *Sewol* in K-Pop," examines how South Korean musicians—BTS, Kim Yoon Ah, Lee Seung-hwan,

Lucid Fall, Red Velvet, and others—have created works to document and memorialize the victims. Thinking creatively about what constitutes activist art in a national context in which elements of the performing arts sector are highly commercialized and even supported by the state, this chapter analyzes how popular music can serve as a public memory archive and how mourning the *Sewol* through popular music aims to heal the public trauma.

Chapter 5, "Performing Diasporic Healing: *Sewol* Activism in Korean American Communities," examines various forms of *Sewol* activism by Koreans and Korean Americans in North American cities and beyond, such as newspaper advertisements, in-person and online demonstrations, fundraising, theatre productions, and relay fastings. Seeing these acts as performances of communal consciousness, I explore how they enabled diasporic communities to channel their helplessness, rage, and sorrow into collective action. Through their strategies of peaceful nonviolent activism to support the *Sewol* families and survivors in searching for the truth and achieving legal redress, these members of the Korean diaspora formed and strengthened community bonds. Furthermore, their continuous activism extended into interests in and activism for other current events in Korea and issues affecting Asian Americans.

In the epilogue, I consider the legacies of the *Sewol* ferry disaster and the activist performance cultures considered in this book in the context of another more recent disaster in South Korea—the 2022 crowd crush in Itaewon. In the massive collective responses to this tragedy, I see the ongoing legacies of *Sewol* performance activism working to channel traumatic experiences into action for social change.

CHAPTER 1

Redressive Theatre

The Sewol *Mothers on the Stage*

"Park Geun-hye is a bitch!" Yi Mi-gyeong shouted out during a performance of theatre troupe Yellow Ribbon's *Living and Dying Next Door*. Yi, who played the role of Se-chan in the production, is not only an actress; she is also the mother of Yi Yeong-man, one of the 250 Danwon High School students who died when the *Sewol* ferry capsized off the southwestern coast of South Korea on April 16, 2014. Se-chan's line, which addressed former South Korean President Park Geun-hye with visceral anger and disappointment, is a commentary on how Park personally, along with her administration, bungled the handling of the *Sewol* ferry disaster and its aftermath. Through the speech act of calling Park "a bitch" during her performance, Yi held the former leader personally accountable for the potent combination of malfeasance and mistreatment that had characterized the government's response to the *Sewol*.

This scene of *Living and Dying Next Door* provides a window onto two developments in the theatre world that have shaped the politics of performance and the ways performance has sought to shape politics around the commemoration of the *Sewol*. First, it documents the close collaborations that have been forged in the theatre world between creators and performers of theatre and those most affected by the disaster, namely the family members of victims. Second, it calls attention to the *Sewol* parents' activism that has formed in the wake of the disaster, particularly the activism of mothers, who in addition to publicly mourning their lost children have also gone beyond displays of privately held grief to express anger and demand political and social changes. Examining these developments in tandem, this chapter analyzes performance pieces adapted from or related to testimonies by the *Sewol* mothers and considers how these performances commemorate the *Sewol* by reconfiguring the meanings of witnessing and redress. To do so, it examines two performance pieces adapted from testimonies by the *Sewol* mothers—*Talking About Her* (2016) and *VEGA* (2016)—and another set of works in which mothers acted as the main performers: Yellow Ribbon's *His and Her Closet* (2016), *Living and Dying Next Door* (2017), *Talent Show* (2019), *Memory Trip* (2021), and *Continuing, Drama* (2023).

In response to the disaster and its mishandling by the South Korean government, Korean activists and artists mobilized collaboration with the victims' families to produce activist theatre productions that center not only the trauma of those most affected by the disaster but also their ongoing lived experiences and wishes. Mothers in particular have become highly visible in these productions. While mothers have long been common figures of grief and sympathy after disasters, the *Sewol* performance community has come to include and represent the mothers not only as victims but also as active participants whose grief is transmuted through performance into communal healing and political activism. This chapter reveals how these works, utilizing the memories and testimonies of the mothers as well as the meaningful objects related to their children or the disaster that they provide, have come to constitute a kind of *collaborative public counter-memory* that works against state cover-ups and unempathetic accounts, centering demands for change in commemoration practices and transforming the meaning of *Sewol*. Through the use of memory and testimony, these performances—especially through the activation of mothers who have traditionally been viewed as passive mourners—move commemoration from the private realm into the public realm, where redress, the performances of *Sewol* mothers argue, must necessarily be a communal project that involves legal redress and social change.

THE *SEWOL* PARENTS' ACTIVISM AND THE RISE OF DOCUMENTARY THEATRE

The *Sewol* parents' activism emerged under unexpected circumstances. Since the disaster, the parents have endured indescribable sorrow and trauma. They regret having been unable to protect their children and are angry with and disappointed in the South Korean government and media.

At the same time, individual parents experience their own kind of grief, and this grief tends to be different between fathers and mothers. Anthropologists Hyeon Jung Lee and Yesung Lee attribute the differences between the grief of fathers and that of mothers to societal gender roles.[1] Fathers often feel guilty about having spent more time at work than with their children. Indeed, after the *Sewol* sank, many of them were too grief-stricken to return to their jobs. By contrast, bereaved mothers often blamed themselves for allowing their children to go on the trip, for instance, and regretted not being able to see or touch their children's corpses. They frequently reported symptoms of depression and somatization.

As gender studies scholar Judith Butler has argued, gender is a performance based on cultural norms.[2] Most Korean mothers are bound by societal constructions of gender roles, and motherhood is shaped by the "interrelated actions played by a number of dominant actors around woman herself."[3] Anthropologist Desintha Asriani describes how being a mother in Korea is increasingly contested, however, as Korean mothers navigate the dichotomy of stay-at-home mother and working mother and negotiate their social status, gender role, capital, and space. As such, a Korean mother's performance of meeting her family's needs often determines, or at least substantially mediates, the social recognition of being a mother.

In the 1960s, South Korea transitioned from a traditional to a modern patriarchy, which resulted in the rural collective family enterprise transforming into the urban nuclear family.[4] Cultural anthropologist Haejoang Cho explains how this modernization enabled Korean mothers to "instrumentalize their children, deploying them in competitive status games . . . which reinforces the materialism and instrumentality of society in general."[5] In this sense, anthropologist Nancy Abelmann views Korean mothers as "critical agents in the production of family class and the work of class mobility."[6] Thus, rather than their individual selves, Korean mothers' labor activities are associated with their familial selves, and their role as wife and mother becomes their primary responsibility.[7]

How are Korean mothers seen in spaces of activism and politics, then, and how might those acts align or conflict with "the social recognition of being a mother"? Answers to this question have changed over time and across different societal contexts. Sociologist Jeong-Lim Nam examines how Korean women's political activism as mothers or wives in the 1980s aimed at challenging existing gender roles.[8] Korean mothers and wives were not visible in labor demonstrations and had discouraged their husbands from participating. In the 1980s, however, mothers and wives actively participated in democratic movements and engaged in advocacy on various social issues, including "workers' survival rights, sexual violence against activists, environmental concerns, and basic human rights." During the Chun Doo-hwan dictatorship, street broadcasting led by women helped strengthen interest and participation in forming a citizen-led army.[9] These women participated in the production and distribution of banners, handouts, and posters; posted flyers explaining the reality of the martial law army's atrocities; and encouraged citizen participation. Such activities helped inform citizens of the situation and outlined guidelines for action. Many women also participated in providing supplies: for example, they donated blood, collected rice, and raised money in each village to collectively prepare food and drinks for the protestors. The mothers' and wives' activities relied on grassroots struggles because there was no formal organization that represented their interests. In some arenas, it was women who stepped in to provide crucial organizational labor that powered activist movements in the late twentieth century.

In the twenty-first century, Korean mothers became more visible in several political movements. For example, in the protests opposing US beef imports in 2008, young mothers joined in, some attending with baby strollers to "make a statement about the threat of contaminated beef and to deter police violence."[10] Mothers' bodies in these protests worked to represent both current society and future generations while also calling attention to differentials in power between authorities and the public.

The *Sewol* mothers' activism is similar to previous movements in that formerly no organized network represented mothers of disaster victims, and in that they relied on support from each other and the local community. The *Sewol* mothers' activism also extends previous forms of activism by expanding their work from the streets to stages. In the wake of the disaster, performance—particularly participation in documentary theatre productions—has served as a means of bringing grieving mothers together and providing them with a wider stage to share their experiences and even make demands.

Sewol mothers' participation in performance activism often grew out of communal activities they engaged in immediately following the disaster. Soon after the sinking, craft workshops became a support system for bereaved mothers with posttraumatic stress disorder (PTSD).[11] In these workshops, the mothers made artwork and items featuring yellow ribbons. These activities gave the mothers something to concentrate on other than their grief. The programs also helped ameliorate the impacts the trauma of the sinking was having on mothers' memories. Sometimes in the wake of these craft workshops, several mothers also met with film directors and playwrights and offered their testimonies for use in films, documentaries, and plays. The result has been a fluorescence in documentary theatre focused on the *Sewol.*

In Korean theatre, it was difficult to find documentary theatre before the early 2000s, but this genre has increased rapidly since then.[12] First, documentary theatre is a theatrical representation of actual events, revealing the realism of the events reproduced on stage. Second, the realism of the play is emphasized by composing the text based on specific research on actual events (conducting interviews with people involved or witnesses, citing reports and statistical data, transcripts, etc.). These documentary plays tend to subvert conventions by citing or displaying reliable materials directly or indirectly, or by raising questions about events by revealing published lies or hidden sides. Third, an author's autobiographical story is reproduced theatrically, and private documents owned by the individual are used. Fourth, real people appear as performers, resisting the fictional form of theatre and using the realism of autobiographical narratives as a theatrical strategy. Experimentation with documentary theatre does not have a long history in Korea, so the genre is referred to interchangeably as "documentary theatre," "contemporary documentary theatre," and "new documentary theatre."[13]

Theatre scholar Gim Bang-ok states that there has been a shift in Korean theatre since the *Sewol* ferry disaster.[14] This is different from the political theatre of the 1980s or the trend of postmodern theatre after the 1990s. Performances that focus on sociopolitical issues and that reconstruct them based on information, personal memories, and documents, rather than relying on fictional worlds or conventional representation, are attracting attention. Old-fashioned political satire has disappeared, and instead we are seeing theatrical experiments that seek to approach new perceptions and truths through concrete data, in-depth analysis, and diversification of perspectives.

According to theatre scholar Yang Geun-ae, post-*Sewol* plays attempt to examine the collective depression and pain caused by the disaster, along with the wider problems of Korean society.[15] She sorts *Sewol* theatre into four categories: (a) plays that directly or indirectly represent the *Sewol* ferry disaster; (b) plays that do not mention the *Sewol* ferry disaster but are reminiscent of the disaster or the pain of its aftermath; (c) plays that deal with domestic and foreign disasters or accidents that occurred in the past; and (d) plays that consider the problems of humanity and capitalism through questions about the nation.

Seong Ji-su's dissertation examines fifty-five *Sewol* plays from the immediate aftermath of the *Sewol* to August 2017.[16] First, works that directly represent the *Sewol* ferry disaster depict the shock and sorrow of those who experienced it, or attempt to give meaning to such emotions. For this reason, most works deal with the *Sewol* disaster from the perspective of the *Sewol* families, or attempt to answer the question "What does the *Sewol* mean to us?" using theatrical language from the perspective of a performer or citizen. In addition, works like these tend to include scenes that reproduce the sinking of the *Sewol* in various ways. Second, works that borrow the *Sewol* disaster as a clear reference but without covering the disaster in its entirety tend to avoid mentioning the *Sewol* ferry disaster; instead, they link the *Sewol* to other disasters at home and abroad. There are also many adaptations of existing plays that are not related to the *Sewol*. Finally, some works were created with a clear plan to promote them in relation to the *Sewol* ferry disaster so the audience would recognize the connection when viewing the performance. Seong classified such works as *Sewol* plays due to their planning and promotion strategies, performance location, and period.

In their participation in documentary theatre performances (several of which I will analyze in more detail later in this chapter), mothers engaged in testimonial activities that can be said to reflect conventional gender roles. But I argue that these are important ways that these mothers stepped outside the boundaries of traditional motherhood to demonstrate the communal scope of their grief and transform this more-than-private grief into political activism. The *Sewol* mothers' activities are reminiscent of the resistance movements in Argentina by the Mothers of the Plaza de Mayo, which were examined by performance studies scholar Diana Taylor.[17] While the mothers' performative gender role can be viewed as emblematic of essentialist notions of motherhood, Taylor contends that "they shifted the site of their enactment from the private sphere—where it could be construed as essentialist—to the public—where it became a bid for political recognition and a direct challenge to the junta."[18] While these programs are arguably gendered, I contend that the *Sewol* mothers' activities are one of many strategies and tactics that they use to reach out to other South Koreans. According to communication studies scholar Jinah Kim, the *Sewol* mothers "challenged the essentialist idea that mothering is personal, individual, and biologically predetermined and put forth a vision of motherhood as a figure of political agency that is necessarily intersectional with other social identities" and "created informal, extranational political networks and protested the idea that somehow they had failed to create a safe world for their children."[19] In the light of Taylor and Kim's research, I argue that the *Sewol* mothers extend motherhood activism in Korea. They express positive energy as active resistance through craft workshops and theatrical performances, extending representations of motherhood politics. By transgressing from conservative practices of mourning and remembering and by actively participating in performative works including stories that were censored or silenced, the mothers center the *Sewol* families' perspective that counter official versions of the incident and imagine different forms of familial and national community. We can see this through closer analysis of individual performances adapted from their testimonies and input.

LISTENING TO AND SPEAKING FOR THE MOTHERS: *TALKING ABOUT HER* (2016)

Written and directed by Yi Gyeong-seong and performed by Creative VaQi, *Geunyeoreul malhaeyo* (Talking about her) premiered on April 14, 2016, at the Namsan Arts Center. The performance was inspired by and adapted from interviews with five *Sewol* mothers who lost their daughters in the *Sewol* ferry disaster—Bak Eun-hui (mother of student victim Yu Yeeun), Bak Yu-sin (mother of student victim Jeong Ye-jin), No Hyeon-hui (mother of student victim Bak Ye-seul), An Yeong-mi (mother of student victim Mun Ji-seong), and Shin Myeong-seop (mother of student victim Hwang Ji-hyeon). From late 2015 to early 2016, the performance creators cautiously asked the women about their lost daughters. Although they were still grieving, the mothers welcomed the creators' questions. The mothers talked about their daughters as enthusiastically as if they had just left for a school trip and would return home at any moment. But inside, the mothers were struggling to make sense of the disaster. They asked the performance creators to tell the stories of their daughters onstage because "the kids can't speak now" and "we have to speak on their behalf."

The performance consists of interviews with the *Sewol* mothers but also reflects on the difficult processes of interviewing them. Yi and the actors contemplated how to approach the mothers and have them tell their stories without making the mothers into a spectacle. During the first act, the performers are the interviewers. Standing apologetically with his hands clasped, a male performer stands alone and hesitantly asks a series of questions about the mothers and their lost daughters: "How and when did you move to Ansan? What was Ye-eun like? What was Ji-hyeon's voice like? Do you remember Ye-jin taking her first steps? What was Ji-hyeon's favorite food?"

During the second act, two male and three female performers sit in a row and talk about their meetings with the mothers, without mentioning them by name. "I was surprised to see how young she was. Before then, I would refer to her as so-and-so's mother. But when I met her, she seemed like my older sister." "She says 'hmmm' a lot as if she is thinking what to say beforehand. She doesn't just talk with her mouth; she talks with her whole body. She uses a lot of hand gestures." The performers mimic the way the mothers talked and moved. Although the performers do not reveal the mothers' names, they do name the daughters, so the audience members can identify the mothers if they care to.

During the third act, each performer reenacts the testimony of a bereaved mother. From here, the play is not only about the mothers but also about the daughters whom they miss dearly—their characteristics, dreams, and hopes. "I can't brag about my daughter, but since you are here today to listen, I might as well brag about her! My Ye-seul was perfect. I was so thankful. Whenever I looked at her, my heart swelled with happiness." "She never complained about my cooking and ate everything." "My Ye-eun did her best at everything." "My Ye-jin was a huge fan of TVXQ's

Yun-ho. Her dream was to become a K-pop star." When listening to the mothers' detailed stories about their daughters, performer Seong Su-yeon says that she felt closer to them. "The unfamiliar names and faces came together. Hwang Ji-hyeon, Jeong Ye-jin, Bak Ye-seul, Mun Ji-seong, and Yu Ye-eun were no longer students from the large photo collage I saw at the altar. I felt like they were people I actually knew."

In the final act, Seong Su-yeon calmly and slowly recites the names of 304 passengers who perished on the ferry. The thirty-minute recitation is a ritual that memorializes each victim. At the end of the performance, a prerecorded testimony from one of the mothers is played for the first time. "I don't want the children's deaths to be in vain. If our society could change, their deaths won't be in vain.... The children can't speak. We have to speak for them." By interviewing the mothers and reenacting their testimonies, *Talking About Her* becomes a memory archive and a space for grief. When listening to the mothers' stories about their daughters, the mothers' sorrow and wish to reveal the truth about the *Sewol* is transmitted to the audience members through the performers.

Performances like *Talking About Her* help to compose narratives from the *Sewol* families' perspective. In this sense, the performance presents a story that moves away from that of mainstream media. After the *Sewol* capsized, mainstream journalism and media in Korea shaped the ways the Korean people understand the disaster. Rather than investigating the systemic causes or conditions surrounding the disaster, Korean mainstream news focused more on the legal punishment sentenced to the captain and crew of the ferry and how much compensation the victims' families would receive from the government. Due to such reporting, many Koreans view the *Sewol* ferry disaster as an event that has been concluded, as the ferry's captain was sentenced to life imprisonment and the victims' families received financial compensation from the government. However, the *Sewol* is not an event that has been concluded. Rather, the disaster includes the aftermath of the sinking—the systemic failures of the ferry service itself, the bungled rescue operation, the Park administration trying to downplay government culpability and hindering the SIC's investigation, and surveillance of the victims' families and supporters. In other words, the performance depicts the *Sewol* as an ongoing disaster.

This kind of performance becomes a public counter-memory that activates stories that are silenced. In addition, performance spectatorship can elicit empathy that can be conducive to forging more caring community bonds. *Talking About Her* elicits remembering and links it to redressive demands, thereby reconfiguring what it means to witness, commemorate, and memorialize. Furthermore, *Talking About Her* illuminates specific performative strategies Korean activists and artists have utilized to commemorate the *Sewol.* These strategies include intense collaboration with survivors of various kinds, centering survivor goals and an ethics of consent to promote witnessing rather than spectacle.

Black Jaguar's intermedial performance *VEGA,* which I examine next, does not reenact the mothers' testimonies but uses sound and visual media to tell their stories.

WITNESSING MEMORY AND TESTIMONY: *VEGA* (2016)

Black Jaguar's *VEGA,* which premiered on February 13, 2016, is an intermedial performance that interweaves words and images from three *Sewol* mothers. After the disaster, Black Jaguar, a multidisciplinary Korean artist known for creating intermedial works on social minorities, saw the student victims being reduced to "Danwon High School students," which she found distressing because of the ways it flattened the individual victims. She felt a kind of responsibility to talk about them through her work, and to do this she connected with their mothers to learn more about them.

VEGA consists of three mothers' prerecorded testimonies interspersed with Black Jaguar's stories. Visual images are projected on a screen on the glass wall of the gallery. The performance space is divided into three places: first, Space Haebang, where the audience is watching; a garage directly across from Space Haebang, where Black Jaguar performs; and in the streets, where some audience members watch the projection or use streaming apps. Space Haebang is a small gallery that accommodates no more than twenty people. The audience members sit close to each other. Black Jaguar wanted the audience members to be seated in uncomfortable chairs in a cramped studio while listening to stories that most Koreans did not want to hear. She hoped that the experience would create a sense of community.

Except for the glass wall where the audience members face Black Jaguar, the other three walls are exhibition spaces. A Danwon High School uniform and drawings of women praying hang on the wall. The drawings might remind the viewer of the mothers of *Sewol* victims, who spent countless hours at the Jindo Gymnasium and Paengmok Port waiting for their children. There are also some personal items—old baby clothes, socks, and a toothbrush—hanging from the ceiling. Yeong-man's mother had lent her son's keepsakes to the exhibition, and these are his items.

The bells chime. Black Jaguar sits in an open garage across from Space Haebang. She sits on a yellow flowered blanket, with a purple-and-white-checkered blanket covering her legs. These blankets had been used by the *Sewol* mothers at the Jindo Gymnasium and Paengmok Port. Black Jaguar and the viewers sit still, listening to the mothers' testimonies from the speakers. The act of sitting still and listening echoes the mothers waiting at Paengmok Port. Black Jaguar moves as little as possible, only making eye contact with the audience. The act of embodying the mothers' position at Paengmok Port also seems like a ritual.

The night of the premiere was a rainy winter evening, so the windows began to mist. The audience members said that Space Haebang's misty windows made Black Jaguar look as if she was underwater. Cars, motorcycles, and people passed by, sometimes blocking the view of the audience. Black Jaguar later said that she did not plan it, but later it seemed like "a metaphor of our society in which we often lose sight of important issues."[20] Si-chan's mother speaks first, introducing herself and recollecting the moment when she waited for her son at Paengmok Port: "I didn't get to see his face.... The video screen showed him slowly, from his legs. My daughter and I watched all the way up to his chin, but then his father turned the screen away and shouted at us not to look at his face. I asked if I could hold his hand. That still lingers in my mind. I should have held his hand once, but I wasn't able to." During the testimony of Si-chan's mother, the projection shows clips of Ansan. The scenery of the neighborhood conveys a sense of emptiness, like the lives of the bereaved families. After a brief segment by Black Jaguar, the voice of Yeong-man's mother is heard. In a similar manner, Yeong-man's mother also introduces herself and recollects the moment when her son's corpse was retrieved: "I should have taken a good look at him and touched him one last time.... When they told me that the casketing would take place, I thought I would get to see him one last time. But when they told me to go see the body that was laid out, he was all wrapped up, except for his face. I was so shocked!" Just as Si-chan's mother regrets not being able to see her son's face and hold him for the last time, Yeong-man's mother regrets not being able to see her son for the last time. Hyeon Jung Lee and Yesung Lee note that many *Sewol* mothers feel regret about not touching or seeing their child's body, and some even feel resentment toward their spouses. Furthermore, the mothers felt that they had failed in their role as mothers due to their inability to save their children from the sinking ferry and hold or touch their children's bodies one last time.

During the testimony of Yeong-man's mother, the projection shows photos of Yeong-man's room and possessions, mainly books, clothes, and photos. The room is absent its owner, who can never return. Because of this knowledge, which the audience shares, the objects represent the unrealized dream or future left behind. In place of their owner, the objects become memorials, performing and experientially affecting the viewers. Although the photos seem merely to display clean, well-lit bedrooms, the owner's absence reminds the viewer of the image of the ferry sinking, the families' anguish, and the street protests. The owner's absence and the remaining objects seem to ask the many questions that are yet to be answered. This sense of remaining expectation that the unmoved objects elicit reminds the viewer that the fight for the *Sewol* families is still ongoing.

Ye-jin's mother gives the last testimony and talks about her last phone call with her daughter when the ferry capsized:

> It was 9:44 am and she tried to explain the situation. She said that there was a helicopter outside and she was wearing a life vest and had been told to wait...but ten minutes later at 9:54 am, she started to cry. She kept saying she would make it out alive.... I scolded her, "Of course you will come out, why are you talking like it is some kind of task or something?" Then I heard shouting. I think that was when the ferry capsized. The other kids were screaming and my Ye-jin shouted "Why, why?" Then the phone went dead.

In an interview, Black Jaguar said that instead of reenacting the mothers' testimonies she would project their voices through the speakers because reenactments would create a kind of distance between the mothers and the audience, whereas she wanted to create an encounter less mediated by other figures. She believed that the rawness of the mothers' words would create a space of memory and mourning. While oral testimonies are sometimes questioned for their veracity, trauma studies scholar Dominick LaCapra argues that such testimonies and their archives can be valuable for "their distinctive relation to experience or the way events are lived; their role in the reconstruction of events, especially in the absence or paucity of other sources."[21] Because such testimonies are not visible in mainstream Korean media, performances that deliver such stories become invaluable public memory archives that document and remember death, loss, and memory. LaCapra also reminds us that traumatic memory is crucial in forming individual and collective identities. Performances like *Talking About Her* and *VEGA* become a political commentary and help form a communal consciousness and critique about the ongoing investigation.

Both *Talking About Her* and *VEGA* wed acts of remembering this specific tragedy and its individual victims to the political work of demanding government transparency, accountability, and redress with the ultimate goal of creating a safer, fairer, and more caring nation and society. These performances have come to constitute a kind of collaborative public counter-memory that undermines and pushes back against forces of government censorship, media bias, online smear campaigns, and other more subtle forms of misremembering and forgetting that proceeded the initial horror of the *Sewol* and have contributed to the marginalization and further traumatization of various categories of survivors.

SEWOL MOTHERS ON THE STAGE: THEATRE TROUPE YELLOW RIBBON

Founded in March 2016, Yellow Ribbon is composed of six women whose children perished on the *Sewol* (Gim Myeong-im, Yi Mi-gyeong, Choe Ji-yeong, Gim Do-hyeon, Bak Yu-sin, and Bak Hye-yeong) and a woman whose daughter is a *Sewol* survivor (Gim Sun-deok). The troupe works through a collaborative process and aims at creating works that address both *Sewol* and community issues. But it was not an easy journey. After the disaster, the bereaved mothers took classes on coffee and how to become baristas as part of a therapeutic workshop. At the end of the course, the mothers were offered the opportunity to participate in a theatre program. Although the mothers did not know much about or feel very enthusiastic about theatre, they said yes.[22]

In October 2015, when director Gim Tae-hyeon first met the mothers, they were not ready to perform. Their eyes were full of sorrow and they seemed intimidated. Some, who felt too pressured to perform, even quit: "When I first met the mothers, I could see that they felt guilty whenever they smiled. Because the public viewed them as victims, they expected the mothers to be sad all the time. The mothers needed to heal. You need to heal to move forward and uncover the truth. I decided to create a space where they can smile and laugh through theatre."[23] In general, mainstream news coverage in Korea branded families as victims in the public eye. Because of such representations, the public expects them to be sad all the time. But as Gim notes, this does not allow for spaces of healing. Participating in craft workshops and theatrical works helped the mothers to focus on something besides their immediate trauma while also being able to deliver the children's stories and use their agency to bring meaning to the disaster on their own terms.

Gim started workshops in which the mothers read humorous scripts. They especially enjoyed O Se-hyeok's *Geuwa geunyeoui otjang* (His and her closet), because they saw themselves in the character who was mother, wife, and fixed-term employee. Gim and the mothers adapted the play into their first production, which premiered on October 22, 2016, in Ansan, Korea. The play, which is discussed in greater detail below, can also be viewed as a *Sewol* story that takes another form. According to Gim, "The play does not directly represent the *Sewol* ferry disaster, but the audience may be reminded of it. They [mothers] could voice their opinions via hunger strikes, head-shavings, and protests, but I wanted them to deliver their stories via theatre where they could create intimacy and bond with the audience."[24] *His and Her Closet* received much media attention not only because of the plot but also because of the cast. Because the actors were the *Sewol* mothers who were also fighting for justice for their children, the audience could view a performance about people who were not protected by the law. The precarious position of fixed-term employees becomes a metaphor for the *Sewol* families. The performance's message of the need to reveal the truth about the *Sewol* was transmitted to the audience by telling stories of other vulnerable social minorities. In an interview, audience member Yi Ji-hye said that she enjoyed the performance, and after seeing it, in contrast to the sorrow and anger she had felt, she found courage to fight.[25]

In their second play, *Yiuse salgo yiuse jukgo* (Living and dying next door), the troupe asks the audience to think about the kind of neighbors they want to be and the kind of community they want to live in. Gim adapted Ryu Seong's original script by adding the *Sewol* mothers' conversations and testimonies. Approximately 40–50 percent of the original script changed.[26] "I constantly asked questions to the mothers and added their ideas into the script. For example, the scene in the workplace [where the *Sewol* mother is shunned by her coworkers] was adapted from one of the mother's experiences. The mothers also provided ideas during rehearsals, and those were added to the performance as well."[27] While the play was inspired by the *Sewol* ferry disaster and features a family member of a *Sewol* victim, it does not depict the disaster itself. Rather, it stages what happened afterward. The performance creates a space for audience members to hear what happened to the families in their own words and creates an alternative space for mourning and remembrance.[28]

After depicting the families' lives after the disaster, the troupe's third play, *Janggi jarang* (Talent show), portrays the student victims and their dreams before embarking on the school trip. Donning Danwon High School uniforms, the mothers staged stories inspired from their children. And the troupe's fourth play, *Gieok yeohaeng* (Memory trip), looks back at what the families experienced in the past eight years and two administrations. Featuring an inanimate object (the yellow ribbon) as the narrator, the play delineates the families' protests and struggles to conduct a thorough investigation and reveal the truth about the disaster.

Most recently, the troupe's fifth play, *Yeonsok, geuk* (Continuing, drama), portrays how the mothers go on with their lives after the disaster. Through a close examination of the troupe's five plays, we can see the transformation of the mothers and their activism within the shifting circumstances of the *Sewol* movement.

STAGING THE STRUGGLE FOR JUSTICE: *HIS AND HER CLOSET* (2016)

From January 10 to March 18, 2017, performances that criticized the Park Geun-hye administration were held at the Gonggong geukjang beullaek tenteu (Public Theatre Black Tent), a temporary public theatre founded by South Korean artists in Seoul's Gwanghwamun Square. These performances were protests against the Park Geun-hye administration for blacklisting and censoring dissident artists. Theatre scholar Jae Kyoung Kim discusses how Gwanghwamun Square became a significant space for the people's movement, and especially from 2014 to 2017 for the *Sewol* activism and commemoration.[29]

> The square established its early character associated with the people's occupation of the square and then with others visiting it as a memorial site after the *Sewol* ferry disaster. Then, it developed its identity as a dynamic public place starting with the 2016–2017 candlelight protests. Although temporarily united civic organizations initiated the candlelight protests as a result of their anger in response to Park's corruption, it was the countless citizens who voluntarily gathered in the square, developed the way to recover from this difficult situation, and spread hope for making a better nation for future generations.

On January 23, 2017, approximately fifty Koreans crowded into a temporary performance space to attend Yellow Ribbon's performance of *His and Her Closet.* It was the troupe's first production since its founding in March 2016. Among the performances staged at the Black Tent, Yellow Ribbon's *His and Her Closet* received the most attention. Written by O Se-hyeok and directed by Gim Tae-hyeon, *His and Her Closet* depicts the struggles of fixed-term employees in contemporary Korea.

The stage has a yellow closet and three blocks that serve as chairs. Before the play started, Gim Tae-hyeon came onstage. "Because this public theatre was made by us, we can stage stories about social minorities that the government hated," he said. In addition, a former fixed-term employee of Yuseong Corp. came onstage and talked briefly about the contract employees at Yuseong Corp., the labor union, and employees who had been injured at Yuseong Corp. but did not receive any compensation. After his talk, the audience clapped and cheered. During the performance, the audience could hear the traffic outside the tent. Such noises reminded the audience that they were at Gwanghwamun Square. This was significant because the *Sewol* victims' memorial altar had been erected in the square and recently transformed into an exhibition space dedicated to memory and safety.[30]

The play is about a family of fixed-term employees and their relationships with the labor union. The first part is about the father's story. He is an apartment security guard played by Yi Mi-gyeong (mother of student victim Yi Yeong-man). He is proud of his work and calls his uniform his "life partner." He is friends with another security guard (played by Bak Yu-sin, mother of student victim Jeong Ye-jin) who works alongside him. One day the apartment manager tells the two security guards, "The tenants' utility fee isn't much and there aren't any thieves during daytime so we don't need both of you." One of the security guards has to give up his job. When the manager leaves, the two security guards have a comic struggle over who gets to keep the uniform.

The father comes home and tells his wife what had happened. The wife (played by Gim Myeong-im, mother of student victim Gwak Su-in) responds that they "have to pay the increased rent, put some money aside for when the youngest son gets married, and reveal the truth about the *Sewol* ferry disaster," and she is frustrated that that her husband might lose his job. However, the father is more worried about the other security guard because "his health is not good and his family is poorer than us."

The next day, the other security guard calls in sick. Because of his absence, the father gets to keep his job. However, he never forgets his former partner. When he comes home and tells his wife what happened, they argue. "What good is friendship and loyalty when you get fired so often that we have a closet full of old uniforms!," his wife shouts as she takes out the old uniforms out of the yellow closet and throws them on the floor. From the pile, the father discovers an old denim jacket and reminisces about the past.

He reminisces about his first job where he met the other security guard. There had been an emergency at work, and he and the other security guard were asked to take care of a box. If the box went unnoticed, they would be promoted to managers. Unable to contain their curiosity, the two men opened the box and found a burnt uniform that belonged to another employee. The employee must have been injured at work, they realized, and the company was trying to cover it up. This scene refers to numerous cases in which companies take advantage of fixed-term employees who are not protected by labor laws.

At first the two men fought against the labor union in hopes of getting a promotion. They started to feel guilty, however, and then sided with the union. "The [manager's] leather jacket doesn't feel good on me," the father says, and puts on his old denim jacket. Back in the present, the father puts on his uniform and asks the other guard to go on strike with him because it is unfair for him to suddenly lose his job for no reason.

The mother's story is next. The son (played by Gim Do-hyeon, mother of student victim Jeong Dong-su) is getting ready for his first day at work. The mother tells him, "Don't take the lead just because you don't like something." Her warning may refer to the precariousness of job security in Korea. Later the mother goes to her job at a local restaurant. A fellow employee tells her that her son does not want to go to college because "half of college graduates are unemployed." The mother thinks about her past and how she raised three children while working fixed-term jobs.

When her husband gets home, she hands him a nice shirt and tells him to give it to the manager as a bribe to keep his job. "What good are partners and loyalty when your own position is insecure and precarious? Is it wrong to think about your own family?" Her questions show that it is not the individual's fault but the system's.

Finally, the son's story unfolds. At work, some colleagues convince him to go help out at the labor union meeting. At first he is not sure about whose side his beliefs and values align with, but later he goes to the gathering of Sarang Electronics' fixed-term employees. Sarang Electronics seems to represent Samsung Electronics, which is notorious for prohibiting employees from forming or joining labor unions. It was only in November 2019, fifty years after the founding of the corporation, that Samsung finally became unionized.[31]

The labor union gathering in the performance supports several issues, which are portrayed in its platform as interwoven rather than separate issues: for example, revealing the truth about the *Sewol,* recovering the ferry, revising the Special Act, extending the SIC's activity period, opposing THAAD (Terminal High Altitude Area Defense) deployment, opposing the Japan-Korea Comfort Women Agreement, and opposing the blacklist. When one of the labor union members says, "We elected the wrong president and the entire country is a mess," the audience claps and cheers. The member says, "Thank you for coming here to stand with us" and shakes hands with the audience members in the front row. It also seems that they are thanking the audience for taking interest in the *Sewol* disaster.

Later the whole family goes to the labor union gathering. They hold signs that say, "Let's make a world where labor is beautiful" and "We will uncover the truth [of the *Sewol* disaster]," and they end the performance by singing the *Sewol* song together. The performance's message of the need to reveal the truth about the *Sewol* was transmitted to the audience by staging stories of other vulnerable social minorities and social justice causes.

Performance can provide a subversive means of calling out insincere government acts of authority or care. By choosing to address the issue of precarious labor, *His and Her Closet* becomes a political commentary on a society that prioritizes profit rather than safety. This is particularly significant to the *Sewol* families because the *Sewol* ferry disaster was not an accidental event; rather, it resulted from both the neoliberal state, which abdicated its duty to protect citizens, and private businesses that exchanged safety for profit. Chonghaejin Marine Co. bought the ferry, which was no longer in use after eighteen years of service, and illegally refurbished it to allow more passengers and cargo than legally permitted, ultimately impacting the ferry's load balance.[32] According to the *4.16* Sewol *Ferry Disaster Report,* investigators learned that the overloaded cargo and lack of water in the ballast tanks made it difficult for the ferry to recover from its sharp turn. In addition, the captain and majority of the crew were temporary employees with contracts that ranged from six months to a year who had little experience with the ferry. Investigators also discovered that the damage would not have been so disastrous had the watertight doors been able to shut and the cargo stored and secured properly. Despite earning $500 million in profit in 2013, Chonghaejin Marine Co. allocated only 0.01 percent of that sum to staff safety training.

Performances like *His and Her Closet* do not stop at acknowledging and responding to harm; they also recognize the systemic causes, failures, and erasures that produce such harm. Through the performance's depiction of labor struggle and activism, the audience might be reminded of the *Sewol* families' protests. When labor reform is demanded in the performance, the audience might be reminded that justice for the *Sewol* families requires a thorough investigation that reveals why the ferry made a sharp turn and why the children were not rescued promptly as well as legal redress that punishes those responsible for the ferry's systemic failures and the bungled rescue mission. Embodied performance can surpass language and constitute interventions in public discourse that draw attention to unfair power differentials that exist between authoritative bodies such as companies and governments, on the one hand, and regular people, on the other.

In addition, performance allows participants to not remain stuck in one identity or place, which is important for moving through trauma. *His and Her Closet* allowed performers to both engage with their own trauma and also get to act as other characters; because talking about something traumatic helps one endure grief, doing so with some distance through the means of a theatre performance focused on a labor movement allowed people to process grief without being personally overwhelmed. During a Q&A session at the Seoul International Women's Film Festival on August 27, 2022, Gim Myeong-im (mother of Gwak Su-in) said that performing with the troupe helps reaffirm her identity and will to move forward with the *Sewol* activism. In addition, *His and Her Closet* helps envision possibilities of relationships between *Sewol* families, other disaster families, and the local community, who is reminded through such works to continue to pay attention to the ongoing investigation and see it as a communal issue.

PERFORMING SOCIAL WRECKAGE AND IMAGINING ITS HEALING: *LIVING AND DYING NEXT DOOR* (2017)

At a public lecture held on April 11, 2018, Gim Tae-hyeon, the director of Yellow Ribbon, explained that the troupe aims to heal wounds and deliver "4.16 values" through its performances. The number "4.16" stands for April 16, the date of the incident, and "4.16 values" are the troupe's communal goals of being considerate of neighbors and valuing communities. After their first play, *His and Her Closet,* they staged their second play, *Living and Dying Next Door,* which asks the audience to think about the kind of neighbors they want to be and what kind of community they want to live in.

The brochure for the second play had minor changes with each performance, but the overall design and layout were consistent. The design features photos of the mothers juxtaposed with cartoonish drawings, indicating the comic genre of the performance. For example, the cover shows the eight mothers, each standing on top of different buildings, appearing to be neighbors. Pages 2 and 3 show a brief introduction to the production and credits of the actors and staff members, with photos from the performance in the background:

> The existence of neighbors after the *Sewol* ferry disaster
> Some brought great pain to the *Sewol* families,
> Some gave them strength to overcome the pain,
> What do neighbors mean to the *Sewol* families?
> What kind of neighbors will we be to the *Sewol* families?
> What kind of neighbors should we be to each other?

Pages 4 and 5 introduce the mothers' names and roles. Below their photos, the mothers included short writings addressed to the audience members:

> Bak Yu-sin (Ye-jin's mom) role of Gim Yeong-gwang: I hope the world remembers our children not as those who died unfortunately on a field trip, but as children who changed the world.
>
> Choe Ji-yeong (Sun-beom's mom) role of neighborhood association leader: Through this play, I hope that those who were not interested in neighbors will think again about what a true neighbor is.

Pages 6 and 7 show the synopsis and director's statement. The director's statement seems to speak on behalf of the mothers: "We worked hard to prepare the production despite the difficult schedule of traveling back and forth to Gwanghwamun Square and Mokpo. We made meticulous notes on the script and memorized the lines and movement. The mothers put their hearts together in hope that this will help in finding the truth about the *Sewol*. We ask the audience to sympathize with the actors and become their real neighbors."

I viewed *Living and Dying Next Door* on three different occasions—on July 6, 2017; on April 5, 2018; and, finally, on December 1, 2018, at the final performance. Each performance was staged at different venues. Like Yellow Ribbon's other productions, the play toured all over Korea and was either free to the public or modestly priced so that it would attract a wide range of viewers. The play begins with an elderly man (played by Bak Yu-sin, mother of student victim Jeong Ye-jin) moving into a new neighborhood.

Four doors—numbered 101, 102, 103, and 104—and four walls zigzag across the stage. Each door represents a tenant living in a block of flats in Ansan. The old man asks for help adjusting and settling in the neighborhood, but the other tenants ignore him. After settling in on his own, the old man observes that his neighbors do not get along with each other. Several scenes in the play refer to communities in which the neighbors do not trust each other. However, the old man slowly brings the neighbors together by sharing food and starting a community garden. The neighbors start to open their hearts to the old man, except for the reclusive tenant of unit 104 (played by Gim Seong-sil, mother of student victim Gim Dong-hyeok). The neighbors tell him that her child drowned on the *Sewol* ferry:

NEIGHBOR (in a hushed voice): She's a *Sewol.* She's the family of a *Sewol* victim.
OLD MAN: So what? Why are you whispering?
UNIT 102: It's an uncomfortable subject. Let's stop talking about it.
OLD MAN: Why? I haven't even started yet.
NEIGHBOR: See? It gets uncomfortable if you talk about them.
OLD MAN: They haven't done anything wrong. Why should we whisper behind their backs?

This exchange reflects the experiences of the victims' families and the people around them. Although the bereaved families received assistance from local citizens and NGOs, they were the subjects of gossip, hate speech, rumors, and surveillance by the Park Geun-hye administration. Korean right-wing media and parties that aligned with the Park administration's policies tapped into identity politics to produce hate speech. Both the right-wing media and right-wing politicians denounced the *Sewol* victims and their families. Because most of the Danwon High School students came from Ansan, a working-class suburb, the victims' families were associated with the political left. Several scenes in the play show the spread of hate speech through gossip, media, and anonymous text messages. In the opening scene, several neighbors gossip about the tenant of unit 104: "I heard that they [victims' families] received a large sum of compensation from the government." "Something like 10 or 20 hundred million won." "They can afford to quit their jobs." "I heard that they bought an apartment with the payment and moved away." "I don't know why they are still making a fuss." In another scene, several characters receive anonymous text messages about the victims' families: "Requesting special law and compensation for a field trip accident is ludicrous!" "The father going on hunger strike didn't even live with his daughter and he used to be a member of the labor party!" The tenant of unit 104 describes overhearing her coworkers gossip about her, saying things such as "It is unfortunate for the dead children, but their families struck it rich." "Nobody has ever received such a huge compensation in the history of accidents. And it's not like they died fighting for the country." Many audience members may have heard the right-wing media and political parties publicly denounce the families, and some may even have received such text messages. As the majority of the audience was not composed of the victims' families, staging moments in which the families become targets of hate speech and rumors helped the audience learn about the families' ongoing hardships and the current state of the investigation.

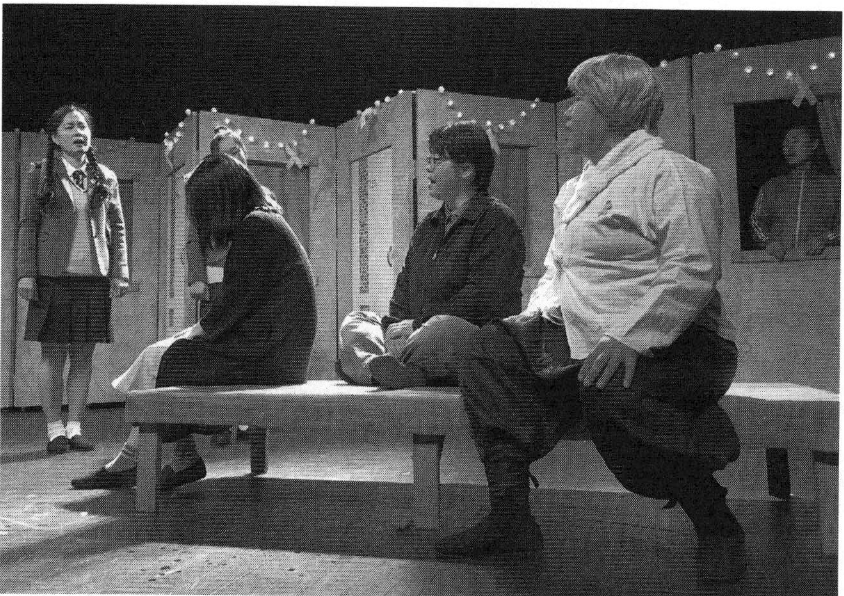

FIGURE 1.1. A scene from theatre troupe Yellow Ribbon's *Living and Dying Next Door*. In this scene, the *Sewol* mothers are singing about the aftermath of the disaster, providing an alternative space to mourn and remember the tragic incident and the victims. Directed by Gim Tae-hyeon. Photo by Areum Jeong.

Near the end of the play, it is revealed that the old man is secretly living with a son who was paralyzed in an accident. When his son has a medical emergency, the tenant of unit 104 is the first to help. The neighbors later join forces to help her rebuild her life. Ultimately, the play ends on a happy note.

The situation of communal disorder presented through this performance reflected the sad realities of dealing with neighbors and society after the sinking. At the Beyond Trauma Symposium, which was organized by the Ansan Mental Health Trauma Center, Young-Hoon Ko, the head of the center, and social work scholar Ji-Young Park each presented their recent study on the mental and physical conditions of the *Sewol* survivors and victims' families.[33] After conducting interviews and a qualitative study of the survivors and victims' families, Ko's and Park's research found that despite widespread public support, these families experienced much conflict with their own community. In addition to the spread of hate speech mentioned above, there were many arguments and clashes between the *Sewol* families and Ansan residents on issues regarding the families' protests and future plans. For example, many local residents are resistant to the idea of a memorial park, which the *Sewol* families are currently planning to construct in Ansan. Ko's study showed that more than 80 percent of the *Sewol* families experienced stress within their social relationships, and this was the biggest reason that families moved away from their home communities in Ansan. Park explained that many families experienced a sense of isolation and then, later, severance from their significant relationships with colleagues, friends, and neighbors.

Conflicts with the local community and the stress and trauma of having to relive the *Sewol* each time they participated in the investigation eventually brought about distrust toward the South Korean government and society. In a KBS interview broadcast on April 19, 2018, Choe Ji-yeong, who plays one of the neighbors, said that she moved from Ansan to Gangwon Province "because of [her] neighbors and everything was too much."[34] A program shown on EBS on April 17, 2018, reported that Choe now lives alone in a desolate area near the mountains.[35] Thus, the families' hardships, often exacerbated by social distrust and dislocation, are still ongoing.

Considering this, one might say that in providing a happy ending, the play might be seen as diminishing the reality of the families' actual lives.

That said, the play was reviewed positively by media and news outlets, who interpreted it as staging a world that the *Sewol* families wish to live in, one where they can exist harmoniously with the local community in relationships of mutual support, despite the conflicts they have experienced. In any case, it is clear that the staging of this performance created, at least temporarily, its own community of caring neighbors.

During the play, there were several moments when I saw the mothers getting choked up. However, they swallowed back their tears and focused on their performance. In those moments, I heard other audience members sniffling and stifling their sobs. After the performance, many audience members stayed back to talk to the mothers. They cried, hugged the mothers, and offered words of encouragement: "We stand in solidarity. Do not lose hope." According to many reviews on social media, it was heartbreaking to see the mothers talk about the disaster onstage, because it was not fictional; it was partly autobiographical, and they were narrating their own personal experiences. This kind of performance does

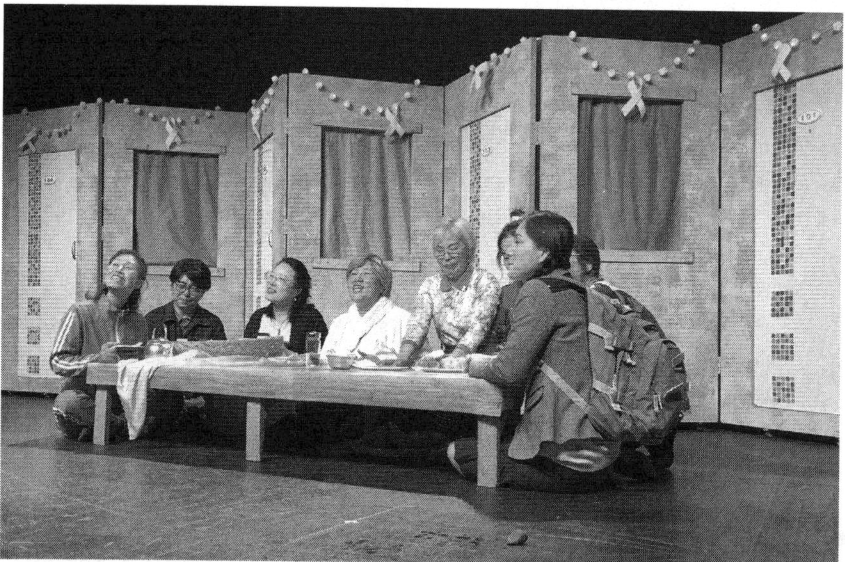

FIGURE 1.2. A scene from theatre troupe Yellow Ribbon's *Living and Dying Next Door.* In this scene, the *Sewol* mothers ask the audience to think about the kind of neighbors they want to be and what kind of community they want to live in. Directed by Gim Tae-hyeon. Photo by Areum Jeong.

not stop at documenting what happened; rather, it creates a space for audience members to hear what happened to the families through their own words. It also becomes a place for the families to heal and connect with the local community that artistic performance works can bring into being. Ultimately, this play shows, the wreckage of the *Sewol* ferry disaster comes in many forms: the trauma of loss, conflict with the local community, harassment from right-wing media and parties, a sense of betrayal and disappointment toward the government, and so on. By staging such moments of social wreckage that followed the physical wreckage of the ferry, the play strives to heal wounds—including those inflicted by society after the initial trauma—and to rebuild communities.

STAGING THE CHILDREN OF ANSAN: *TALENT SHOW* (2019)

Yellow Ribbon's third production, *Talent Show,* premiered on April 5, 2019, in Ansan, Korea. The play is a fictionalized account of five high school girls preparing a talent show in anticipation of their upcoming class trip. Inspired by Gim Sun-deok (mother of student survivor Jang Ae-jin), who wrote about her daughter's talent show during a free-writing session, the troupe decided to stage the children's stories for their third production.[36] While the troupe's previous plays had been adaptations, *Talent Show* is the troupe's first original production. Playwright Byeon Hyo-jin incorporated stories about the children's lives into the script.[37] To assume the role of high school students, the mothers wore Danwon High School uniforms.

The cover of the brochure shows the faces of seven mothers attached to drawings of school uniforms. They seem to be posing for a photo in front of a grassy background, indicating the theme of the play. On the lower left corner of the brochure is a blooming forsythia bush, hinting that the play is set in springtime. Pages 2 and 3 show the synopsis, the mothers' names and roles, and a brief introduction to the production by the playwright:

> I wrote this because I wanted to breathe life into the children through five students who were united by friendship as they prepared for a talent

> show on a school trip. This is the third work of Yellow Ribbon. I feel that the way the main character, A-yeong, holds the hand of Ga-yeon, who extended her hand first, and prepares to show off her talent with her friends is similar to our theatre company. There are various reasons, but in the end, we want to express our commitment through the girls who stand on stage with one goal. Without solidarity, there is no theatre.

The school bells chime, signaling the start of the play. A-yeong (played by Gim Myeong-im, mother of student victim Gwak Su-in) is a high school student in Ansan, a city in Gyeonggi Province, just southwest of Seoul. She views Luffy, the character from the Japanese manga *One Piece,* as her oldest imaginary friend. In several scenes, Luffy (played by Gim Dohyeon, mother of student victim Jeong Dong-su) comes to life and even offers advice to the lonely A-yeong. A-yeong observes her classmates and decides that they do not have anything in common with her; Ha-neul (played by Yi Mi-gyeong, mother of student victim Yi Yeong-man) is interested in music, Ji-suk (played by Gim Sun-deok) cares about her appearance, and Baek-hui (played by Jo Ok-hyeong) likes to swear. One day, Ga-yeon (played by Bak Yu-sin, mother of student victim Jeong Ye-jin), the class president, announces a class trip to Jeju Island the next month and tries to recruit students for the talent show. After much hesitation, A-yeong agrees to participate. The girls rehearse a cover dance to "Catallena," by the K-pop girl group Orange Caramel. For the first time, A-yeong feels a sense of belonging. When her parents cannot afford to send her on the school trip, her new friends take part-time jobs to help earn the money that A-yeong needs. The play ends with the girls eagerly leaving on their trip. While the scene is cheerful, it is also full of foreboding for the audience: When one of the students yells out, "Mom and Dad, I'll be back in three days," the audience, thinking about the *Sewol,* knows that this is not necessarily true.

Talent Show required the performers to embody students who, although fictional characters, are based on real children. To don Danwon High School uniforms and represent their children was very difficult for the mothers. In an interview with *Korean Theatre,* Gim Myeong-im said, "It breaks my heart, but I think of my son every moment on stage."[38] More so than its previous two performances, *Talent Show* engaged with directly representing those whose lives and futures were lost, asking not only the audience but also the closely related performers to focus on their lives and subjectivities. As Dori Laub reminds us, this kind of engagement has risks, as the "act of telling might itself become severely traumatizing, if the price of speaking is *re-living:* not relief, but further retraumatization."[39] Referring to theories about how the human brain does not process traumatic events in the same ways that it does other experiences, Laub explains, "Trauma survivors live not with the memories of the past, but with an event that could not and did not proceed through to its completion, has no ending, attained no closure, and therefore, as far as its survivors are concerned, continues into the present and is current in every respect."[40] In some ways, *Talent Show* might be seen as a meditation on living without closure rather than a representation of closure being already accomplished. In relation to Laub's idea of trauma's timelessness, the *Sewol* survivors and families have not found closure; their trauma is ongoing, and is even being experienced as reliving their children's last weeks and the

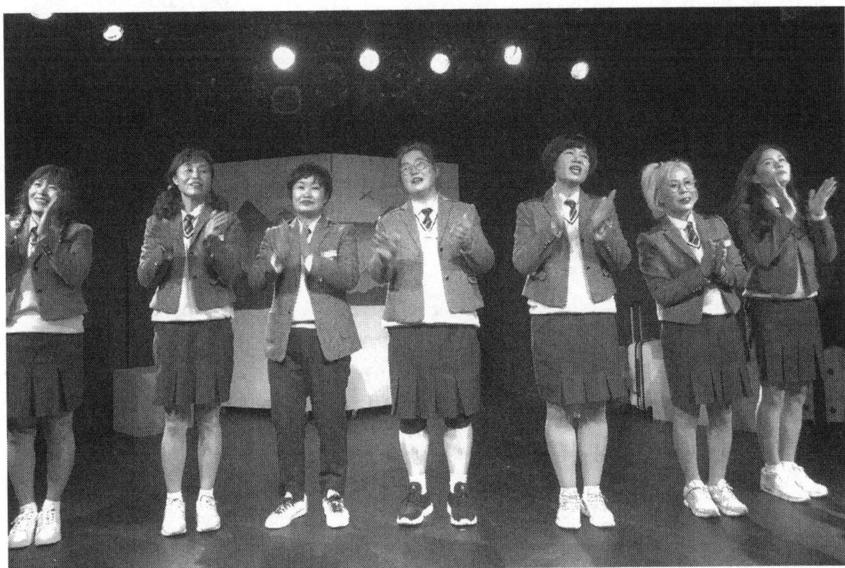

FIGURE 1.3. A scene from theatre troupe Yellow Ribbon's *Talent Show.* In the play, the *Sewol* mothers wear Danwon High School uniforms and portray the student victims before they embarked on the school trip. Directed by Gim Tae-hyeon. Photo by Areum Jeong.

foreboding moments when it was possible to imagine everything turning out differently. Sharing such scenes with an audience brings back a sense of immediacy to the *Sewol* families' ongoing fights to tell their children's stories and achieve justice. Choe Ji-yeong (mother of student victim Gwon Sun-beom) discusses the troupe's purpose, commenting that that the mothers continue the troupe's work so they can shed light on the disaster: "We want to meet people and deliver stories about our children through theatre."[41] By staging something that seems impossibly traumatic, *Talent Show* asks the viewer to remember the victims and raise awareness about the *Sewol* activism, therefore helping the mothers confront their trauma and go on with their lives. Gim Do-hyeon claims that she was able to smile again and fight for truth after joining the troupe.[42]

A TRIP DOWN THE *SEWOL* MOTHERS' MEMORY LANE: *MEMORY TRIP* (2021)

Premiered on May 29, 2021, Yellow Ribbon's *Memory Trip* depicts the *Sewol* mothers' journeys from 2014 to the present. For approximately fifty-eight minutes, the play narrates what the mothers have experienced during the past seven years. The play opens with Yi Mi-gyeong introducing herself as a yellow ribbon. By animating this significant object, the play centers the yellow ribbon as a somewhat naive character, creating a cheerful and even comical atmosphere, which can throw into sharper relief some of the more dramatic and menacing incidents experienced by the mothers.

Yellow ribbons, of course, are what many *Sewol* mothers busied their hands in making immediately following the disaster. Cultural anthropologist Nan Kim looks at how the color yellow came to define activism and dissident identity in South Korea, tracing how yellow objects have been circulated in "layered metaphorical assemblages that constituted new forms of public memory and new practices of political mobilization."[43] She sees yellow ribbons as "the things that acted as visual and material synecdoche for interrelated historical narratives"[44] and notes that they were a "public sign of remembrance and sympathy as well as an emblem of dissent among those who had defied the repression under Park."[45] Throughout the play, the mothers play roles of victims' families, politicians who used the disaster for their own interests, and local citizens who protested against the *Sewol* memorial park in Ansan. By staging some of the mothers' unforgettable moments, the audience can learn about and remember what the families experienced throughout the Park and Moon administrations.

Despite the cheerfulness of the yellow ribbon, *Memory Trip* includes heartbreaking scenes. One of these is when the mothers reminisce about the morning their children departed for the school trip seven years ago. Six mothers each tell their child to have fun on the school trip as they wave goodbye, shouting, "I miss you." While viewing the play, I found the most chilling part to be in the final act, when the yellow ribbon, played by Yi, has a conversation with the *Sewol* mothers who are protesting in the streets, trying to have a meeting with Park Geun-hye. After introducing herself as a yellow ribbon, Yi tells the mothers, "You won't be able to meet the president. The president doesn't want to meet you." When another mother asks, "When will all of this be done? When will it be the day when the truth is revealed and all those who are guilty are punished so I can face my child?" the yellow ribbon answers, "That day will come. It will come for sure." The yellow ribbon looks at the exhausted mothers, who are huddled together sleeping on the streets, and speaks in a low voice:

> "It will take a long time. A very long time. You will spend many more nights in the city square and on the streets. The calluses on your feet and palms will never heal. The people's lies and schemes will try to swallow you. You will fall down hundreds and thousands of times. The people you fight against are much more evil and merciless than you think they are. You will shed tears several more times than tears you shed before. But your voice will become stronger and you will learn how to fight and win. You will experience things you never did and meet people you never met before. Some will leave you, but some will stay by your side till the end. And when that day comes, everyone will know that the mothers and the *Sewol* victims changed our society."

As the play comes to an end, the yellow ribbon cheerfully tells the audience that we must remember what happened, and that is why we should continue the memory trip.

During the Q&A, director Gim Tae-hyeon commented that this play was the most difficult of all the plays troupe Yellow Ribbon had performed. Bak Hye-yeong (mother of student victim Choe Yun-min) added that it was so difficult to perform this play that sometimes she did not want to go on stage. She was inspired to perform, however, by the audience members who cry and laugh and think about the *Sewol*. Bak Yu-sin (mother of student victim Jeong Ye-jin) said that it was especially difficult to see the other mothers swallow back their tears while performing. For many mothers, performing their own experiences from the past seven years is traumatic because they have to relive the experiences that caused them so much sorrow.

LIFE GOES ON: *CONTINUING, DRAMA* (2023)

Yellow Ribbon's fifth production is titled *yeonsok, geuk* in the Korean language. While *yeonsokgeuk* translates to "soap opera," the title separates the term into *yeonsok, geuk*—*yeonsok* meaning "continuation" or "continuing," and *geuk* meaning "drama" or "play"—perhaps to include other interpretations as well such as the mothers' lives after the disaster. After much consideration, I translated the play's title into *Continuing, Drama,* which alludes to how the mothers' lives continue to go on without their children after the disaster.

In contrast to the previous productions' brochures, which feature cartoonish drawings, the brochure for the fifth production takes a calmer and more somber tone. The cover juxtaposes the smiling faces of seven mothers with blurry scenery photos such as raindrops, the sea, and a night view. Page 2 shows a brief introduction to the production and the mothers' names and roles. Page 3 contains the statements by playwrights Ryu Seong and Byeon Hyo-jin:

> Ryu Seong's statement: *Continuing, Drama* began with the idea of focusing on the mothers' stories, but could not be separated from their children's stories. But *Continuing, Drama* is special because it is composed of stories drawn from the mothers themselves. In other words, the mothers are both actors and writers of each episode.
>
> Byeon Hyo-jin's statement: With the upcoming tenth anniversary of the *Sewol* ferry disaster in the present in which the October 29 disaster

> (Itaewon crowd crush) is unresolved, I wrote this play because I wanted to convey how the mothers today feel and look.

The playwrights' statements reveal how the production was inspired by the mothers' stories and how the mothers' testimonies played an important role in crafting the play.

The play premiered on May 5, 2023, and I viewed the performance on May 27, 2023. Throughout the play, each mother remembers precious moments with her child, expresses her longing, and reminds viewers of their current and future tasks.

In the segment "Yo-sak, Do You Want to Go on an Adventure?," Dong-su's mother reminisces about playing mobile games with her son: "I liked the fact that I was just spending time with you, rather than playing games. Because we were friends both in reality and in games." Addressing her son by his game nickname, Dong-su's mother describes how she copes with her loss by connecting with a remnant of the time she spent with her son: "I still play the game I played with you. You are still on my friend list. It has been so long since you have been online that you are at the end of the list. My friend Yo-sak. Yo-sak, do you want to go on an adventure? Dong-su, *eomma* is bored. Let's go on an adventure with *eomma*."

Dong-su's mother does not forget to remind the viewer of her primary responsibility: "Dong-su, whatever *eomma* does, she does it until the end. I am good at playing games and even better at fighting. In the game, you become a tank and protect *eomma*, but if something happens to you, *eomma* will fight until the end." The resolved message to her son reveals her unrelenting will to fight for legal redress.

In the segment "My mother Gim Myeong-im," Su-in's mother imagines conversing with her son who perished. Played by Yeong-man's mother, Su-in describes his mother as if he is looking down from heaven: "Hello, my name is Bak Su-in, 2nd grade, class 7, at Danwon High School. Today I am going to talk about my mom, who people don't know much about. She is quiet, kind, and shy. Well, people know her as that kind of person. But that is not everything about my mom." By focusing on the mothers' characteristics and stories, the play helps audience members imagine the mothers as individuals with their own goals. This kind of depiction goes against the media's tendency to reduce the mothers to "*Sewol* mothers" and the ways it flattens the victims' families.

Su-in's mother also provides testimonies of the difficulties she experienced after the disaster: "That is the most difficult. I mean smiling. Since Su-in is no longer around, *eomma* feels like she cannot smile anymore. No one will say anything if you cry, but what will people think if you smile? Why is that mother smiling like that when she lost her child? Wouldn't they think so?" This might remind the viewer of the troupe's second play, which portrays the conflicts between the *Sewol* families and local residents and the stress and trauma the mothers had experienced.

At the end of the segment, Su-in's mother imagines a conversation with her son.

> "Su-in, you have been very upset because of *eomma,* right?"
>
> "No. People may not know *eomma,* but I know *eomma.* I learned a lot from *eomma.* My *eomma* was the best *eomma* to me. I was really happy to be born as *eomma*'s son."

While such an exchange between a *Sewol* mother and her child is impossible to achieve, it is through performance that this kind of impossibility can be imagined. It reminds the viewer of the mothers' lived experiences and wishes.

In the segment "Some Night," Sun-beom's mother recollects her activism of the past nine years: "*Eomma* went on a march. *Eomma* shaved her head. *Eomma* went on a hunger strike. *Eomma* put on a play. *Eomma* made butterflies. And *eomma* lives with yellow hair."

In addition to *Sewol* activism, she describes how she stands in solidarity with families of other disaster victims:

> "Sun-beom, *eomma* met the Itaewon families today. When I looked at those people, I felt like I looking at myself. It is frustrating and painful because we are the same. My mind sways dozens of times a day. When I feel like giving it all up, I become scared of myself. Don't worry, though. *Eomma* made a promise to my son. Son, do you trust *eomma*? You do, right? *Eomma* will never give up. One butterfly a day.
>
> "To the bereaved families of the October 29 Itaewon disaster, this is Choe Ji-yeong, Gwon Sun-beom's mother. I know that no matter what I say now, you will not hear or feel it. I fully understand that. There may be a long way to go. Time and time again, it will feel like the world is falling apart and you might not want to hold anyone's hand. Still, if you

> stretch out your hand, I will remain within your reach. I know mothers, and parents never give up. And the world we hope for will come. So let's fight together until the end. Let's go together."

The *Sewol* parents' will to stand in solidarity with families of the Itaewon crowd crush was born not only of their personal experience and trauma but also because the *Sewol* families received much support from families of other disasters, which I detail in the next chapter. Just as Sun-beom's mother narrates her experience of meeting the Itaewon families, the *Sewol* families assisted the Itaewon families in tasks to seek redress, as they have already undergone everything that the Itaewon families will come to experience.[46] By lending support to someone who is going through another disaster that could have been prevented, Sun-beom's mother shows empathy and the performances of care the troupe portrayed in their second production.

Similar to the other mothers, Sun-beom's mother calmly states her will to continue with her activism: "What a night, kids. It is a night when the sky is all yellow and butterflies are flying around. On nights like this, I do not hear people saying they wish we would stop, or feel the pressure of having to do something more. I just think, oh, the yellow dye looks good. Then my dark heart will ease a little. My yellow dye looks good today. Then I guess I should finish my job, right?" Her soliloquy reveals that after ten years of activism, the mothers have become stronger and now know how to live with their trauma. Just as the Yellow Ribbon says in the fourth production, the mothers have "become stronger and learned how to fight." This is also noticeable in the stories of Yeong-man's mother, in the next segment, who chooses to pursue her dreams in addition to the *Sewol* activism.

In the segment "I Really, Really Want to Do So Many Things," Yeong-man's mother asks the audience, "Would you like to hear my bucket list?" as she describes how her life continued after the disaster:

> "Every day when I open my eyes, I miss my child so much. In times like that, it would be nice if he could appear and show me his face, even if it is just in my dream. I have not been able to see him these days. But a long time ago, he appeared in a dream, and that dream was so sad.... A dream that cannot be drawn, touched, held, or seized. Even in my dream, the happy moment is short-lived. I dream, knowing you will leave again. Out

of regret, I endlessly cup your face, hug you tightly, and take a picture with you, feeling happy for a moment. Instead of holding on to you, I send you off and tell you to come visit again. And then I wake up feeling sad that it was just a dream. I cry silently while thinking about the happy moments, trying not to forget them. If you appear in my dreams again, I wish I could just hold you tight so you don't leave. Every day, I dream a dream that cannot come true.

"I never imagined that I would become a person like this, singing and reciting poetry onstage. At first, after losing my Yeong-man, I had so much anger in my heart. I was more hardworking than anyone else, but why did this happen to me? I was so angry and resentful of going through such an unimaginable misfortune that I cursed and complained, hoping the whole world would be ruined. I was angry at this irresponsible country that did not protect the lives of its citizens, but actually I was angry at myself. If I had been a better person, I would not have lost Yeong-man. Isn't it because I am not a rich mother, a powerful mother, which is why I lost Yeong-man? I blamed, resented, and hated myself. Then I met you who became another special member of our family, who always supports the bereaved families, who suffers and accompanies us, and who always stays by our side. If it weren't for the comfort and warmth you gave me, I wonder if I would have been able to survive this. I think that the greatest gift my Yeong-man gave me when he left was you, precious people.

"So I came up with a stage name after my Yeong-man passed away—Like the Sun. What this means is, that just like you, who always shine brightly like the sun, I should always shine brightly on those around me, so I named myself Like the Sun.

"*Eomma* will live like the sun. I will never hide in the dark again, I will never be overcome by sadness, and I will never cry in despair. I will shine brighter than anyone else and live happily. I want to listen to the voice of my heart, pursue my dreams every day, and live the new life that my Yeong-man has gifted me. I will find my passion and pursue my dreams. Until the day I go to your side, *eomma* will live a more fulfilling life than anyone else in the world. Like the sun."

Despite the trauma of losing her child, Yeong-man's mother reveals her desires and is determined to pursue her dreams. By doing so, she challenges the stereotypical idea that disaster families should merely grieve and mourn.

In the segment "Practicing Memories," Yun-min's mother and sisters describe how they remember a family member who passed away.

> "After the accident, I became very confused because Yun-min, who shared the same room and slept in the same bed as me, disappeared. Is it okay to be hungry? Is it okay to sleep? Is it okay to eat? Is it okay to meet a friend? Is it okay to laugh? Is it okay to cry? Every place and every object in my house is filled with memories of Yun-min. That is why I miss you so much. Is it okay to do that? On the day of Yun-min's funeral, *eomma* told us that when you miss Yun-min, you should not avoid it. If you avoid crying or being sad, our Yun-min will be remembered as a sad child. Then she will gradually be forgotten. So, let's talk about everything."
>
> "Let's talk about our memories of Yun-min often and remember her fondly. Only then will our Yun-min will be with us forever."
>
> "I was so grateful that *eomma* said that. Because I know how to live from now on. That is how I was able to endure it."

Testimonies of siblings of *Sewol* victims are not as common as those of parents. These young people have undergone much stress and trauma, as they were subject to hate speech and rumors while having to put on a brave face for their parents.

In the play's last segment, "Actor Gim Sun-deok's Solidarity/Story (or Journey)," Ae-jin's mother describes survivor's guilt and how she stands in solidarity with the mothers of the *Sewol* victims.

> "How great it would have been if we had met and put on a play merely as a hobby.
>
> "We constantly save each other, both onstage and in real life. Save and save again. That is why Gim Sun-deok, who is both a family member of a *Sewol* ferry survivor and a member of Yellow Ribbon, can be onstage again.
>
> "One day in 2014, Ae-jin said, *eomma,* I never thought something like this would happen to me. *Eomma* didn't know either. I am sorry. *Eomma,* why didn't my friends come back? *Eomma* does not know either. I am sorry. *Eomma,* I need to know the truth. *Eomma,* please join us. Please help reveal the truth until the end. Yes, *eomma* knows what she has to do from now on.
>
> "This was a promise to Ae-jin, a promise as a mother who lives in this

> world, and a promise to the mothers of the troupe. A promise that would not have been easy to keep if I had been alone. I want to live well, eat well, and speak well next to the mothers, who reached out to me, who felt the nervousness of my first performance with me, who consoled me not to cry onstage, and who danced and sang and ran around with excitement."

Gim Sun-deok bravely finished her soliloquy with tears in her eyes. Her story reveals how families of survivors struggle with survivor's guilt and a different kind of responsibility and trauma. These testimonies are honest and sincere stories written by the mothers themselves. These are not just performances but also living archives and memorials of their activism.

In this chapter we have seen how the *Sewol* ferry disaster became a turning point on the South Korean performance scene and how Korean performance makers struggled to depict the disaster yet ultimately worked with parents, especially mothers, to find a way forward. The chapter has examined two performance pieces adapted from testimonies by the *Sewol* mothers—*Talking About Her* (2016) and *VEGA* (2016)—and Yellow Ribbon's five performances—*His and Her Closet* (2016), *Living and Dying Next Door* (2017), *Talent Show* (2019), *Memory Trip* (2021), and *Continuing, Drama* (2023)—and showed how theatre and political activism intersect with each other, serving as a memory archive and political commentary, and contributing to social change. While the impact of the theatrical performances and their contributions to social change might not be seen immediately, the audience members who sympathize with the mothers' pain and empathize with their depression and trauma stand in solidarity with the families. Some might even become encouraged to pay more attention to the Special Investigation or attend the families' future activities. In addition, this research analyzed the staging of the *Sewol* mothers and how such representations highlight the gendered role of mothers in South Korea while also showing how activist mothers are challenging social structures by demanding recognition of their trauma and changes that will offer true redress.

In *Talking About Her* and *VEGA*, the interviewers/performers and audience members become listeners to the mothers' testimonies, bearing witness to their trauma. The performances that deliver such stories become invaluable public memory archives that document and remember death, loss, and memory. The artists create a redressive arena that neither glorifies the mothers nor makes them into a spectacle. While both *Talking About Her* and *VEGA* consist of testimonies by the *Sewol* mothers, *Talking About Her* chooses to reenact the mothers' testimonies, and *VEGA* delivers the rawness of the mothers' words. In their testimonies, the bereaved mothers blamed themselves for not taking better care of their children and regretted not seeing or touching their children's dead bodies. The mothers' grief stems from parents' societal gender roles in South Korea, where mothers perform the majority of care labor and find meaning in the achievements of their husbands and children.

Yellow Ribbon's first production, *His and Her Closet,* depicts social minorities, who are not protected by South Korean laws, as a metaphor for the *Sewol* victims and families. The performance's staging at the Black Tent critiques the Park administration's neo-authoritarianism, and it represents vulnerable social minorities' reimagining of justice. While the language of law is lacking, embodied performance can transcend language and constitute interventions in public discourse that contribute to social change. *His and Her Closet* left a deep impact on many audience members because it was the *Sewol* mothers' first theatrical performance. It challenged the popular belief that disaster victims should always grieve and mourn. Although the mothers came together under unfortunate circumstances, they continue to expand motherhood activism in Korea. They express positive energy as active resistance through craft workshops and theatrical performances, extending representations of motherhood politics. While the mothers' activities are arguably gendered, they are one of the many strategies and tactics that they use to step outside the boundaries of traditional motherhood and to transform their grief into political activism. Yellow Ribbon's second production, *Living and Dying Next Door,* documents and critically represents political and social issues, serving as a memory archive that resists the government and media's attempt to erase the *Sewol* ferry disaster. The performance also becomes a political commentary, critiquing the censorship and neo-authoritarian rule of the Park administration. Moreover, Yellow Ribbon's works are based on the aesthetics of and approaches to community art through collaboration and dialogical approach and practice, aiming for a sustainable community. Their performances try to make sense of the disaster, to identify with the victims' families, and to think about how to solve the structural problems of contemporary Korean society. By staging characters based on the student victims, Yellow Ribbon's third and fourth production, *Talent Show* and *Memory Trip,* remind the audience of the families who are fighting for justice. By representing the victims and their mothers through performance, the play conveys the families' struggles to achieve justice, the questions that remain to be answered, and the problems that the South Korean government needs to solve. Finally, Yellow Ribbon's fifth production, *Continuing, Drama,* draws on the mothers' stories and shows the transformation of the mothers and their activism.

Ten years after the disaster, the *Sewol* families are told that they need to accept the past and move on. The families' fight for justice, the memorialization of the disaster, and the staging of the mothers do not conform to public opinion today. Philosopher Walter Benjamin reminds us that history is not the accumulation of "homogenous, empty time, but time filled by the presence of the now" and contends that the remembrance of past events determines how future histories might be shaped.[47] As such, the performances I examined document and memorialize the disaster, engaging with the past so they can determine how past events are recorded and represented. Without the representations of the families' pain and suffering, and their quest for justice, history becomes "homogenous, empty time."

Despite their sorrow, *Sewol* parents have become ardent activists. Even after Park Geun-hye's impeachment, the parents continued to attend events and protest in front of the Blue House, demanding that the Moon Jae-in government and the liberal party keep their promise to conduct a thorough investigation and reveal the truth about the *Sewol.* The parents have also come out in favor of other causes, such as support for wartime comfort women and commemorations of the Gwangju Democratic Uprising. Their tireless participation arose from their determination to create a better society, one that values life and safety.

CHAPTER 2

Memorializing Through Performance

Site-Specific Performances with Objects in Ansan and Paengmok Port

After the *Sewol* ferry capsized, the South Korean people began to view two geographic locations differently than they had before: Ansan, the student victims' hometown, and Paengmok Port, where the families waited for divers to retrieve their children's bodies, became closely associated with the *Sewol* disaster in the public imagination. Ansan, a city located south of Seoul and well-known for its multicultural demographic due to migrant laborers, now represents the *Sewol* and its student victims. It is where the student victims grew up and went to school, and where many of their families continue to live. It is also where the *Sewol* memorial park will be built. Despite the support victims' families have from the local community, the memorial park has been a cause for dispute between the *Sewol* families and other residents of Ansan as well as a lightning rod for conflict on the national stage, where right-wing media and politicians have spread hate speech and rumors about the park for their own interests. Situated on the southern coast of South Korea, Paengmok Port has also become a site of both commemoration and contestation. Emerging immediately after the *Sewol* as a space of collective mourning, even after the children's bodies were found, numerous Koreans visited Paengmok Port to pay their respects, leaving yellow ribbons in memory of the victims. But the subsequent development of the port has sparked clashes over whether and how the *Sewol* should be memorialized there.

In the wake of the *Sewol,* activists and artists created memorials that document the victims—or, rather, their absence—and the people who remember them. While these works emerged across the country, and internationally as well, Ansan and Paengmok Port were central staging grounds for commemorative acts and performances. With the passage of time and government stonewalling threatening to submerge memories of both the tragedy and the protest movements it inspired, activists and artists have sought to memorialize not only the event and its victims but also the demands for accountability and redress the *Sewol* inspired, which they have kept alive through exhibits and performances staged at or near these emotionally and politically charged sites. Documenting and analyzing works that unfolded in Ansan and Paengmok Port, this chapter combines tools of close reading and participant observation to explore how site-specific performances have sought to memorialize and make meaning out of the disaster.

First, analysis of three performances staged in Ansan bring the city to the fore as a space that documents and remembers the disaster and the lives its victims led there before the tragedy. *The Children's Room* is a photography exhibition that showcases the bedrooms of 188 of the students who perished on the *Sewol*. Each room is absent its owner, who can never return. In place of their owners, the objects left behind perform and experientially affect the viewers. This project frames those moments in which the room is stilled in relationship to the performative objects and the photographic medium. Next, the *Sewol* commemorative classrooms document the student victims' absence and remind the viewer that the tragedy is ongoing. *Camino de Ansan,* an annual pilgrimage project that began in 2015, invites the participants to walk the streets of Ansan and asks them to remember the victims and families through embodied performance.

Second, this chapter provides a close reading of performances at Paengmok Port, focusing on how artists have sought to commemorate the lost lives in the space in which the victims' families experienced overwhelming sorrow and trauma in the immediate aftermath of the disaster. In 2015's *Blanket Project,* eighteen Korean artists borrowed a blanket that several victims' families had used while waiting at Paengmok Port for the divers to retrieve their children's bodies. The artists took turns using the blanket to mourn and remember the victims in their own ways, and then created art. They transformed the blanket, which had given the families temporary comfort and a space to rest, into music, performance, and poetry. In Jang Geun-hui's "Laundry Day," the blanket embodies the families' pain and sorrow and the artists' hope for healing and redress.

In analyzing these works, this chapter focuses on the ways site-specific performative works utilize physical objects belonging to victims or their loved ones—namely, childhood artifacts, a blanket, and classrooms—the presence of which call attention to the disaster and its aftermath. Activists and artists go beyond enabling witnessing of the *Sewol* and its tragic aftermath by using objects to materialize ongoing loss and linking this loss to persisting structures of government malfeasance and unaccountability, which are located here in specific geographies. Through their use of objects, the creators of these works counter official narratives about the event and transmute acts of witnessing loss into a form of memorialization that centers concrete demands for truth and redress in the grounded spaces of South Korea's most multicultural neighborhood and the land closest to the site of the *Sewol*'s sinking.

WITNESSING OBJECTS TO COUNTER FORGETTING

How can objects become witnesses and prevent viewers from forgetting events? How can objects perform and make viewers perform? While the use of objects to document and memorialize tragedies is relatively ubiquitous, the activist and artists' responses to the *Sewol* analyzed in this chapter show how physical objects can become invested with counter-hegemonic purposes and affects, producing truth or change in conditions marked by official disavowal of responsibility. Moving away from the notion that matter is stable and passive, scholars have debated how matter can be dynamic and hold agency. Materialism scholar Karen Barad argues that materiality is "always already a desiring dynamism, a reiterative reconfiguring, energized and energizing, enlivened and enlivening."[1] Political theorist Jane Bennett draws from philosopher Bruno Latour's idea of "actant," a source of action that can be human or not, or a combination of the two.[2] Thus, matter acts and is not necessarily a channel for human action. And through its interaction with humans, the materiality of objects can be viewed as dynamic acts in meaning-making processes.

Gender studies scholar Sara Ahmed explains that objects, or our relationships with particular objects, can perform affect:

> We are moved by things. And in being moved, we make things. An object can be affective by virtue of its own location (the object might be *here,* which is *where* I experience this or that affect) and the timing of its appearance (the object might be *now,* which is *when* I experience this or that affect). To experience an object as being affective or sensational is to be directed not only toward an object, but to "whatever" is around that object, which includes what is behind the object, the conditions of its arrival.[3]

Ahmed's notion of affective objects provides a framework in examining how *Sewol* objects act and perform affect. The case studies I examine in this chapter are not stable objects; rather, they are dynamic acts that hold cultural history and memory—experiences of the victims, memories of the families—that affect viewers.

When examining how objects document the *Sewol* and how they become witnesses to the aftermath, particularly in the works of performance artists, it is necessary to look at how objects perform affect based on national tragedies or personal experiences. Communication studies scholar Marita Sturken uses the term "cultural memory" to define "memory that is shared outside the avenues of formal historical discourse yet is entangled with cultural products and imbued with cultural meaning."[4] Sturken distinguishes between cultural memory, personal memory, and official historical discourse, stating that they do not fall within neatly defined boundaries. Cultural memory is inseparable from history. The instability or "changeability of memories" raises issues of "how the past can be verified, understood, and given meaning."[5] By examining the Vietnam War, the AIDS epidemic, and other events in America, Sturken examines how the cultural memory of such events "has been produced through a range of cultural products" and writes that these cultural products are "technologies of memory, not vessels of memory in which memory passively resides so much as objects through which memories are shared, produced, and given meaning."[6] Because memory is articulated through processes of representation, these objects are "technologies of memory in that they embody and generate memory and are thus implicated in the power dynamics of memory's production."[7] Sturken's ideas help me see how objects not only represent the *Sewol* but also hold cultural history and personal memory and are given meaning through the forms and modes of processing loss that they encourage. In addition, Sturken examines souvenirs from tourism sites that commemorate national tragedies. These objects can be viewed as "emblems of the ways that American culture processes and engages with loss."[8] I find Sturken's ideas useful in reconfiguring how objects associated with the *Sewol* victims or their families are memorials to the *Sewol.*

Literary critic and scholar Susan Stewart reminds us that we cherish souvenirs because they hold singular experiences:

> We might say that this capacity of objects to serve as traces of authentic experience is, in fact, exemplified by the souvenir. The souvenir distinguishes experiences. We do not need or desire souvenirs of events that are repeatable. Rather we need and desire souvenirs of events that are reportable, events whose materiality has escaped us, events that thereby exist only through the invention of narrative. Through narrative the souvenir substitutes a context of perpetual consumption for its context of origin. It represents not the lived experience of its maker but the "secondhand" experience of its possessor/owner.[9]

While the objects I examine in this chapter are not exactly souvenirs, Stewart's theorization is useful in viewing the significance of the objects, and how and what they perform. Stewart's theorization of how objects work to narrativize experiences is also important here, especially when combined with scholarship on time. I argue that the objects hold multiple temporalities—of the original owner, of the families who cherish them, of the artist who uses them in performances, and of the audience member who tries to make sense of the disaster. The victims' families, especially, struggle to make sense of the disaster by obsessively investigating, studying, and revising the timeline of April 16, 2014. We might say that the time of the victims' families operates differently from that of other families. Gender studies scholar J. Halberstam theorizes about "queer uses of time and space" that develop according to other logics of location, movement, and identification.[10] Halberstam writes that queerness is "an outcome of strange temporalities, imaginative life schedules, and eccentric economic practices," allowing one to imagine alternative relations to time that move away from normative temporalities.[11] Imagining the time—or, rather, the defamiliarization of time—of the victims' families in relation to Halberstam's idea of queer temporalities allows for an examination of the *Sewol* objects' multiple temporalities and of the families' imaginings of alternative relations to time. Importantly, these non-normative relations contain challenges to official timelines of the disaster and common exhortations that families or the nation needs to "move on."

Performance studies scholar Elizabeth W. Son examines how memorials invite "performances of care," embodied acts that materialize concern and interest by providing for the needs of or looking after what one is caring for—in this case, memorials. In her research on comfort women activism in South Korea and the diaspora, Son analyzes how the bronze statue of the girl evokes the survivors' fight for justice and how the materiality of the statue elicits embodied engagements and performance care.[12] Son's work helps me see how the *Sewol* objects elicit care by families, supporters, and local citizens via spectatorship, written notes, yellow ribbons, theatrical performances, and petitions.

While there has been much academic interest in the psychological symptoms of the *Sewol* survivors and bereaved families, what has been less examined, with only a few exceptions, is how objects and performative works represent the *Sewol* and shape responses to it that seek to engage care in and through arenas of politics, policies, and projects rather than only through personal feelings and relations. Cultural anthropologist Nan Kim looks at how the color yellow came to define activism and dissident identity in South Korea, tracing how yellow objects have been circulated in "layered metaphorical assemblages that constituted new forms of public memory and new practices of political mobilization."[13] She suggests thinking of yellow ribbons as "the things that acted as visual and material synecdoche for interrelated historical narratives," arguing that the yellow ribbons provided a "public sign of remembrance and sympathy as well as an emblem of dissent among those who had defied the repression under Park."[14] Art historian Hong Kal examines how Korean artist Hong Sungdam represents the *Sewol* in his art and analyzes how his paintings translate affect, triggering an empathic response that moves viewers.[15] Theatre critic Yang Geun-ae argues that Korean theatre practitioners sought ways to overcome their sense of depression and helplessness and create a space for communal redress.[16] Theatre practitioner Seong Ji-su's dissertation looks at how the *Sewol* reconfigured Korean theatre, shifting the roles and relationships among audience, creators, and space.[17] Through a close reading of how objects document and memorialize the *Sewol,* I contribute to the growing literature and analyze how art and theatre contribute to *Sewol* activism and commemorate the disaster. In addition, this study will contribute to disaster studies of how material remains become memorials.

ANSAN, THE CITY WITH 250 HOLES IN ITS HEART

Ansan is known across South Korea as a particularly diverse city. It is diverse ethnically and culturally, because beginning in the 1990s migrant workers from China, Indonesia, Sri Lanka, and Vietnam flocked to Ansan to find work. Even before it became known for the *Sewol* ferry disaster, Ansan had been through difficult times. Due to the 1990s manufacturing recession and the 1997 Asian financial crisis, which greatly affected Korea's economy, many domestic workers left Ansan, and migrant workers began to fill vacant positions. By 2009, appproximately 33,000 migrant workers from fifty-six countries were living in Ansan.[18] The Korean government designated the Won-gok-dong area in Ansan, where migrant workers are most concentrated, as Korea's first and only "multicultural village special zone." Ten years after this designation, the number of migrant workers living in Ansan had increased to more than 86,000 from 108 countries.

When the *Sewol* struck, with so many of the victims' families concentrated so heavily in just one city, it created many dilemmas about how to articulate the relationship between Ansan and the disaster. On the one hand, families and supporters often felt an intense need to mark what had happened in local ways and in local spaces, to show how the tragedy had impacted a specific local community. On the other hand, concerns emerged about what it would mean economically and politically for Ansan to be physically connected to the disaster through memorial works and spaces. One place these competing desires and agendas were made visible was in the battle over whether or not to preserve the victims' classrooms at Danwon High School. After disputes between the families of deceased and surviving students, the commemorative classrooms were moved temporarily to the Ansan Office of Education in 2016, then moved permanently to the 4.16 Institute of Democratic Citizenship Education (also located in Ansan) in 2021.

Another, more extensive disagreement centered on the construction of a memorial park.[19] The 4.16 Families for Truth and a Safer Society and NGOs argued that the memorial park should be built within the Hwarang Amusement Park in the victims' hometown, Ansan. However, when some construction associations denounced the memorial park and remarked that the presence of such a depressing "ossuary" would cause land prices to drop, conflicts between the *Sewol* families and Ansan residents arose. The city of Ansan plans to build a 23,000-square-meter memorial park within the 618,000-square-meter Hwarang Amusement Park. The controversial altar would take up only 660 square meters. Victims' families tried to persuade residents who opposed the project. Right-wing politicians denounced the victims' families and the memorial park, however, especially during local elections. For example, the campaign poster of Yi Min-geun, the mayoral candidate of the Liberty Korea Party in 2018, read, "Building a shrine in the Hwarang Amusement Park is a way to make Ansan a gloomy city forever." Even more outrageously, the campaign poster of Yi Hye-gyeong, mayoral candidate of the Bareunmirae Party in 2018, read, "When a dog dies, do we keep it in the house?" This shows how political parties use hate politics based on discrimination and exclusion against underprivileged groups. Although the South Korean government has approved the budget for the memorial park, there is still some local resentment.

A ROOM NO LONGER OF ONE'S OWN: *THE CHILDREN'S ROOM*

The Children's Room is an online photography exhibition organized by *Ohmynews,* a local Korean online news website, and two local *Sewol* NGOs.[20] Sixteen photographers—Gim Min-ho, Gim Shin, Gim Hong-gu, No Sun-taek, Bak Gim Hyeong-jun, Bak Seung-hwa, Seong Dong-hun, Yi Wu-gi, Yi Jae-gak, Yim Tae-hun, Jeom Jom-ppae, Jeong Yeong-gu, Jo Wu-hye, Jo Jin-seop, Choe Hyeong-rak, and Heo Ran—photographed the childhood bedrooms of student victims after the disaster. The homepage introduces the exhibition: "After the *Sewol* ferry disaster, 304 rooms became empty and 304 dreams disappeared. To document this absence, *Ohmynews* prepared the online exhibition *The Children's Room* with the 4.16 Memory Archive and 4.16 Family Committee." Since April 2015, millions of people have viewed this exhibition.

The Children's Room showcases 188 rooms. Each of the 188 thumbnails has the name of a student victim and a view of his or her room, arranged in Hangeul (Korean alphabetical) order. In addition to the photos of the students' rooms, there are brief text descriptions introducing each student and close-ups of his or her possessions, mainly books, clothes, photos, and ID cards, and so on.

On first glance, all of the rooms look alike. But upon closer inspection, what distinguishes each room is a close-up of objects that represent the student's dreams or hobbies. Accompanying short messages written by the victim's family also tell the deceased student's story.

In addition to commemorating the student victims, *The Children's Room* helps viewers imagine them as individual students with their own dreams and goals. In contrast to mainstream Korean media's tendency to reduce all 250 student victims to "Danwon High School students," here the viewer learns not only individual names but also personalizing details. For instance, "(Go) Wu-jae wanted to become an engineer like his father. During his first year in high school, he participated in the International Robot Olympiad's Gyeonggi-wide competition." This text appears next to a close-up photo of a model plane that Wu-jae had built. On student victim Gim Ju-a's desk there is a list of daily goals: "Read more... be more diligent... be on time... get better grades... be good to my parents... always do my best." Pyeon Da-in had kept a timeline of her life, beginning with her date of birth: February 2, 1997. She had imagined herself as someone who "graduates from Seoul National University in 2019, opens her own animal hospital, gives birth to her first child in 2028, second child nine years later, meets her first granddaughter in 2052, and dies in April 2075." Each entry, handwritten in ink in different colors, shows how Ju-a and Da-in imagined particular stages in their lives and expected to meet each goal. However, the students' lives had stopped before they reached their goal of "2016, graduates from high school."

Each room is absent its owner, who can never return. In place of their owners, the objects left behind perform and experientially affect the viewers. The dreams or goals that the objects had represented stopped on April 16, 2014.

The viewer of *The Children's Room* is unable to imagine the future of what these objects had previously represented. As Halberstam's notion of queer temporality helps us understand alternative relations to time, the inability to imagine the future can be seen as a defamiliarization of time. In addition, Judith Butler's notion of melancholia as an internalization of and identification with loss helps us view these objects as objects of melancholia, characterized by unresolved anger and love and the refusal to let go.[21] In these ways, *The Children's Room* helps to contextualize and communicate both the emotions and activism of *Sewol* parents, including their investigatory activism into the timeline of the disaster. Unable to move forward without a thorough investigation revealing why the ferry capsized and why the passengers were not rescued promptly, which Park's administration foreclosed through its hindering of the Special Investigation Commission's efforts, the families became ardent activists and researchers themselves, tirelessly meeting with scientists to discuss possible scenarios and compiling information to reconstruct the timeline of April 16, 2014. For the past ten years, the families have had one goal: to figure out what happened and why. Each time I attended a seminar or talk sponsored by the *Sewol* families and supporters, I received a brochure that delineated the timeline of the incident. In each new brochure, I could see that the timeline had become more elaborate in detail. Until the families learn what happened to their children, they cannot move on; their time remains stopped on April 16, 2014. At the same time, April 16, 2014, is not allowed to be relegated to the past, as these brochures keep in step with the present, showing this to be an ongoing disaster in terms of its unresolved state.

This project frames those moments in which the room is stilled in relation to the performative objects and the photographic medium. According to Susan Sontag, photographs can be both an impartial "record of the real" and a "witness to the real" that holds the photographer's point of view.[22] In a similar manner, *The Children's Room,* with the stillness of its depicted rooms, documents the owner's absence and becomes a visual commentary that memorializes the dead and missing while also calling attention to the time that has passed without resolution. Holocaust and genocide studies scholar Stephenie Young explains how photography organizes and documents death through the "forensic imagination."[23] I borrow Young's idea of a performative moment when the original definition of the document, a teaching tool, is combined with or read through the vehicle of artistic creation, to consider a type of document that returns to its original meaning, "to teach," and is something that opens up discussion rather than shutting it down. By documenting the victims' rooms, the photos reveal the temporal rupture of the dreams the objects represented for their owners. This rupture also draws our attention to the many complications and disturbances surrounding the disaster's temporalities and its unresolved state: the "golden time" that elapsed, the presidential documents that contain information about the immediate hours and days after the incident, the three years it took to raise the sunken ferry from the sea, and the past eight years of censorship by the Park administration and neglect by the Moon administration. The families' tireless reconstruction of the timeline is their way of making sense of the disaster; their participation in this exhibition, especially through the donation of now-beloved memorial objects, was essential to the construction of its meanings. Although the photos seem to merely display clean, well-lit bedrooms that are cared for by families, the owners' absence and the objects that remain seem to ask the many questions that have yet to be answered, while still reminding the viewer that the fight for the *Sewol* families, the keepers of these rooms, who remain present and deserving of care and justice, is still ongoing.

WE WILL ALWAYS REMEMBER YOU: THE *SEWOL* COMMEMORATIVE CLASSROOMS

The *Sewol* commemorative classrooms are ten preserved classrooms at Danwon High School that were used by the students who perished. Since the incident, their desks have been covered with flowers and letters from families, friends, and strangers. When three hundred new students were admitted for the spring semester of 2016, however, the school announced that the commemorative classrooms were no longer going to remain preserved. When the victims' families and local NGOs protested, the other parents demanded that the classrooms be returned to use, arguing that "the school is not just a space for the victims. . . . While it is acceptable to remember and mourn the incident, it is problematic for the current students. Not only is there a shortage of classrooms, but the current students are also suffering from anxiety, depression and guilt, and are not able to receive a normal education."[24] The victims' families and local NGOs responded that they "could not let the school move the commemorative classrooms and remove the remnants of the victims before a thorough investigation is conducted" and suggested adding new classrooms on the third floor and in the basement of the school.[25] In November 2015, the Gyeonggido Office of Education proposed temporarily moving the commemorative classrooms and reconstructing them in a local education center near the school. Yi Jae-jeong, the superintendent of education, declared that classrooms are "a space for students, not a space for mourning" and that the decision was made "for the students and to help Danwon High School move forward."[26] On August 20, 2016, the victims' families and local NGOs moved the chairs, desks, and possessions of the deceased students and their teachers to the Ansan Office of Education, where they reconstructed the commemorative classrooms. Finally, in 2021, the classrooms were moved to the 4.16 Institute of Democratic Citizenship Education (also located in Ansan) as their permanent destination.

My first visit to the classrooms was in April 2018. At a glance, the classrooms seem to look like any others, with course schedules and list of students' duties and rules hung next to the blackboards. As I stepped into the classroom, I could see each desk covered with flowers, letters, photos, scrapbooks, and a visitor book. On the wall hangs a calendar from April 2014. Under the dates for the 15th, 16th, 17th, and 18th are the handwritten words "class trip." For these classrooms, time had stopped on April 16, 2014. Until all bodies are found and a thorough investigation—one that discovers the cause of the disaster and why the students were not promptly rescued—is conducted, the students' remnants remain frozen on that day. The remnants' temporality refers to the many questions that remain to be answered and the current state of the investigation. The classrooms and objects also produce affective responses by illustrating the relationship between the victims and their families and friends, who not only brought memorial items but have also worked to save the students' presence in these classroom from erasure.

Communication studies scholar Chaim Noy reminds us how artifacts at a heritage site perform or validate authenticity and serve as "an authen-

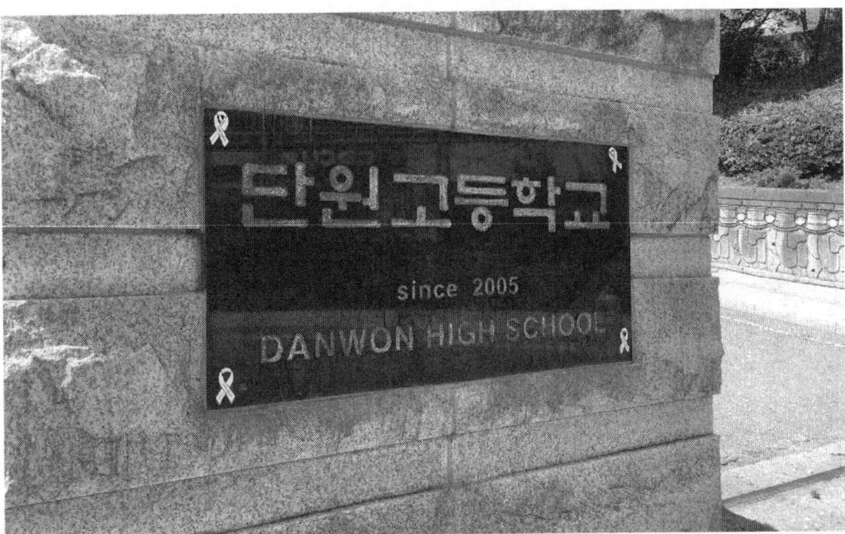

FIGURE 2.1. Danwon High School in Ansan, Korea. Four yellow ribbons are attached to the school's signpost. In addition to mourning the victims, the yellow ribbons came to represent activism and dissident identity in Korea. Photo by Areum Jeong.

ticated/authenticating surface."[27] For Noy, authenticity "often serves as a valuable resource, generating genuine performances and moving experiences," and he refers to performance as "acts that instantiate social identities and agencies."[28] Through a close examination of the artifacts exhibited at a national-military heritage site in West Jerusalem, particularly the commemorative visitor book, Noy argues that the visitor book enables a moving experience among visitors as they write and partake in the commemoration by extending their condolences. Noy's argument is useful in examining the flowers and letters and the victims' photos and personal objects in the *Sewol* memorial classrooms. For example, the letters illustrate the relationship between the victims and their families and friends: "I am so sorry and I love you so much, my child." "I miss you. I hope you are resting in peace." "We will never forget you. We will always remember you." The letters and the preservation of the chairs, desks, classroom equipment, and personal items reflect the victims' families' ongoing struggle to remember the victims. The objects produce affective responses in the viewer, who is reminded of the tragic loss. During my visit, I saw other visitors walking slowly and silently in the classroom, leaning forward to get a closer look at the photos of the deceased students and to read the letters from the families. Many visitors were crying silently, tears streaming down their faces. Later, when I talked to them, they commented how they clearly remember the day of the incident, how everything seemed surreal, and how depressed and traumatized they were just by viewing the objects. These classrooms create an open intersubjective space, inviting the viewer to experience, to walk in the classroom, read the letters from families and friends, and sign the visitor book. Through these activities, the viewer may try to make sense of the disaster and situation, because we do not know what really happened. In these classrooms we do not see the ship sinking, we do not hear the passengers' request for help, we do not see the families waiting for their children at the harbor, and we do not hear the students' anguished cries when their bodies submerged. Those are neither seen nor heard. What we see is a clean, well-lit classroom, with

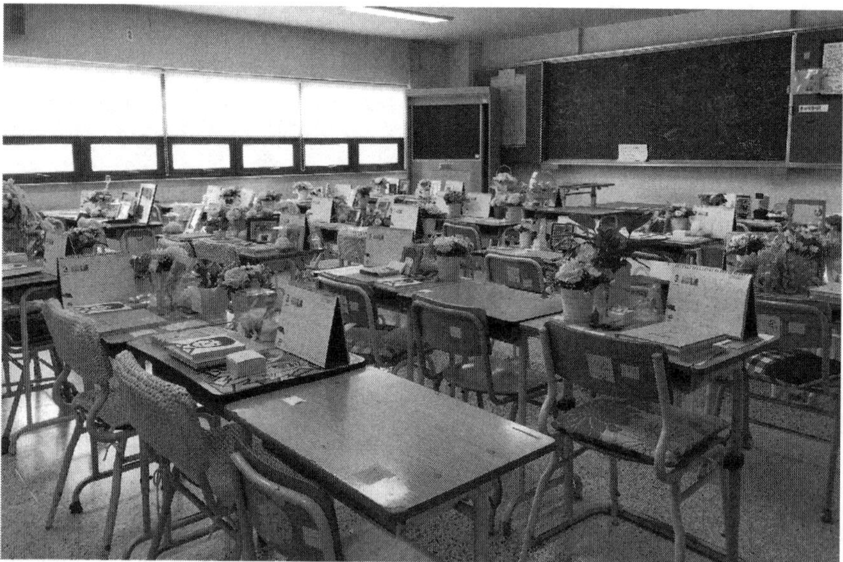

FIGURE 2.2. The *Sewol* commemorative classrooms are the ten classrooms at Danwon High School that were used by the students who perished. In August 2016, the classrooms were temporarily moved to the Ansan Office of Education. Photo by Areum Jeong.

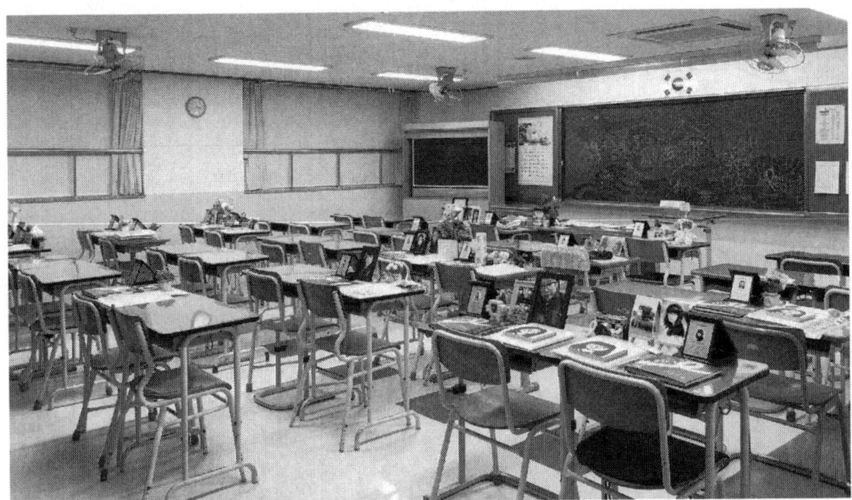

FIGURE 2.3. The *Sewol* commemorative classrooms were moved to the 4.16 Institute of Democratic Citizenship Education in 2021 as their permanent destination. Photo by Areum Jeong.

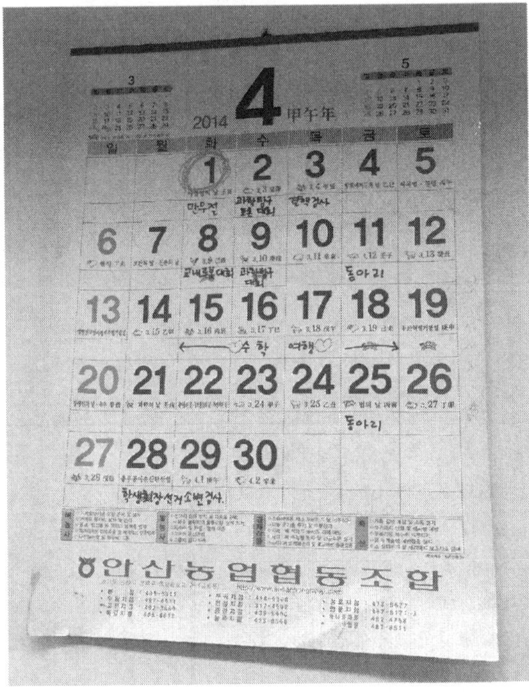

FIGURE 2.4. In one of the commemorative classrooms, a calendar from April 2014 hangs on the wall. Under the dates for the 15th, 16th, 17th, and 18th are the handwritten words "class trip." Photo by Areum Jeong.

glossy photos of smiling students and their remnants. The staging of the classroom stands in for the wreckage of the ship itself through objects that perform affect.

These classrooms function as memorials that document, record, and remember death, loss, and memory. While disaster studies scholar Scott Knowles states that memorials are usually constructed after the disaster investigation is concluded, the *Sewol* memorials are culturally specific in that they were installed shortly after the incident occurred and while the investigation was still ongoing.[29] These memorials are meaningful because their visibility to the public becomes an important factor in moving the investigation forward. Because Park's government tried to hinder the investigation, the families had to rely on public support to continue with the protests and proceed with the investigation. Projects such as the commemorative classrooms, which serve as both an artistic document and a memorial, create a commentary about how to document and memorialize the dead and missing for an audience, creating a public discourse, an alternative forum. The classrooms embody the image of *Sewol* victims, or rather their absence, in the public imagination, and they do so in different ways than the private rooms of *The Children's Room* by emphasizing the victims' identities as public school students—children supposed to be under the protection of public institutions when they died. The classrooms offer an ongoing educational message: Remembering is crucial.

CHOREOGRAPHING AND DOCUMENTING THE SPACE OF THE HOMETOWN: *CAMINO DE ANSAN*

While *The Children's Room* exhibit and preserved classrooms invite visitors into the spaces of *Sewol* victims, *Camino de Ansan,* an annual pilgrimage project that begun in 2015, invites the participants to remember the victims while choreographing and documenting the space of Ansan through site-specific embodied performance that repeats every year. In doing so, it creates a dynamic form of memorialization in which the city itself is made into a memorial space that can promote reflection on the *Sewol.*

Cultural anthropologist Victor Turner examines pilgrimage as a ritualized performance and "liminal phenomenon" where participants are united by "communitas."[30]

> We can envisage the social process involving a particular group of pilgrims during their preparations for departure, their collective experiences on the journey, their arrival at the pilgrim center, their behavior and impressions at the center, and their return journey, as a sequence of social dramas and social enterprises and other processual units to be isolated by induction from an appropriate number of cases in which there is a development in the nature and intensity of relationships between the members of the pilgrimage group and its subgroups.[31]

Turner suggests that pilgrimage enables the participant to perform in alternative positions and help construct communal consciousness. Pilgrimage can also be examined in light of performance studies scholar Diana Taylor's idea of the repertoire—ephemeral forms of embodied knowledge and practice that extend beyond the archive. In the following, I examine how *Camino de Ansan* can be viewed as a pilgrimage that uses the repertoire's bodily ways of knowing to transmit knowledge.

During each *Camino de Ansan,* participants walk approximately ten kilometers of Ansan, during which there are short breaks and drinks, snacks, and emergency medication are available to the participants. Summarizing the purpose of the event, Go Ju-yeong, the producer, and Yun Han-sol, the director, comment that the pilgrimage "is another form of remembering" and shows that "you shouldn't stop grieving."[32] The project's committee is composed of a collective of local artists from design, sound art, and theatre (Green Pig, JAT Project, Shim Bo-Seon, and Unmake Lab). Each group is in charge of selecting and leading participants through a particular area in Ansan. Importantly, this is an ongoing event: Since its start in 2015, it has been held repeatedly, with organizers ascribing evolving emotions and meanings to each successive iteration. When I participated in 2019, before the event, the committee posted this announcement of the pilgrimage on social media:

> In 2015, we were angry. In 2016, we were powerless. In 2017, we were hopeful. In 2018, we were fearful again. In 2019, we ask ourselves what the *Sewol* ferry disaster means and how we experience and walk Ansan.

> In a rapidly changing city, memories are fading and promises are broken. It's time to take a step forward again.
>
> It's been five years since the *Sewol* ferry disaster occurred. Please participate in *Camino de Ansan* to gather our small steps, reinforce our memories, and move forward.[33]

On May 5, 2019, I arrived at Exit 2 of Ansan Station. There was a small booth set up outside the exit where pilgrims could check in. I received a pair of gloves, a pamphlet, a black umbrella, and a bottle of water. I also received a mission card. Mine read, "Hiccup when you walk by flowers." At 1 p.m., the organizers gathered and encouraged the participants to prepare for the walk by doing some stretching exercises. The organizers then silently raised two fingers, signaling the participants to form two lines. No one gave verbal instructions or asked the participants to turn off their electronic devices. The participants were free to walk and chat as much or as little as they wished. Most people walked in silence. From

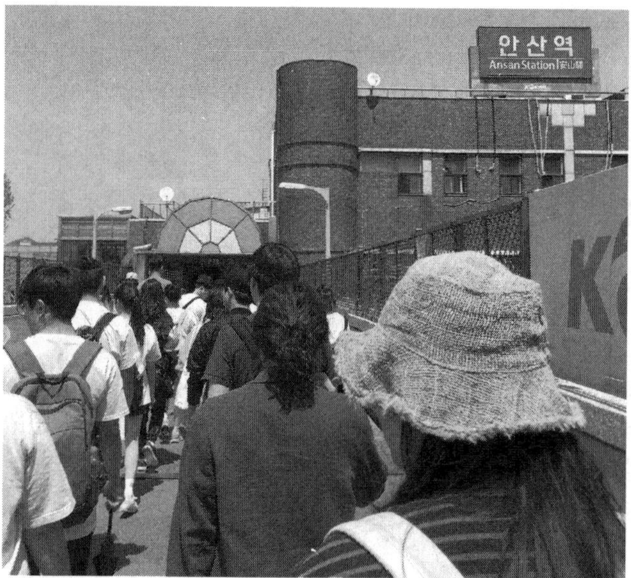

FIGURE 2.5. *Camino de Ansan* is an annual pilgrimage performance that began in 2015 as a means of reflecting on the *Sewol* ferry disaster. The pilgrimage starts at Ansan Station. Photo by Areum Jeong.

time to time, I would have a quiet conversation with one of the *Sewol* mothers behind me.

For approximately six hours, we walked along mountain trails and through markets, parks, apartments, and schools. We walked through neighborhoods that were home to migrant workers. We walked through both abandoned neighborhoods and newly built apartment complexes. We walked in twos and fours, or sometimes in a single file. The organizers would communicate with their umbrellas and gestures. They rarely spoke. Sometimes we would hold the umbrella of the person in front of us, creating a human train. This might have been done to avoid traffic. At these times, and when we followed narrow paths, I had to take small steps to keep from stepping on the heels of the person in front of me. Often the pilgrimage line would curve into the shape of a question mark. While marching along those lines, I would ask how we could remember Ansan.

The pilgrimage also visited the commemorative classrooms and the site of the memorial park. The commemorative classrooms seemed to confirm the victims' absence. The land where the memorial park would be built was empty except for the grass.

From time to time, we saw high school students in their uniforms. They rarely engaged with the participants. Sometimes we would see them close by; sometimes they would go about their business from afar. They reminded us of the students who had died. These were streets that the victims might have walked with their families and friends. Now the people who walk those streets remember the victims.

While the goal of the missions described in the cards were not overtly explained, I think their intention was have the participants remember and repeat a certain action. Sometimes, I would forget to hiccup when passing by flowers unless I heard someone else do it. The hiccups were like an effort to remember the *Sewol.* Each step I took was one of memory and mourning, and an effort to remember the victims and their families. I was reminded that the *Sewol* is not in the past. It is so much more than a disaster that happened on a class trip; it prompted the Korean people to question community, education, government, law, and violence in South Korea. Other pilgrims demonstrated that they too were thinking in broad terms about the disaster and what it meant. For instance, one performer wrote "Time does not make anything disappear" on a wall with chalk, reminding us that the *Sewol* is not something to be forgotten in time.

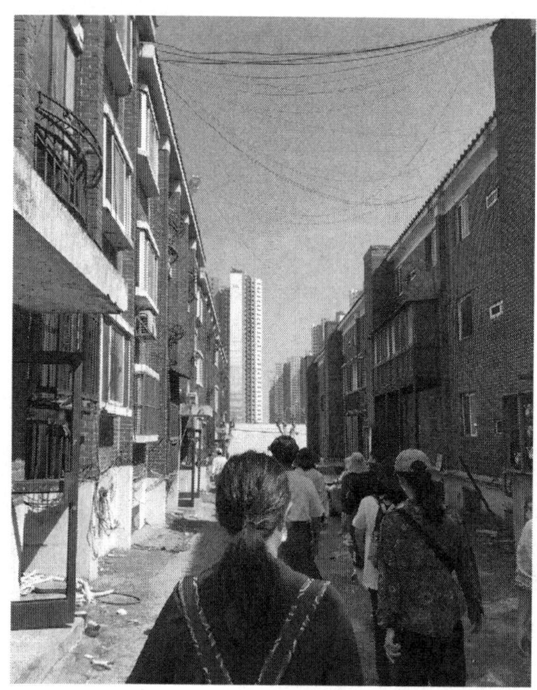

FIGURE 2.6. During *Camino de Ansan*, the participants and I walked through both abandoned neighborhoods and newly built apartment complexes. Photo by Areum Jeong.

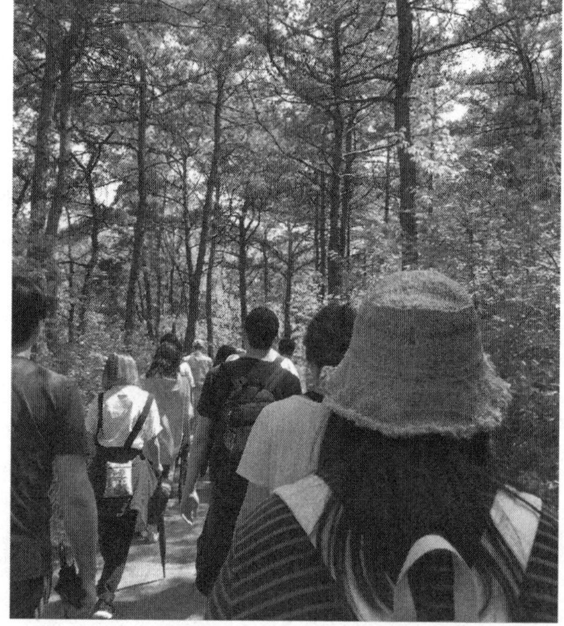

FIGURE 2.7. During *Camino de Ansan*, the participants and I walked along mountain trails and through markets, parks, apartments, and schools. Photo by Areum Jeong.

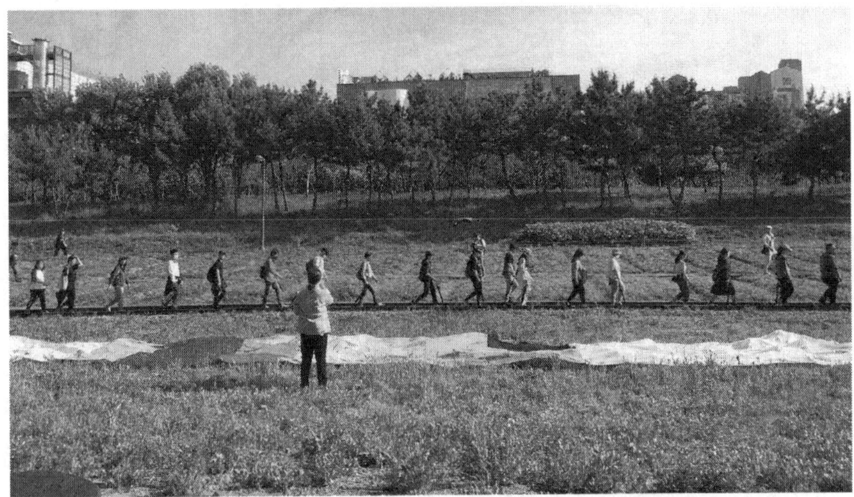

FIGURE 2.8. The pilgrimage also visited the land where the *Sewol* memorial park would be built. Photo by Areum Jeong.

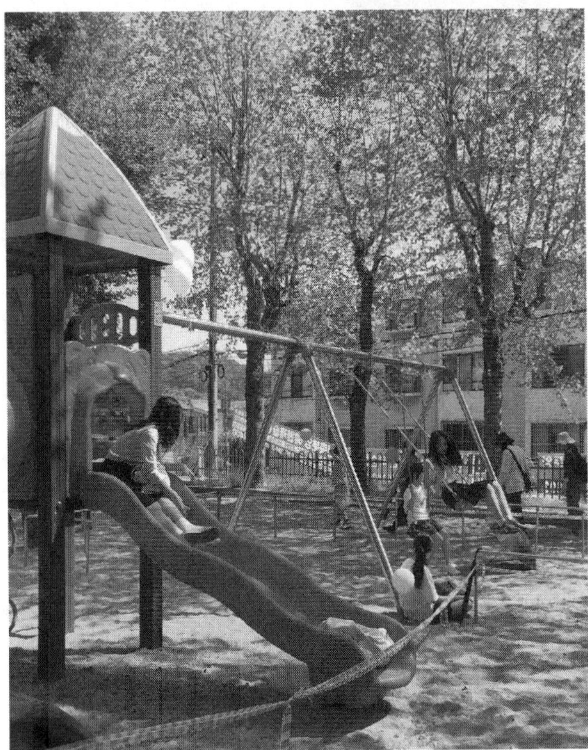

FIGURE 2.9. During *Camino de Ansan*, the participants and I saw high school students in their uniforms. Photo by Areum Jeong.

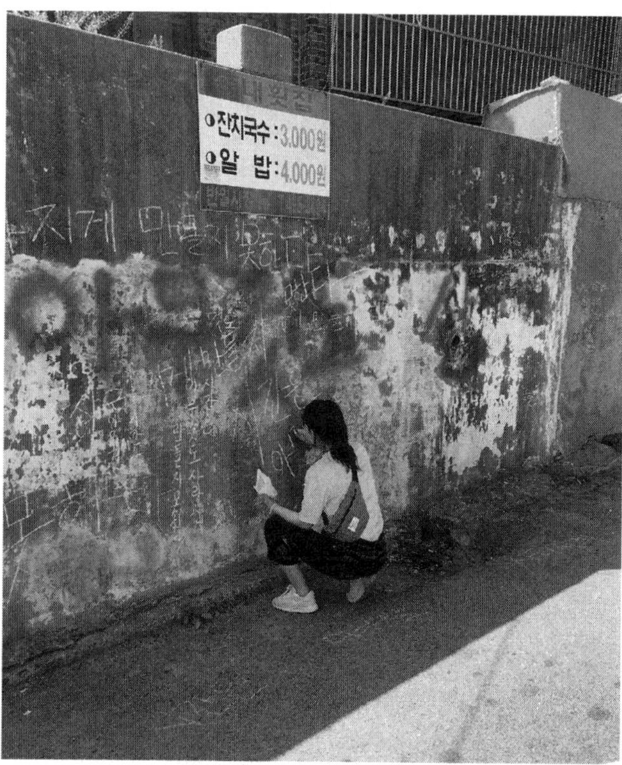

FIGURE 2.10. A performer writes "Time does not make anything disappear" on a wall during *Camino de Ansan*. Photo by Areum Jeong.

PAENGMOK PORT, THE SADDEST PORT IN THE WORLD

Paengmok Port, in Jindo, South Jeolla Province, is where the *Sewol* victims' parents waited for divers to retrieve their children's bodies. At first, immediately after the disaster, the survivors and families of the missing stayed at Jindo Gymnasium.[34] The families here were desperate for information, such as an accurate list of survivors, the possibility of further rescue, the search progress, and future plans, but there was no on-scene commander who could responsibly deliver such information.[35] On the night of April 16, the families of the missing began to move to Paengmok Port. To directly observe the search-and-rescue situation, they boarded a boat and went out to the accident area. Some of the families who moved to Paengmok Port returned to Jindo Gymnasium, but many families of the missing remained at Paengmok Port.[36] Even though the port environment was worse than the gymnasium, the families thought that they could more quickly obtain the results of the search and identification of the missing persons by being closer to the scene.[37]

Meanwhile, social conditions at the gymnasium deteriorated. Frequent clashes between the victims and public officials forced the officials to take off their uniforms, making it difficult to find anyone in uniform other than military surgeons and volunteers. As the distrust of the government and public officials became extreme, it became impossible to distinguish who was who in the crowd.[38]

Amid this disorderly and chaotic scene, the families of the missing became increasingly worried and suspicious of their surroundings. Undercover reporters pretending to be family members of the missing were discovered writing articles without the family members' consent. Plainclothes police officers and intelligence officers from the National Intelligence Service (NIS) surveilled the families of the missing and reported to their superiors. Families of the missing said they could not trust each other, as anyone could be an intelligence officer or a spy.[39] Back at the port, things similarly unraveled. Families clashed with reporters, who took close-up photos of the arriving bodies and transport process, while police did not effectively intervene.[40] Later a police line was installed, but that alone could not control the reckless reporters, who entered the temporary morgue pretending to be family members of the missing and continued their unethical coverage by recording the cries of the victims around the morgue.[41] The media, in short, added to the chaos and trauma for many families.

In the aftermath of the disaster, Paengmok Port became a site for visits and commemorations. Koreans trekked to Paengmok Port to pay their respects, leaving handwritten notes and yellow ribbons on the rails. A large yellow ribbon was painted on the red lighthouse at the end of the port, where it remains today. Below the ribbons are tiles with messages from local residents. A makeshift memorial altar holds the victims' photos. All these objects become witnesses to the wreckage of the *Sewol,* and in their public display, they also created witnesses out of those who viewed them. These memorials create open intersubjective spaces for those left behind and those who have experienced anger and loss. These objects represent unhealed wounds, depression, and national trauma. Ten years after the sinking, however, the memorials have rusted and the ribbons have become frayed and faded. The deterioration of the memorials reflects neglect from the government and from residents.

Before the disaster, Paengmok Port had been slated to undergo a massive redevelopment scheme. Jindo's Paengmok Port development project, passed in 2012, called for construction and developments that would induce connections with industrial, leisure, and tourist facilities. In the wake of the *Sewol,* this plan was suspended, and in the meantime, the spontaneous memorials were assembled. Then, in early 2019, the National Emergency Response Committee announced that the port development project had resumed.[42] Following this, many of the facilities and installations that were constructed at Paengmok Port after the disaster were subsequently demolished. The decision to resume the development plan and destroy the memorials did not go uncontested. In 2018, the 4.16 Family Council announced a plan to create a small memory space to recall the search work and hold memorial events. In late 2018, the council received signatures from 3,380 organizations and individuals who agreed with the creation of the memory space at Paengmok Port. They requested meetings with the head of Jindo and the governor of South Jeolla Province but did not receive an answer. Jindo is concerned that the memory space will permanently associate the region with the disaster, which will be bad for real estate prices, tourism, and the city spirit. The 4.16 Family Council insisted on creating a memory space, even a small one. However, Jindo sent an official letter to the 4.16 Family Council requesting the demolition of the facility so that the construction could resume.

Helping us understand such spontaneous memorials such as those created by mourners and visitors at Paengmok Port, Nan Kim reminds us that such objects have been circulated and recirculated in layered metaphorical assemblages that constitute new forms of public memory.[43] Therefore, these assemblages at Paengmok Port and the imagined port project should be seen as charged sites where public memory of *Sewol* is being constructed and contested. Recognizing this, artists have made this a space of performance, where they seek to commemorate the victims and remember the sorrow and trauma the families experienced in the immediate aftermath of the disaster.

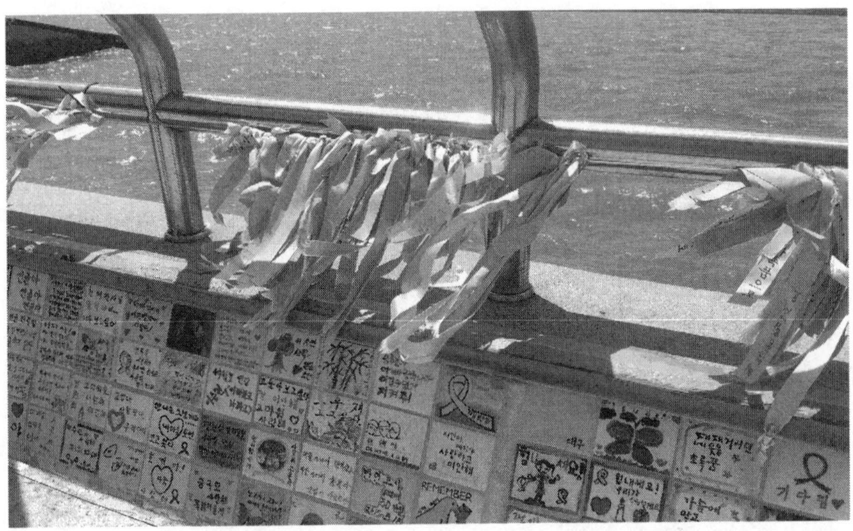

FIGURE 2.11. Koreans trekked to Paengmok Port to pay their respects, leaving yellow ribbons on the rails. Photo by Hieyoon Kim.

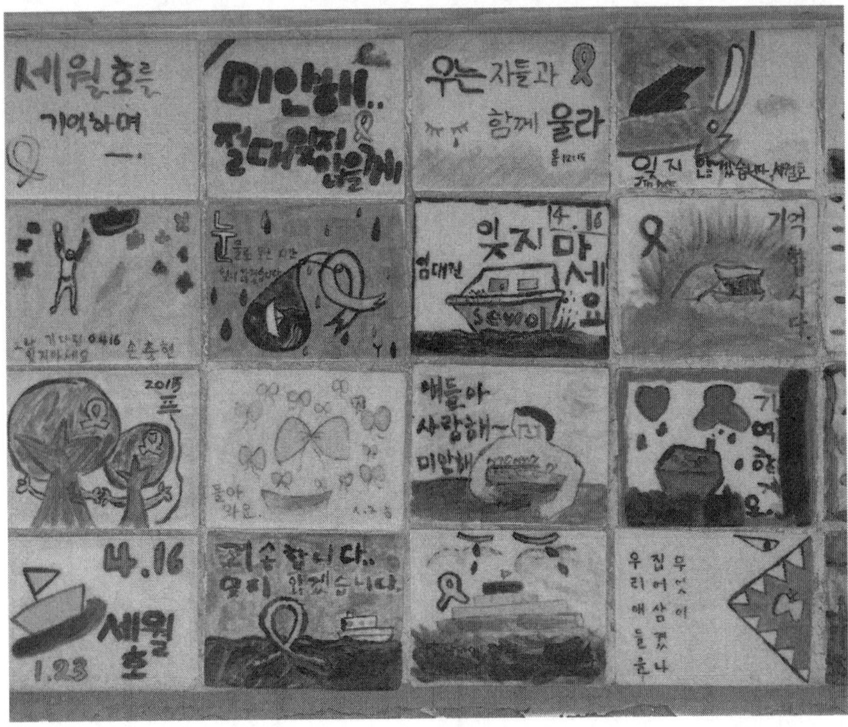

FIGURE 2.12. Below the yellow ribbons are tiles with messages from local residents. Photo by Hieyoon Kim.

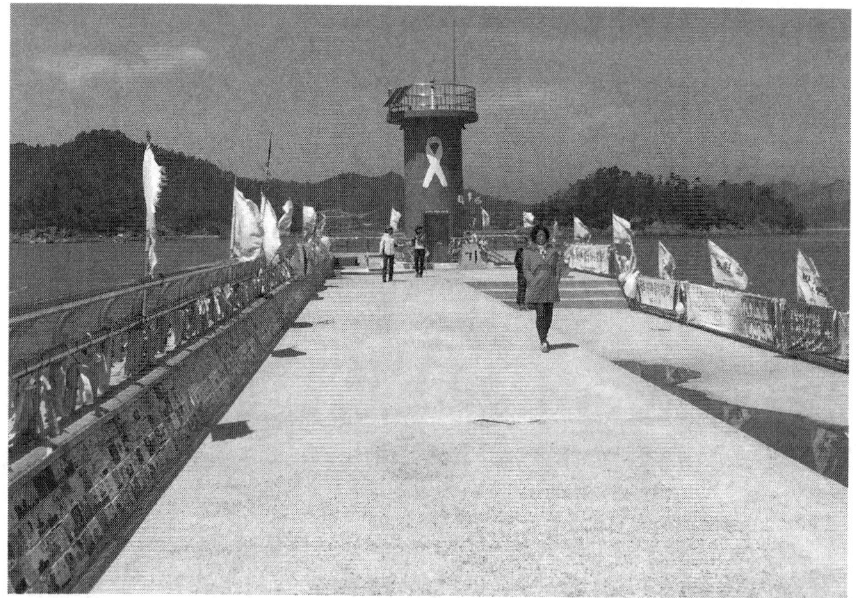

FIGURE 2.13. A large yellow ribbon is painted on the red lighthouse at the end of the port. Photo by Hieyoon Kim.

PERFORMING MEMORY AND REDRESS: *THE BLANKET PROJECT*

In 2015, eighteen performance artists and teams—Yu Gi-tae, Choe Seong-ho, Gim Ju-eun, Hong Han-sol, Jeong Ho-gyeong, Go Jae-wuk, Gim Jin-a, Jo Seong-ji, Gim Ye-ji, Jo Byeong-hui, Indie art hall Gong, Gim Bo-ram, Ro Wa-jeong, Black Jaguar, Gim Jaemini, Mitgeurim, Han Jong-seon, Munmun, Takeout Drawing, Valet Parking, Jang Geun-hui, and Space Heem—borrowed a blanket that several *Sewol* victims' families had used at Paengmok Port in 2014. For a year, *The Blanket Project* lent the blanket to eighteen activists and artists, each of whom did something with or to the blanket and documented how the blanket had been used. The activists and artists used the blanket to mourn the disaster, each imbuing it with their own memories about the disaster.

For example, Valet Parking, a group of four performers—Gang Ha-jeong, Bak Eun-ji, Yi Jin-won, and Jang Deok-yeong—held the blanket while standing ankle-deep in the water at Paengmok Port. "We held the blanket and stared at the sea for six hours. As time passed, the weight of the blanket transformed into bodily pain. During the six hours, we could not say a word."[44] Here we can see how performers utilized the object on site to embody the mothers' pain and sorrow in waiting for their children.

In another iteration, "Laundry Day," performance artist Jang Geun-hui created a work that involved filming the victims' mothers washing the blanket behind the *Sewol* memorial altar at Paengmok Port. The mothers reminisced about how cold it had been when they were waiting for the children and how they had wrapped themselves in the blanket. The following is a transcript of the mothers' conversation.

> "Seeing this blanket [reminds me of] Jindo Gymnasium..."
>
> "We didn't know this would happen. It was better when I didn't know you. It would have been better if you were just another *ajumma* to me..."
>
> "If only we could wash the world clean, too. Let's wash it!"
>
> "When I smell this blanket, it reminds me of the scent of Paengmok Port. I can just smell it. The gritty scent."
>
> "I don't want to see this blanket. It reminds me of when I first got there all nervous waiting for the children. It reminds me of my first night there when we slept on top of paper boxes. The next day, it rained and because it was April, I was wearing light clothes. I was so cold. I received a raincoat and wore that all the time. I couldn't even change my clothes."
>
> "I was in the family waiting room most of the time. Waiting for the children to arrive, to see their names pop up. I waited there until my child arrived. I had this blanket around me all the time."
>
> "I had a strange feeling when I woke up that morning, like my son was going to arrive. My family from Ansan came. My siblings from other provinces came, too. They all came, but my son didn't arrive yet. Most of his classmates arrived. My son arrived in the evening. I was thankful to him because the family was able to see him. We hugged each other and they congratulated me. It's actually not something to congratulate. Back then, we were scared that we might not find him. It felt like a long time. When he arrived, it was only April 21. But it felt like we waited for years and centuries. I was so scared. It was hell."[45]

As this transcription attests, the blanket holds many painful memories of when the mothers arrived at Jindo Gymnasium and Paengmok Port to wait for their children's bodies to be recovered, and when they were waiting for their children's names to appear on the screen. The blanket brings out the fear, hope, sorrow, and longing the mothers had felt during that time. In this sense, the blanket becomes an affective object that holds trauma. By transforming the blanket into performances that represent the mothers' grief and hope for justice, the artists stand in solidarity with the victims' families.

In relation to Sturken's idea that objects are "technologies of memory in that they embody and generate memory," the blanket in both Valet Parking's and Jang's performances holds the cultural history of the *Sewol* and personal memory of the bereaved mothers.[46] Similar to the ways the AIDS Quilt represents "testimonials of and to specific individuals" and "the sharing of personal memories to establish a collectivity," *The Blanket Project* can be seen as a memorial that commemorates the victims, creating a community of shared loss.[47]

The blanket also holds multiple temporalities—of the mothers, of the artists who create new relationships with it through their performances, and of the audience member who tries to make sense of the disaster. In addition, the space where the two performances take place serves as an important element. Because they take place at the Paengmok Port and memorial altar, both performances show artists' efforts to reconfigure the meaning of the space by charging it with potent references to the traumatic event that happened there and its aftermath. Henri Lefebvre argues that space is not just a container; rather, the body "produces itself in space and produces that space," and space "governs" the living body.[48] He states that the "release of energy . . . modifies space or generates a new space."[49] Then the body, which produces space, is also produced by space.[50] In addition, memory is often perceived to be located in specific places of objects. Pierre Nora reminds us that "memory attaches itself to sites, whereas history attaches itself to events."[51] The performance space for both works, the Paengmok Port and memorial altar, is saturated with the histories of the *Sewol,* the families' grief, and the Korean people's trauma. In relation to Lefebvre and Nora's idea of space, the performances imbue the space with an alternative experience and story, thus re-creating the spatial energy.

Like many of the *Sewol* mothers' activities and their participation in craft workshops and theatrical performances discussed in the previous chapter, the act of washing the blanket is also gendered. But by performing this act so publicly, and for a filmed piece of performance, these mothers can be seen as stepping outside the boundaries of traditional motherhood and transforming their grief into political activism. By expressing positive energy and resilience as active resistance through performance, they are able to make claims on the space of the port, expressing ideas about the meanings of the site now, which can also speak to the debates over its memorialization. While developers may want to wash the site clean of its associations with the *Sewol,* the mothers' own performative acts of washing associate the space with their families and communities, which express ongoing desire for physical memorialization of their children and activism in this space.

While *The Children's Room* reveals the temporal rupture of the dreams that the objects once represented, *The Blanket Project* shows how the *Sewol* blanket also holds multiple temporalities—of the mothers whose time stopped on April 16, 2014, of the artists who create new relationships with it through their performances, and of the audience member who tries to make sense of the disaster.

SEEKING HOPE AND TRUTH ON THE ROAD

Throughout the aftermath of the *Sewol,* families and activists have visibly mobilized across the country to demand access to information and accountability from the government. In July 2014, the *Sewol* families rode the Hope Bus across Korea for twelve days to collect signatures for a petition to request the *Sewol* Ferry Disaster Special Act ("Special Act").[52] The Special Act was passed by the South Korean National Assembly on November 7, 2014, was signed into law on November 19, 2014, and took effect on January 1, 2015. The nationwide petition was essential to the enactment of the Special Act, which founded the *Sewol* Ferry Disaster Special Investigation Commission (SIC).[53] However, Park's government and the ruling Saenuri Party made it as difficult as possible for the SIC to do its job. Gim Yeong-han, a senior presidential secretary for civil affairs, described this difficult process in his journal in late 2016. According to Gim, the Blue House, facing growing criticism, blamed the Special Act for the national divide and believed that the SIC was a vehicle of leftists. Apparently, the Blue House's perception of the SIC was shared with government agencies, including the Saenuri Party and Ministry of Oceans and Fisheries.[54] Although the SIC was created by law and had the authority to investigate, it was unable to exercise its authority and perform its activities properly because the government frustrated its efforts.[55]

After Park was removed from office, the investigation by the Moon administration also stalled. In October 2020, the 4.16 *Sewol* Citizens' Council and other organizations submitted a petition to the National Assembly's national consensus.[56] The petition requested an amendment to the Special Act for the investigation of truth of social disasters and the construction of a safer society. It also requested the release of all presidential records related to the *Sewol.* Before Park was impeached, for reasons that were not made clear, she ordered presidential records related to the *Sewol* to be sealed for thirty years.[57] As these papers might hold important information about the disaster and the government's handling of it, the families urged the Moon administration to open the sealed records. This petition was an urgent act on the families' part because the Special Investigation Committee on Social Disaster was going to be shut down on December 11, 2020, the end of its original mandate. The committee could not conduct the investigation without the right to investigate, and it could not see the sealed documents. To be successful in opening the records, the petition had to receive 100,000 signatures within a month. It would then be reviewed by a standing committee under the jurisdiction of the National Assembly.

On October 6, 2020, Yun Gyeong-hui, mother of student victim Gim Si-yeon, and several families boarded a bus with the words "4.16 Truth Bus" and a large yellow ribbon painted on its side as it stood in front of the Blue House.[58] The Truth Bus traveled 3,100 kilometers across twenty-seven cities for twenty-one days, to Gwangju, Busan, and Wonju. From dawn to dusk the families met with citizens and discussed the *Sewol* investigation and corrected misinformation. For instance, a citizen whom Yun had met in Pyeongtaek, Gyeonggi-do, asked, "Why are the *Sewol* families here?" After listening to Yun's explanation that the investigation had made little progress, he said, "I thought the investigation was going well. I am so sorry to hear that."[59] Such exchanges were common along the trip, reflecting the lack of accurate information circulating among the public. Along the way, survivors of other disasters provided crucial support, without which Yun said that she would not have been able to complete the arduous journey. In Daejeon, she was comforted by the mother of Gim Dong-jun, a young man who had died after being bullied in his workplace. In Jeju, the father of Yi Min-ho, a young man who had died in a workplace accident, held signs with Yun. Families of other people who had not been protected by the system offered condolences and stood in solidarity with the *Sewol* families. Perhaps they understood what it was like to lose a family member and not get justice. If the *Sewol* families received justice, it might give hope to many other families who were fighting similar battles. The efforts of Yun and the *Sewol* families paid off. On October 31, 2020, the petition reached 100,000 signatures. "Investigating the truth and punishing those who committed crimes will not bring our children back," Yun said. "But we need to disclose the truth to make a safer society and make sure this doesn't happen again." In the same way that the AIDS Quilt constructs, in Sturken's words, "a collective, cultural memory that is fractured, multifarious, and diverse,"[60] the Truth Bus brought together communities in which loss and memory are shared, communities in which various families struggle to achieve justice.

In 2014 the families fought against the Park administration to have their voices heard. In 2020 they struggled to connect with the Korean people and inform them about the situation of the investigation. The Hope and Truth buses became a means to publicize the families' quest for justice. The transformation from the Hope Bus to the Truth Bus shows the sociocultural and political shift in the families' journey. The families who had found hope after Park's removal and Moon's election have been disappointed by the Moon administration's inaction. They insisted that the government investigate the truth about the disaster. The buses' mobility across time and national space represents the families' determination and will to push ahead with the investigation, reimagining justice by drawing direct parallels between both administration's failures to meet their standards and picturing their platform as an issue that resonated far beyond Ansan.

At the same time, the spectacle of these painted buses also called attention to the glaring absence of an object—the sealed documents, whose lack of visibility these campaigns brought to the fore. The sealed documents evoke the Park administration's neo-authoritarian rule, the Moon government's neglect, and the families' continued struggles for transparency and justice. The documents, which might contain information on the immediate hours after the incident, also stand for the temporal rupture in investigating the truth, as they are sealed until 2047. Whereas previous projects discussed in this chapter utilized emotionally charged sites and objects to evoke public response and advocate for continued memorialization, the mobile bus campaigns take the activists' fight on the road, connecting *Sewol* families to other Koreans around the country and showcasing the ways their campaign might be seen as a national one representing people's rights to government transparency and redress. Because of its links to citizen petitions, these performances straddle the realms of performance and politics, and in doing so they enact demands that the *Sewol* be commemorated not only emotionally and physically but also through material changes in laws and policies.

In this chapter we have seen how objects document the *Sewol* and how they not only become witnesses to the aftermath in Ansan and Paengmok Port but also serve as inducements to memorialize the disaster in the face of forces that want to hide or erase it. In addition, these objects embody acts of activism, moving the viewers to remember the victims and stand in solidarity with the families. *The Children's Room* and *Sewol* commemorative classrooms remind the viewers of the student victims' absence and the many questions about the *Sewol* that have yet to be answered. *Camino de Ansan* commemorates the disaster through embodied performance, walking the space of Ansan. *The Blanket Project* uses a blanket from the *Sewol* families to create performances that mourn the victims and seek redress, each imbuing the object with their own memories about the disaster. The site-specific performances of Ansan and Paengmok Port represent the families' ongoing struggle for justice and the changes in political climate in South Korea. The Hope and Truth buses' mobility represents the families' ongoing struggle for justice amid changes in political climate in South Korea that have yet to provide full transparency.

In December 2021, President Moon Jae-in announced that he would pardon Park Geun-hye and release her from prison.[61] Moon and his administration received much criticism for this decision, as there still has not been a thorough investigation of the *Sewol* and the presidential records that Park sealed remain unopened. It was quite shocking to hear that the liberal party—the "Candlelight Government," which vowed to reveal the truth about the *Sewol*—was even considering pardoning Park when the bereaved parents were still protesting and sleeping outside the Blue House, struggling for justice. It was also a slap in the face to the millions of Koreans who marched and protested in late 2016 for a more just and safety-conscious society. Whether the investigation will move forward and reveal the truth about the *Sewol* is beyond the scope of this chapter. That said, the remnants of the *Sewol*—the objects, performances, and protests—will continue to represent the families and supporters' fight for justice and revive public interest in the truth about the *Sewol*.

I close this chapter with a poem written by A-yeong, the main character of Yellow Ribbon's *Talent Show*. A-yeong's poem describes Ansan, with its working-class residents, and the children of Ansan who grew up too fast because of their parents' daily struggles:

> Ansan's Morning Hurts
>
> The neighborhood where the sun sets every day,
> Ansan's morning hurts.
>
> I feel Dad's rough whiskers when he comes home at dawn after the night shift,
> I feel sad when I hear Mom snore after returning from work,
> and we get ready for school.
>
> Although spicy kimchi soup, salty fish cakes, and a hot bowl of rice do not see me out,
> I know Ansan,
> the neighborhood where the sun rises every morning.
> I know the rough whiskers and snores.
>
> I'm OK, I'm OK.
> I get by in this neighborhood every day,
> so it doesn't hurt me anymore.

CHAPTER 3

Reimagining Justice

The Sewol *in South Korean Theatre and Performance*

On March 4, 2017, South Korean activists laid out 304 life vests—thirty-eight rows of eight vests—on Gwanghwamun Square in Seoul. A yellow ribbon was attached to each life vest. Below the life vests, the activists wrote each *Sewol* victim's name in yellow chalk next to a white chrysanthemum. It seemed that the activists wanted to represent each *Sewol* victim as an individual. When the activists moved among the life vests, their shirts and jeans became covered with dust from the yellow chalk.

Below the rows of life vests was a small air pump attached to a speaker and megaphone. This street performance was intended to remind the viewer of the coast guard officers who lied about having injected air into the ferry's air pockets right after it sank. The sound of the air being pumped in sounded like a foghorn. Whenever the foghorn was heard, the activists stopped, turned, and stared at the air pump. This disruption, and even the moment of silence, evokes the students who perished on the ferry and did not return home alive. The activists' performances represent collective mourning and trauma.

Why were the activists performing at the city square in South Korea's capital? After the sinking of the *Sewol,* former South Korean president Park Geun-hye promised that she and the government would conduct a thorough investigation. However, instead of trying to identify the cause of the incident and why the students had not been rescued, Park's administration refused to cooperate with the survivors and victims' families; furthermore, she obstructed the *Sewol* Ferry Disaster Special Investigation

Commission's efforts. When the people marched in the streets to criticize the government's refusal to accept responsibility for the disaster, Park's administration had the police suppress the protests by force, even arresting the grieving families. In addition, Park's administration surveilled the victims' families and labeled them as the political left or *jongbuk*—someone who sympathizes with North Korean ideology. Such political conditions might have encouraged Korean artists to commemorate the disaster and continue critiquing the government. In addition, Park's administration denied grants and other opportunities to dissident artists. In October 2016, it was revealed that Park's administration had censored prominent artists such as Hong Sung-dam and Bak Geun-hyeong and blacklisted 9,473 other artists.

Enraged artists responded to the Park administration's mishandling of the disaster, obfuscations, and blacklisting with various kinds of public theatre that were enacted in symbolically important national (and international) spaces. With these performances, which often emphasized themes of embodiment in the face of erasure or censorship, they called attention to these systemic injustices, contributed to the archiving of information the government had tried to censor, and creatively fashioned spaces for dissent and protest to take place even in the face of blacklisting. Foremost among these was the Public Theatre Black Tent, in which people were free to create art and voice their opinions. This chapter also examines Jayoung Chung's *Empathy,* an audience participatory performance that premiered on June 24, 2017, at the Asia Culture Center; and Bak Sanghyeon's *From Pluto,* the first chronological *Sewol* play that premiered in May 2019 at the Namsan Arts Center. The very act of staging such works highlights the artists' use of performative strategies against the regime. Together these performances contributed to wider activism around the necessity of political and legal reforms for delivering justice.

POLITICAL AND LEGAL UNDERMINING OF THE *SEWOL* FERRY DISASTER SPECIAL INVESTIGATION COMMISSION

What can citizens do when the government fails to protect the people in need? What can we do when the government is abusing its authority? The

Sewol Ferry Disaster Special Act ("Special Act") was passed by the South Korean National Assembly on November 7, 2014. It was promulgated on November 19, 2014, and went into effect on January 1, 2015. The Korean people's nationwide petition was essential to the enactment of the Special Act.[1] The National Assembly announced the reason for the enactment of the *Sewol* Special Act as follows:

> On April 16, 2014, the *Sewol* ferry sank off the coast near Jodomyeon, Jindogun, Jeollanamdo, causing 304 people on board to die or go missing. Therefore, there is a need to reveal the cause of the incident and follow-up measures, support the victims, and establish safety measures to prevent disasters. The purpose of the Special Act is to stipulate the formation and operation of the Special Investigation Commission ("SIC"), ensure the SIC's activities, and request a parliamentary vote to appoint a special counsel.

The scope of the SIC's investigation included matters regarding the investigation of the *Sewol* ferry disaster; the reform of law, policies, practices, and system that enabled the cause of the *Sewol* ferry disaster; the investigation on the poor rescue efforts and government responses to the *Sewol* ferry disaster; the investigation of the victims' defamation of character by impartial media reports and social media network postings; the establishment of comprehensive measure for a safer society and prevention of disasters; and the inspection of victim support measures.

The South Korean government claims that the SIC was formed on January 1, 2015, when the Special Act went into effect. However, the SIC director and other members were not recognized as government officials, so they did not have the authority to launch an investigation. Thus, the SIC was not officially formed in January 2015 in any meaningful capacity, and the government's argument regarding the SIC's activity period is farfetched. This is especially important because the SIC's mandate was only for one year. Article 7 of the Special Act spells out the SIC's activity period thus: "The commission shall complete its activities within one year from the date when the commission's composition is completed. However, if it is difficult to complete the activities within this period, the period of the activity can be extended for six months." To form a commission, the commission's personnel and material resources must be established.

Therefore, "the date when the commission's composition is completed" would signify "when the personnel and material composition of the commission is substantially completed." The SIC's personnel composition consisted of commission members and investigators. "Material composition" meant securing an office and getting a budget approved by the cabinet. Because the budget was allocated on August 4, 2015, the SIC argued that this was the day that the SIC was launched. Due to the large number of investigation projects, the eighteen-month investigation period should have ended on February 3, 2017. However, the government forced the SIC to end its investigation in June 2016.

In the eleven-month period, the SIC faced many obstacles because the government and the ruling Saenuri Party made it extremely difficult for the SIC to do its job. This was also described in the journal of Gim Yeong-han, a former senior presidential secretary for civil affairs, in late 2016. According to Gim, the Blue House blamed the Special Act for the national divide and believed that the SIC was composed of leftists. Apparently the Blue House's perception of the SIC was shared by government agencies, including the Saenuri Party and the Ministry of Oceans and Fisheries. Although the SIC was created by law and had investigative authority, it was unable to exercise its authority.

The government curtailed the SIC's authority via the Special Act Enforcement Decree. On March 27, 2015, the Ministry of Oceans and Fisheries announced the Special Act Enforcement Decree without any explanation. The preannouncement of the legislation held content that violated the purpose of the Special Act: for example, dispatching government officials closely associated with Park's party and regime to occupy the key SIC posts. If the Enforcement Decree was to be enacted as proposed, it was expected that the dispatched officials would take full control of the SIC, thereby reducing the authority of commission members. In response, the SIC demanded that the ministry withdraw the Enforcement Decree, claiming as they did so that the Enforcement Decree could violate the purpose of the Special Act's legislation, reduce the scope of the SIC's activities, and infringe on the authority of the other SIC members. The SIC also argued that the Enforcement Decree could interfere with its investigation activities and undermine the SIC's independence.

Despite these state concerns, on May 11, 2015, the government passed and implemented the Enforcement Decree with only minor revisions. Because the SIC could not waste precious time, the commission members decided to establish the SIC according to the Enforcement Decree. But they also sought ways to operate independently. For example, the SIC decided not to request dispatch for the three government officials, including the administrative support director, because those positions could influence the SIC's activities. The SIC director and members decided that leaving the three posts vacant would be helpful in keeping the SIC independent.

The SIC budget also limited what the commission could do. The SIC sent the budget proposal to the Ministry of Economy and Finance several times and even visited the office in person to discuss the budget, but the ministry never responded. Then, on August 4, 2015, a cabinet meeting approved the SIC's funding and allocated 8.9 billion Korean won instead of the 16 billion Korean won initially requested. In other words, the requested total budget, which was for the SIC investigation activities such as digital forensics and scientific research, was cut by 44 percent. The budget was also decided seven months after the Special Act went into effect. With such a reduced budget, it would be difficult to conduct a comprehensive scientific investigation into the *Sewol* ferry disaster.

Even after the SIC was finally launched on August 4, 2015, the investigation was not smooth. For example, the government did not cooperate with the SIC in collecting data on the disaster. The Blue House and the National Intelligence Service did not submit any data on Park Geun-hye's activities on the day of the incident. The court, prosecution, and Board of Audit and Inspection also did not send data to the SIC. And although the SIC discovered that there were 1 million Coast Guard frequency communication recordings, only 7,100 were handed over to the SIC. The Ministry of Oceans and Fisheries was very reluctant to provide data on the salvage of the ferry, and eventually provided less than 50 percent of the requested data. When the Shanghai Salvage Company tried to retrieve the ferry, the Ministry of Oceans and Fisheries refused to allow the SIC investigators to board the barge. The SIC tried to investigate the sunken ferry by themselves, but because of budget constraints, it could do so for only five days.

Despite such difficulties, the SIC discovered some previously unknown information about the disaster, especially during the investigative hearings it held. The first hearing took place from December 14 to

16, 2015, at the Seoul YWCA; the second from March 28 to 29, 2016, at the Seoul City Hall; and the third from September 1 to 2, 2016, at Yonsei University. The second hearing identified errors in the AIS data, confirming that the *Sewol* was unsafe to begin with. The hearing also revealed problems in the ferry salvage process. The third hearing disclosed that the ferry's cargo congestion explained why the ferry tipped over after its sudden turn, though there is still no explanation as to *why* the ferry suddenly turned. The third hearing also revealed that the coast guard lied about having injected air into the ferry's air pockets. In addition, the third hearing revealed that the Korean Broadcasting System (KBS) president had regularly intervened with the news, showing that many news reports on the *Sewol* ferry disaster were biased.

On December 9, 2016, Park Geun-hye was impeached. Although the *Sewol* was not included in the several reasons for her impeachment, the judge mentioned that Park had violated the obligation to faithfully execute her duties as president (Article 69 of the Constitution and Article 56 of the State Public Officials Act):

> A true leader of a nation should swiftly ascertain the situation when a national crisis strikes.... Such a crisis occurred on April 16, 2014, the day of the *Sewol* ferry tragedy. All the citizens who were watching the situation unfold, not to mention the victims and their families, were desperately hoping that the respondent, as the president, would at least display the smallest amount of leadership to protect the people. However, the respondent remained in the presidential residence and did not go into the office until that evening, for no particular reason. As a result, despite the fact that an unprecedented large-scale disaster had occurred and a "serious" crisis alert, the highest of its kind, had been issued, the defendant realized the gravity of the situation extremely belatedly, and maintained an insincere attitude without displaying any leadership as president to understand the situation and support the rescue operation. The respondent failed to appear before the public for eight hours when the lives and safety of over four hundred of the nation's people were faced with a grave and pressing threat.... Therefore, the respondent failed to faithfully perform her duties... and thus violated the obligation to faithfully execute the duties of the president as specifically provided by Article 69 of the Constitution and Article 56 of the State Public Officials Act.[2]

Performance studies scholars Joshua Takano Chambers-Letson and Elizabeth W. Son provide a framework for understanding how the South Korean government abused the legal system and excluded its most vulnerable citizens in need. Drawing on theories by Carl Schmitt, Giorgio Agamben, Aihwa Ong, Jasbir K. Puar, and Tavia Nyong'o, Chambers-Letson's work is helpful in understanding how the "seemingly universal guarantees of juridical subjectivity do not apply to all people all of the time."[3] In the case of the *Sewol,* state negligence and biased media coverage moved the bodies of the student victims and their supporters beyond the bounds of deserving national protection. Elizabeth Son, meanwhile, examines the Women's International War Crimes Tribunal on Japan's Military Sexual Slavery and analyzes how the tribunal provided ways for survivors to offer testimony.[4] Son argues that the performative strategies used in the survivors' testimonies "questioned the given frame of international adjudication handed down by postwar tribunals and their inattention to gender-based crimes."[5] These works are useful in viewing how the Public Theatre Black Tent's performative strategies criticized the Park Geun-hye administration's censorship of South Korean artists who express dissident opinions, and how performance can reimagine justice.

PERFORMING ACTIVISM IN GWANGHWAMUN SQUARE: ASIA'S FIRST HOLOGRAPHIC "GHOST RALLY" AND THE PUBLIC THEATRE BLACK TENT

Park's administration started to censor artists in 2013, even before the *Sewol* ferry capsized in 2014. On August 8, 2013, Gim Gi-chun, chief of staff to the South Korean president, ordered his secretaries to deny grants to artist Hong Sung-dam.[6] Hong Sung-dam is well-known for his political work, especially Sewol *Owol* (2014), which depicted the *Sewol* ferry disaster and linked it to Park Geun-hye and her government.[7] In September 2013, the Blue House issued instructions regarding "the need to correct the leftist behavior of the city's cultural assets" to the Ministry of Culture, Sports and Tourism. In response to the films *The Attorney* (2013), *Project Cheonan Ship* (2013), and the National Theater Company of Korea's *The Frogs,* Gim Gi-chun remarked that the political left was taking over the cultural scene. On December 20, 2013, Gim told his secretaries, "anti-government and antinationalist groups have become the hotbed for leftists to support pro–North Korean forces" and ordered them to "conduct a complete survey of support by the current government and prepare measures against it." Here, "conducting a complete survey" can be read as instructions for preparing a blacklist.[8]

In October 2014, when the Busan International Film Festival screened the documentary *The Truth Shall Not Sink with* Sewol (2014), festival director Yi Yong-gwan was asked to resign and the festival was audited by the Board of Audit and Inspection. Jo Yun-seon, former head of the Ministry of Culture, Sports and Tourism, asked the Saenuri Party to denounce the documentary.[9] Jo also ordered her staff member Gang Il-won to buy up all the tickets before the screening and post negative reviews of the documentary online.

Suspicions about the government surveilling and censoring arts and culture arose when theatre critic Gim Mi-do reported that Bak Geun-hyeong's play *All Soldiers Are Unfortunate* was initially selected for funding by the Arts Council Korea, but members of the council reconvened the jury members and demanded that the funds be rescinded.[10] When the jury refused, the committee visited Bak personally to urge him to cancel his performance and even to sign written confirmation that he was forfeiting the funds. In addition, in October 2015, Arts Council Korea interrupted a performance at the Seoul Performing Arts Festival because references to the popular clothing brand North Face and to a school trip evoked the *Sewol* ferry disaster.

After the *Sewol* ferry disaster, demonstrations demanding a thorough investigation escalated into nationwide protests. In 2015, there were three times as many arrests by the Korean police at street protests than in 2014. *Kyunghyang Shinmun,* a nationwide newspaper, stated that the Park Geun-hye administration had abused its power after the *Sewol* ferry disaster and that the police's abuse of power had violated citizens' rights to freedom of assembly and demonstration.[11] In early 2016, when government discipline strengthened and street protests were banned, activists expressed themselves in other ways, turning to performance strategies and modalities that were responsive to this regime of growing censorship, to which performance works drew critical attention.

On February 24, 2016, Asia's first holographic "ghost rally" was held in

Seoul's Gwanghwamun Square. This virtual protest, in which organizers projected life-size images of marchers, took place after the South Korean police rejected an application for a demonstration near the Blue House. Demonstrations outside the Blue House had been banned after violent protests over the government's handling of the *Sewol* disaster. Although police said their refusal of a permit had nothing to do with freedom of speech, many did not believe their statements, which sowed further institutional distrust.

Inspired by the hologram demonstrations in Spain, Amnesty International asked potential participants to send messages, photos, and audio or video recordings through a messaging app. Such performances were made possible through careful planning via social networking sites. At the site were the organizers, who set up the projection, and journalists, who were waiting to photograph the holographic protest. A transparent screen was set in front of an old palace gate in the city square. Holographic figures marched and chanted, "Promise us democracy! Promise us freedom of assembly!" Gim Hui-jin, director of Amnesty International Korea, said, "The [South Korean] situation has become so restrictive that only ghosts like these may freely march on the street."[12] Many Koreans posted about the holographic protest on social media accounts, expressing their support for the organizers. They commented that the holographic protest was a refreshing tactic, while lamenting that South Korea's political conditions limited popular protest to virtual reality.

Such performative strategies by the *Sewol* activists allow us to imagine the efficacy of the digital body. While activists were prohibited from physically protesting at the city square, the digital bodies were able to overcome such limitations, enabling performance to circumvent legal boundaries and become sites of possibility. Thus, the holographic protest defied the Park administration's neo-authoritarian rule and state censorship and created an alternative space in which to raise voices and reconfigure bodily performances of mass protest. Rather than discussing whether virtual protests can be as effective as physical ones, I view the holographic body as one with its own performative presence.

One year later, in early 2017, the performative possibilities of political action were again altered, in Gwanghwamun Square. On October 12, 2016, *Hankook Ilbo,* a nationwide newspaper, reported the blacklisting of 9,473 artists. After months of protests, artists founded the Public Theatre

Black Tent on January 7, 2017, and opened the temporary public venue with theatre company Gorae's *Red Poem* on January 10, 2017.[13] The Black Tent staged various performances on social issues until March 18, 2017. According to Yi Hae-seong, the director of Black Tent, "The biggest significance and value of Black Tent is that artists of all genres, including theatre, dance, mime, and music, gathered to perform, and workers and citizens worked together to create a public theatre. Art, labor, and citizens created a special synergy in the process. That power changed society and expanded genres and individuals."[14] Among the many works that took place at the Black Tent, one particular street performance caught my attention. The "We Are the Constitution" performance, held on March 4, 2017, mourned the *Sewol* victims and represented activists' defiance of government censorship and surveillance. The performance consisted of three segments, the first two titled "Life Vest" and "Breath" (with which I opened this chapter). In the final segment, "We Are the Constitution," ladders of different heights were placed above the rows of vests. On top of the ladders, the activists recited the preamble of the Constitution of the Republic of Korea together:

> We, the people of Korea, proud of a resplendent history and traditions dating from time immemorial, upholding the cause of the Provisional Republic of Korea Government born of the March First Independence Movement of 1919 and the democratic ideals of the April Nineteenth Uprising of 1960 against injustice, having assumed the mission of democratic reform and peaceful unification of our homeland and having determined to consolidate national unity with justice, humanitarianism and brotherly love, and To destroy all social vices and injustice, and To afford equal opportunities to every person and provide for the fullest development of individual capabilities in all fields, including political, economic, social and cultural life by further strengthening the basic free and democratic order conducive to private initiative and public harmony, and To help each person discharge those duties and responsibilities concomitant to freedoms and rights, and To elevate the quality of life for all citizens and contribute to lasting world peace and the common prosperity of mankind and thereby to ensure security, liberty and happiness for ourselves and our posterity forever, Do hereby amend, through national referendum following a resolution by the National Assembly, the Constitution, ordained and established on the Twelfth Day of July anno Domini Nineteen hundred and forty-eight, and amended eight times subsequently.[15]

Next, the activists took turns reciting parts of the constitution that the government seemed to be violating at the time:

> Article 1. (1) The Republic of Korea shall be a democratic republic. (2) The sovereignty of the Republic of Korea shall reside in the people, and all state authority shall emanate from the people.
>
> Article 10. All citizens shall be assured of human worth and dignity and have the right to pursuit of happiness. It shall be the duty of the State to confirm and guarantee the fundamental and inviolable human rights of individuals.
>
> Article 21. (1) All citizens shall enjoy freedom of speech and the press, and freedom of assembly and association. (2) Licensing or censorship of speech and the press, and licensing of assembly and association shall not be recognized.
>
> Article 34. (1) All citizens shall be entitled to a life worthy of human beings. (6) The State shall endeavor to prevent disasters and to protect citizens from harm therefrom.
>
> Article 37. (1) Freedoms and rights of citizens shall not be neglected on the grounds that they are not enumerated in the Constitution. (2) The freedoms and rights of citizens may be restricted by Act only when necessary for national security, the maintenance of law and order or for public welfare. Even when such restriction is imposed, no essential aspect of the freedom or right shall be violated.
>
> Article 69. The President, at the time of his/her inauguration, shall take the following oath: "I do solemnly swear before the people that I will faithfully execute the duties of the President by observing the Constitution, defending the State, pursuing the peaceful unification of the homeland, promoting the freedom and welfare of the people and endeavoring to develop national culture."
>
> Article 103. Judges shall rule independently according to their conscience and in conformity with the Constitution and laws.
>
> Article 119. (2) The State may regulate and coordinate economic affairs in order to maintain the balanced growth and stability of the national economy, to ensure proper distribution of income, to prevent the domination of the market and the abuse of economic power and to democratize the economy through harmony among the economic agents.[16]

The performance, along with the other two segments, can be viewed as criticism of the South Korean government's failure to protect the people in need. As Chambers-Letson argues, the notion of law universally protecting the people is flawed; the Special Act, which seemingly protects and supports the SIC's aims, did not help the people in need. Under the pretense of passing the Special Act to help the victims' families, the government tried to use the Special Act and other institutional and legal systems to hinder the SIC's efforts in uncovering the truth. In this sense, both the holographic protest and the "We Are the Constitution" performance created spaces not just for memory and mourning but also for the reimagining of justice. When the language of law is lacking, and especially when law is being used to stifle public criticism of powerful institutions, embodied performance can transcend language and constitute interventions in public discourse that contribute to social change.

PUTTING ONESELF IN OTHERS' SHOES THROUGH PERFORMANCE: *EMPATHY* (2017–2018)

Jayoung Chung's *Empathy*, an audience participatory performance that commemorates the *Sewol* victims, premiered on June 24, 2017, at the Asia Culture Center, a government-sponsored organization that promotes Asian art and culture through various productions, programs, and research in Gwangju, Korea. Incorporating dance and prerecorded oral narratives, *Empathy* aims to rethink the relationship between the performer and the viewer. Chung felt the need to create this performance after meeting the mothers of the *Sewol* victims in 2014:

> My experience of holding the mothers' hands led me to create a performance that shared their pain. The holding of hands and the shoes are important in this performance. Empathy means sharing one's pain, putting oneself in others' shoes. The *Sewol* mother gave me her shoes for this performance. Our bodies hold electricity. As you have seen in the performance, the performers' touch brings upon sound. It signifies that when we touch each other, it lights up the darkness and breaks the silence. The place mats were made of conductive thread. The contact of skin enables sound and light. It signifies that we can make light and sound when we hold hands.[17]

The stage is bare, except for the two place mats with thin cords crisscrossed on the surface. Underneath the place mats, Chung had created two areas with conductive tape on the ground. She also reconstructed the shoes to carry an electrical current. As human bodies hold electricity, any two people who touch each other, either barefoot on the place mats or wearing the conductive shoes, can function as a switch that lights up the dark venue and turns on prerecorded sounds. As Chung defines empathy as "sharing one's pain and putting oneself in others' shoes," the act of physical contact becomes important in the performance. The bodies become the vessel through the performative act of literally taking off one's shoes and stepping into the other's, and the holding of hands. The tactile encounter between the person and the object is important in the performance because it signifies the audience member's agency to connect with the other.

The performance opens with a black-and-white image of the sea projected on the screen, accompanied by the sounds of waves crashing on the shore. Interweaving dance and visual media, the performance com-

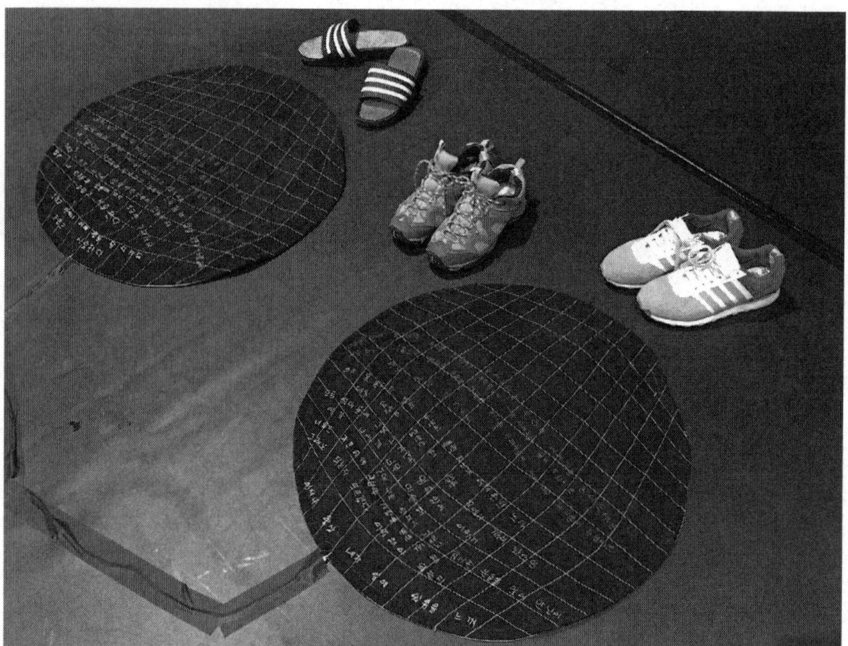

FIGURE 3.1. Underneath the place mats, Jayoung Chung had created two areas with conductive tapes on the ground. She also reconstructed the *Sewol* mother's shoes to carry an electrical current. Photo by Areum Jeong.

prises three segments in which three performers take turns taking off each other's shoes and offering them to the audience. When the performers touch each other, the dark stage lights up and we hear a prerecorded voice through the speakers:

> "Hi, baby. How are you? We haven't seen each other for four years now. I want to see you. Each day feels like a trance and I want to wake up from it. The mothers' time has stopped on that day. I met a lot of people because of you and I received a lot of attention and love, but I don't know if I'm worthy of it. I feel you at my side all the time. We are going to build a memorial park in Ansan, so wait a little. Please look after your father and brothers. I love you."

Empathy stands out from other *Sewol* performances in that it involves audience participation: The spectator voluntarily becomes the actor. By using such theatrical devices, Chung asks viewers to engage physically with the show's material. The staging of these oral testimonies demands a certain type of interaction. In *Empathy,* the spectator becomes a *spect-actor* and is not limited to the role of passive audience member. In order to light up the stage and hear the mothers' voices, the audience members are encouraged to step into each other's shoes and touch each other's hands. By enabling the audience members to step into the shoes of the *Sewol* mothers both during and after the performance, *Empathy* offers a space for community engagement, for individuals to try to make an effort to understand one another. *Empathy* challenges audiences' ways of relating to the mothers by making the audience aware of their roles as agents of commemoration.

Throughout the performance, the mother's prerecorded testimony does not merely function as a narrative; rather, it can be viewed as an Austinian speech act that performs affect—mainly grief, sorrow, and trauma—and provides information on the aftermath of the incident. While the testimony consists of a narrative that conveys the mother's sorrow and vulnerability about the loss of her child, the testimony does not convey destruction or weakness. In relation to Butler's idea of vulnerability becoming a means to connecting and engaging with the audience, the mother's frank and sincere testimony becomes a powerful performance through her exposure of vulnerability and endeavor to document and memorialize the incident through performative acts. The testimony enables the audience member to access stories of the victim's childhood, the mother's memories of her child, and the families' condition after the tragedy. Through her testimony, the audience is able to imagine such moments and engage with the mother and the tragic incident. Although we can never fully understand or identify with the mother's grief, the act of putting the shoes on signifies consolation and support. The audiences' actions are especially significant because they bring awareness to each other. The enhanced awareness and shared empathy produce a sense of belonging to a community of memory and mourning. Moreover, the staging of this performance at a theatre sponsored by government funding proffers an alternative vision of a national community, in contrast to the exclusionary and hypernationalistic one created by the administration.

When the performance came to an end, the director and performers invited the rest of the audience to come up to the stage and try stepping in the shoes. Several audience members lined up. When they each stepped in the shoes and touched hands with the performer, we could hear the testimony again. Those who did not participate during the performance might have been motivated to do so after the performance because they wanted to produce their own experiences of viewing these testimonies. In light of gender studies scholar Sara Ahmed's idea of how objects—or, rather, our relationships with objects—can perform affect, the three pairs of shoes used in *Empathy* are performative. These objects do not function as insignificant items or materials. Rather, these objects carry the experiences of the families' memories and sorrows. The shoes hold the histories of the mothers and the performers and carry the experiences of audience members as they step into them in order to express their empathy toward the victims. The shoes hold multiple temporalities—of the mothers who mourn the children's death, of the artists who utilize them in performances, and of the audience members who try to make sense of the tragic incident.

COMMEMORATING THE CHILDREN WHO BECAME STARS IN THE SKY: *FROM PLUTO* (2019)

Myeongwangseongeseo (From Pluto), written and directed by Bak Sang-hyeon, premiered in May 2019 at the Namsan Arts Center. Bak is a director, playwright, and professor at the Korea National University of Arts. His previous plays *Saikopaeseu* (Psychopath; 2012) and *Chijeong* (A love affair; 2015) were staged at the Namsan Arts Center. Initially called the Drama Center, the Namsan Arts Center, built in 1962, is Korea's oldest modern theatre.[18] Yu Chi-jin, a renowned Korean director and playwright, established the center with a $65,000 grant from the Rockefeller Foundation. In 2009, the venue was renovated and renamed the Namsan Arts Center. In 2016, the Center, which staged mostly American and British plays, expanded its programming to include local experimental productions.

Bak was inspired to create *From Pluto* after meeting five *Sewol* families on December 22, 2014. Though partly fictional, the plot is largely based on information on the *Sewol* ferry disaster and testimonies from victims' families and supporters. Bak consulted the *Sewol* archives, visited the commemorative classrooms, and studied several Korean publications, such as O Jun-ho's *Documenting the* Sewol *Ferry*. While many productions represented the *Sewol* metaphorically, this is the first play that depicts it chronologically. The play, a reenactment of the disaster and its aftermath, also documents the event. Bak had not intended to create documentary theatre, however.[19] His purpose was to confront the *Sewol* disaster, but he found he could not do so because he did not have complete information about what happened. When writing the students' lines, Bak wondered what they would have said, and whether he could really speak for them. During rehearsals Bak ordered controlled, restrained acting. The cast members rehearsed for two and half months and spent much time contemplating the disaster. Bak commented that the play was his way of remembering the victims and an expression of the prayers and wishes of the families and friends left behind.

The play begins on April 14, 2014, the day before the class trip. It stages the incident chronologically with testimonies from the victims' families, survivors, and supporters, and portrays the aftermath of the incident based on public opinion and true events. In addition, the play also directly portrays the victims in several fictional scenes. In one scene, the students have a party in the ferry's steering house. The members of the broadcasting club introduce each student: for example, "She is our class president, but after the ferry's captain took off, she is our captain!" When introduced, each student comes forward and delivers a short statement: "I want to breathe fresh air." "Do you think my last text message was delivered to my parents? If only I could see them one more time." "Mom, please remember to take your medicine. Dad, don't drink too much. Be well." "Mom, I'm sorry I complained about your cooking." "Mom and Dad, don't worry. I was actually really scared, but it was not that painful." "Why didn't we go out when the ferry started to sink? Why didn't we?"

Between these statements, members of the broadcasting club repeatedly instruct some students, "Stay where you are. Don't move," while other students dance and have fun. This evokes the instructions given to the students as the ferry sank. The students' playfulness is in sharp contrast to their wistful words. Suddenly the venue becomes completely dark except for some lights floating in the background. The students stand still. A male adult's voice is heard: "Here you all are. Let's go home. I'll take you all home." The voice belongs to one of the divers who retrieved their bodies. This fictional scene was a heartbreaking reminder that the students the actors represent are gone. This scene represents the unrepresentable. Instead of depicting the students awaiting help as trapped and frightened, this scene portrays them as happy and full of life. This is how their families and friends wish to remember them. Perhaps it was represented this way because we do not know what really happened. We do not know why the ferry made a sharp turn and what caused it to sink. We do not know why the students were not rescued sooner, and we do not know why the Park administration demonized the victims' families and supporters and hindered the investigation.

The play also portrays the aftermath of the incident. In a scene set in a church, we see parents reacting to Captain Yi Jun-seok's thirty-six-year prison sentence. The priest asks them to pray, to ask God to please take away their hatred toward the captain and crew. One bereaved parent described seeing his child's corpse. He asks, "How do we accept this, God? What is God's will?" The parents discuss the Bible and then begin arguing. "If there really is a God, God would have saved the children," says one mother. I was reminded of the many Korean pastors who stated, "God gave Korea an opportunity by drowning the young students," or "The poor students should just have gone to Gyeongju. I don't know why they took a ferry to Jeju Island and created this commotion."[20] These pastors were not the only ones who made cruel and insensitive remarks toward the *Sewol* victims and families.

In addition, by citing the words of the supporters, the play reminds the viewer of the many unresolved issues. In another scene, we see several divers attend a funeral, perhaps that of the diver Gim Gwan-hong, who was diagnosed with PTSD and took his own life. The divers talk about their trauma and what it was like to search for the students' bodies. "Back then, I thought, Thank God I can do this [dive and search for the students]," one diver says. "I still have nightmares about that," says another. For three months after the sinking, twenty-five civilian divers spent more than twelve hours a day searching for the bodies of the *Sewol* victims; eventually they recovered nearly three hundred bodies from the sunken ferry.[21] During that time, they performed excessive labor in recovering the bodies, without any government body providing direction and oversight to protect their safety and well-being. Although many divers are still living with physical pain and PTSD, they have not been compensated by the South Korean government. Two divers have died by suicide.[22] Han Jae-myeong was diagnosed with osteonecrosis, a bone tissue disease caused by interruption of the blood supply. Eight divers are unable to work due to physical injuries they sustained during the search. When Gim Sang-woo was inside the submerged ferry, luggage fell on his head, and he had to undergo surgery on his neck. He is still unable to work as a diver. These volunteer civilian divers are not eligible for workmen's compensation, however; furthermore, those with osteonecrosis cannot receive any kind of compensation or disability assistance. After diver Gim Gwan-hong's death, seventy members of the National Assembly proposed the Gim Gwan-hong Act to compensate divers, but the Judiciary Committee still has not passed it. This scene again reminds the viewer that numerous *Sewol* supporters who have been diagnosed with health issues have been denied government care. Recovery from the *Sewol* is still ongoing.

In her review, theatre critic Gim Bang-ok wrote that the play not only questions whether or not the *Sewol* could be represented but also shows how it has become unavoidable *not* to question political issues represented in Korean theatre today.[23] Although it might not have been Bak's initial focus when writing and directing *From Pluto,* the play also becomes a political commentary on the *Sewol* families' struggles, the supporters' troubles, the unanswered questions, and ongoing issues of health and safety of families and rescue personnel that need to be addressed by the South Korean government.

As we have seen in this chapter through a close examination of the *Sewol* Ferry Disaster Special Act and the *Sewol* Ferry Disaster Special

Investigation Commission's activities, the South Korean government and legal system failed the families of the students who perished on the *Sewol.* We also looked at how political street performances resisted government censorship and surveillance, and the chapter analyzed how these performances provided a means of public discourse that advocated for social change.

Each *Sewol* performance becomes an act of documenting the tragic incident and letting the *Sewol* families and supporters know that they are not alone in their struggles. The very act of observing, documenting, and analyzing such past and present histories is crucial in remembering what happened and creating a forum for social change and the search for truth. Jayoung Chung's *Empathy* stages not only the aftermath of emotional and material wreckage but also the people who fight to remember the *Sewol* ferry disaster. In addition, the range of witnesses is extended to the spectator by viewing the mothers' testimonies and victims' remnants. In each performance, the spectator attends to the *Sewol* families' stories and bears witness to the acts of redress.

Although many performances have memorialized and mourned the people who died on the *Sewol,* nearly all of them have mentioned the victims only indirectly. Perhaps the artists thought it would be too exploitative or traumatizing to depict them. Or perhaps they questioned their right to do so when the families' grief was still fresh. Interestingly, Bak Sang-hyeon's *From Pluto* stages the students either directly or metaphorically. *From Pluto,* a reenactment of the disaster and its aftermath, depicts the student victims directly and raises the question of whether the *Sewol* can be represented. By representing the victims of the *Sewol* ferry disaster, *From Pluto* conveys the families' struggles to achieve justice, the rescue personnel and supporters' ongoing difficulties in recovering, the questions that remain to be answered, and problems that the South Korean government needs to solve.

The Black Tent performances, *Empathy,* and *From Pluto* document and critically represent political and social issues, serving as a memory archive that resists the government's and media's attempts to erase the *Sewol* ferry disaster. The performances also become a political commentary, critiquing the censorship and neo-authoritarian rule of the Park Geun-hye administration. The performances try to make sense of the *Sewol* disaster, to identify with the victims' families, and to think about how to solve the structural problems of contemporary Korean society. The hopes for social change echo those of the "4.16 Human Rights Manifesto" written by the *Sewol* families:

> We declare our rights to dignity and safety through loss, mourning, and fury. We promise we will not abandon the practice of remembering the *Sewol* ferry disaster and uncovering the truth and establishing justice. We also pledge that we will pay attention to other disasters in this world and stand in solidarity. We will not hesitate to raise our voices against social structures and powers that undermine dignity and security. This declaration is not a final one; it will be completed in the process of many of us talking, shouting and acting. Let's hold hands together. Let's act together.[24]

In February 2020, I visited the *Sewol* memorial hall at Gwanghwamun Square.[25] As I stepped inside the memorial hall, I could see the clean and

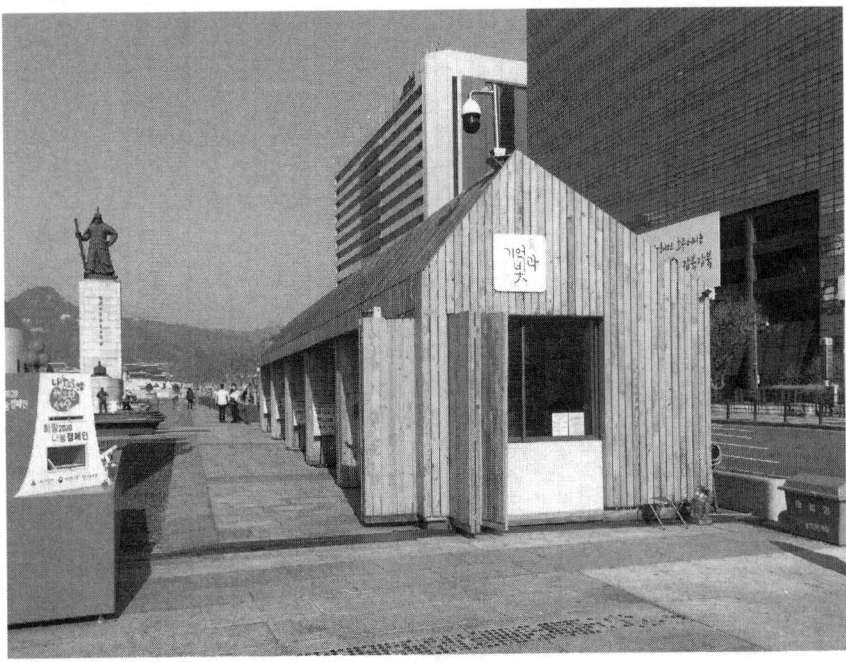

FIGURE 3.2. The *Sewol* memorial hall at Gwanghwamun Square. The city government removed it from the square in July 2021. Photo by Areum Jeong.

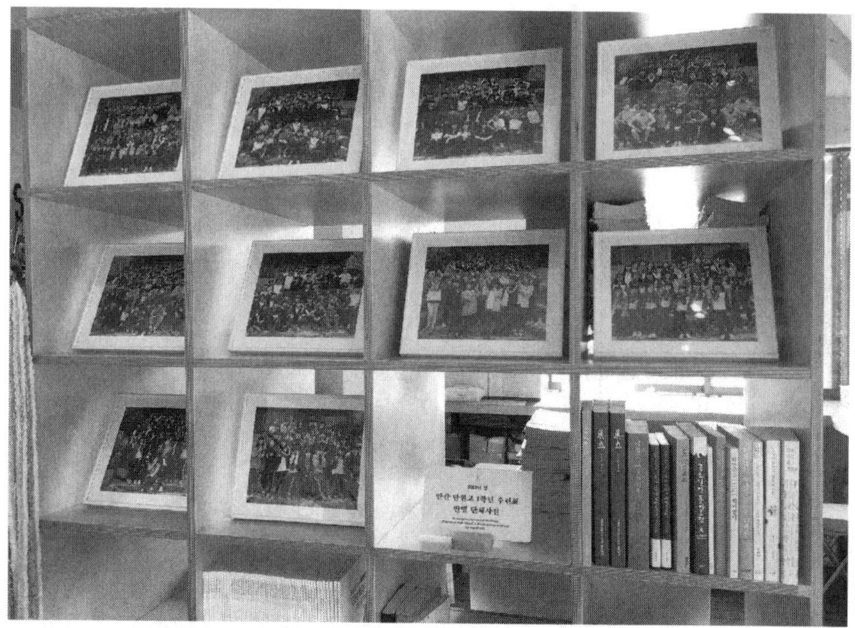

FIGURE 3.3. The clean and well-lit exhibition space of the *Sewol* memorial hall at Gwanghwamun Square showcased photos of the student victims and written testimonies of the victims' families and friends. Photo by Areum Jeong.

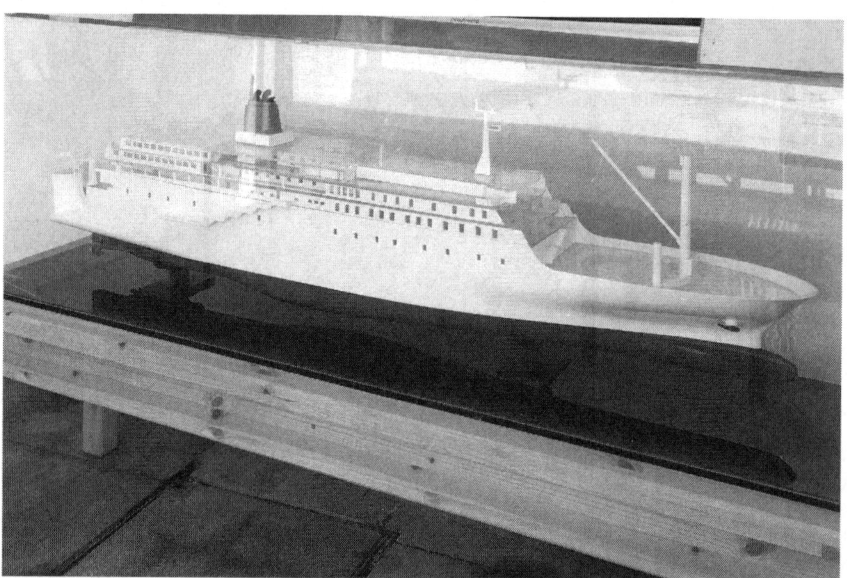

FIGURE 3.4. The *Sewol* memorial hall at Gwanghwamun Square also held a replica of the *Sewol* ferry. Photo by Areum Jeong.

well-lit exhibition space showcasing photos of the student victims and written testimonies of the victims' families and friends. There was also a replica of the *Sewol* ferry, representing another form of wreckage and functioning as a memorial that documents and preserves death, loss, and memory. Inscribed on the wall was this Korean sentence: "We must change after the *Sewol*."

CHAPTER 4

Singing for a Spring Day

The Sewol *in K-Pop*

In May 2017, Angela Pulvirenti, an Italian fan of K-pop group BTS, created a video that analyzes BTS's "Spring Day" music video; Pulvirenti's video garnered more than 115,000 views and nearly seven hundred comments.[1] "Spring Day" is a well-known song in South Korea, and many Koreans associate the song with the *Sewol* ferry disaster victims due to its lyrics about missing a loved one and its music video, which seems to allude to the students victims and the ferry disaster, which I will explain further in this chapter. Pulvirenti was shocked to learn about the *Sewol* after viewing the "Spring Day" music video, understanding it as a tragedy "caused by the corruption and the negligence of the Korean government, the shipping industry... that could happen not only in Korea but in other places, too."[2]

Through Pulvirenti's video, other international fans of BTS learned more about the *Sewol,* as seen in numerous comments. In addition to creating the analysis video, Pulvirenti studied articles, investigative reports, and videos about the *Sewol.* She even visited Korea to meet with the *Sewol* families in September 2019, and organized with other fans to create commemorative projects. Pulvirenti's experience is one of the many examples that show how popular music has the power to reach millions of viewers. After the *Sewol,* many K-pop fans and some performers directed their affective labor in ways that brought attention to the *Sewol* as a traumatic event and made K-pop an arena where emotions and political feelings about the disaster could be expressed and around which community could be forged.

Through an examination of K-pop works that audiences have

interpreted as referencing the sinking of the *Sewol,* this chapter explores how popular music can serve as a public memory archive and offer alternative spaces for memory and mourning. In the aftermath of the *Sewol,* it argues, lyrical and visual motifs of K-pop performances that trigger certain affects and create empathy among listeners/viewers have created spaces for revisiting the disaster, questioning the actions and inactions of authorities, and commemorating the victims in ways that link honoring their lives with calls for change. While different in many ways—scale, budget, audience, venue, distribution, and so on—from the artistic works discussed in the previous chapters, K-pop performances have provided vast popular audiences with a forum for remembering and making meaning out of the disaster.

In the 1970s and 1980s, many South Korean songs expressed dissent against the Park Chung-hee and Chun Doo-hwan dictatorship. During protests against the authoritarian regimes, activists would sing *minjung gayo,* a term coined in the mid-1980s to distinguish this genre of expressly political popular music. While this trend never disappeared from the protest scene, popular music became increasingly synonymous with K-pop, whose meteoric growth has propelled and been propelled by the industry. Nevertheless, although K-pop is a primarily a commercial arena, its artists responded to the sinking of the *Sewol* and its aftermath of injustice, reaching millions of Koreans and global audiences with their performances.

While many K-pop fans and the industry might prefer that artists and their content be devoid of politics, contemporary K-pop music has never seen a shortage of songs that deliver sociopolitical messages. In the 1990s, Seo Taiji and Boys, one of the most influential acts in contemporary Korean popular culture, sang songs that addressed issues such as the impacts of Korea's competitive education system ("Classroom Idea") and the plight of runaway teenagers ("Come Back Home"); the latter became so popular that it motivated many Korean runaway teens to return to their homes. First-generation idol groups such as H.O.T. and SechsKies also sang about school bullying ("The Warrior's Descendant"), the education system ("School Byeolgok"), and preventable disasters ("I yah!"). In October 2016, Ewha Womans University students sang Girls' Generation's "Into the New World" during protests against the university and the Park administration's rampant corruption and incompetence.[3] Capturing nationwide attention, these students' protests spread, combining other complaints with anger over the *Sewol.*[4]

As these examples attest, K-pop gives the younger generation a voice to call out pressing concerns and issues in Korean society. And despite commercial and political pressures that encourage noncontroversial content, various K-pop artists have represented and responded to such concerns in their music. There are many examples in which K-pop idols raise issues about diversity, environmentalism, feminism, or mental health in their works, and fans becoming inspired to support the idols' messages through collective action. In this sense, it is possible to view K-pop as artists as performing activism in and through their music, and to see K-pop as a potentially activist arena of popular culture. Indeed, in terms of the sheer number of fans they reach, K-pop idols can be viewed as some of the most influential activists in the world.

In the wake of the *Sewol* ferry disaster, many of the biggest names in K-pop, such as BTS, Kim Yoon Ah, Lee Seung-hwan, Lucid Fall, and Red Velvet, have made direct or indirect references to the *Sewol* tragedy in their work. Some musicians addressed the sinking of the ferry in media interviews or on social media platforms; meanwhile, other apparent references were more subtle, leading South Korean audiences themselves to posit that connections were being made to the disaster. That many K-pop artists have generational connections to a large proportion of the victims suggested that they might feel more strongly about commemorating them and standing in solidarity with their families and supporters.

"IS THE SONG ABOUT THE *SEWOL*?"

Performances that commemorate the *Sewol* are not just for the victims' families but also for the rest of the Korean society. Since the disaster, a growing corpus of research has shown that the Korean people suffered from the trauma and its aftermath. The research of Hyekyung Woo and her team at Seoul National University indicates how this trauma was reflected in everyday speech and social media.[5] Examining data from March 2014 to June 2014 on social media platforms, Woo examined emotional utterances in reactions to the *Sewol* by analyzing keywords associated with the human-made disaster and with suicide; the finding was that keywords associated with suicide were common in the population.

Historian Nan Kim describes how the Korean people were traumatized by the incident:

> I had been living in Seoul that spring, and during the days and weeks in the wake of the *Sewol* disaster, a palpable sense of depression was all but ubiquitous. What surprised me was how common it became for everyday conversations to start with expressions of not only sorrow but also guilt over the loss of so many young lives. I remember asking a friend what she made of this spontaneous and pervasive guilt complex. On top of anger at those responsible, she described an anguished sense of regret for having tolerated the kind of society that had allowed this disaster to happen and a feeling of personal responsibility for not having done enough to fight corruption.[6]

This "ubiquitous" depression is one of the tragedy's main legacies. When Koreans view images of capsized boats or yellow ribbons, they have a strong visceral reaction of grief and anger. In a similar sentiment, sociologist Cho Han Haejoang writes,

> The *Sewol* Ferry Disaster has dredged up acute feelings of sadness and anger within the Korean people. . . . It has forced people to take the small moments of self-awareness that have formed from gazing into the black hole of despair and transform them into public speech. Shuttling back and forth between the public and private spheres, the surviving families and mourning citizens are recovering the practices of empathy and mourning that were either suppressed or excluded from the phallocentric political sphere.[7]

This sinking of the *Sewol* became a turning point in South Korean history, forcing the public to question issues of community, education, government, law, and violence and leading to massive popular protests and movements. Many participants in this moment of reckoning and change sought solace and community in Korea's most popular music genre, K-pop.

Popular music has the power to amplify stories and to build a public memory archive because of the reach of popular music through its wide circulation. Popular music also has affective power and can move people to action in unique ways. In the case of responding to the *Sewol,* specific characteristics of K-pop amplify these qualities, including its enormous popularity, the central role of its fandom, and the ways it produces and mediates mass affect. According to statistics released by the Korea Foundation, there are more than 200 million fans of Korean pop culture around the globe.[8]

Since its origins in the late twentieth century, fan practices have been central to the production of K-pop as a cultural and artistic phenomenon and behemoth global industry. The K-pop group BTS, one of the most popular musical acts in the world, calls their fandom "ARMY," a fitting moniker for the powerful role fans have played in powering their success. Highly organized and complexly networked, K-pop fandom is a community that mobilizes its resources, especially digital media and technology, to set and achieve communal goals. Today everything from the careers of individual idols to the fate of an entire multinational industry relies on the labor that K-pop fans perform in service to the music and entertainment they love. This in turn makes K-pop artists particularly responsive to fans' needs and desires. For decades, fans of K-pop have found encouragement, happiness, and a sense of community through the special connections they forge with idols and the broader K-pop fan base. Meanwhile, K-pop's success in Korea and around the world would not have been possible without the creative contributions of an enthusiastic, diverse, and seemingly ever-growing fandom. From promoting specific idols and groups, to generating enthusiasm for the industry more broadly, fans massively influence the business of K-pop and its cultural significance. K-pop fan practices and activities constitute a central productive force, shaping not only K-pop's explosive global popularity but also K-pop's cultural and social impacts and horizons of possibility, which include its cultural politics.

In a way, these K-pop fans perform a kind of *materialization of affective labor.* Affective labor, as scholars have theorized, refers to kinds of work that produces, maintains, and manages emotions, feelings, and experiences, including the kinds of intensely felt individual and collective experiences of enjoyment and belonging K-pop elicits in its legions of fans worldwide.

Music, scholars have shown, has capacities to elicit empathy; in the case of the *Sewol,* a listener's empathy might facilitate affective responses in identifying with music that mentions the victims of the *Sewol* and their families, and this in term can lead to personal and collective actions. Emery Schubert suggests that "musical and social processing draw upon shared neural resources" and that music is a "social stimulus capable of recruiting empathy systems."[9]

Words and images can produce affect and generate empathy. Patrik N. Juslin and Daniel Vastfjall argue that composers and performers encode affective gestures into the music, and listeners decode those gestures through mimetic, mirroring processes.[10] Moreover, according to Hauke Egermann and Stephen McAdams, the greater the listener's empathy, the more likely the listener will exhibit an affective response.[11] Therefore, for instance, people who already know about the *Sewol* and care for how its victims were treated are more likely to exhibit an affective response when listening to songs about it. Artists' use of evocative words and images—for example, references to goodbyes, the sea, or the color yellow—can help to elicit such responses.

Because the *Sewol* has become politically contentious, many musicians would rather not discuss the meaning of some songs that seem to refer to or comment on the disaster. For many musicians, having to explain whether a song is or is not about the *Sewol* might present a dilemma stemming from sociopolitical issues pertaining to the arts. When a musician claims to have written a song about the *Sewol,* it becomes a new story. While some listeners may compliment musicians' critical gaze on social issues and courage to state the intention behind the song, some may dismiss such musicians as "leftist celebrities" or otherwise. As previously discussed, Korean artists whose works commemorated the tragedy and demanded government accountability were denied grants and funding by the Park government. This kind of pressure set the tone for popular artists and industries as well, and with regard to K-pop, it is important to remember the close connections that have evolved between the industry and state support. At the same time, though, hugely commercially successful artists are of course less economically constrained or directly financially reliant on government support.

This chapter's analysis does not take a position for or against musicians who do or do not explain the meaning of songs that audiences have linked to the *Sewol*; instead it focuses on examining how and why Koreans associate certain songs and performances with the *Sewol* as well as on the broader significance of K-pop performances in relation to representation, activism, and commemoration. I examine several songs and music videos that Koreans associate with the *Sewol.* I then show that musicians who say their songs are about the *Sewol* tend to commemorate the victims by borrowing words and phrases from *Sewol* activists, victims' families, and citizens who stand with them. By contrast, musicians who will not say whether or not the song is about the *Sewol* tend to use visual imagery to generate empathy. Songs about longing, sadness, and sorrow might or might not have been written with the *Sewol* in mind, but perhaps more importantly, these songs can take on specific popular resonances through the workings of fan labor that connects them to the *Sewol.* Taken together, works across both categories illustrate how and why K-pop performances become sites of remembrance and meaning making.

SONGS AND MUSIC VIDEOS THAT MENTION THE *SEWOL*

f(x)'s "Red Light"

f(x) was a girl group that was managed by SM Entertainment. Its members were Victoria, Amber, Luna, Krystal, and Sulli (now deceased). SM Entertainment's producing director Lee Sung-soo described "Red Light" as "a song that criticizes the *Sewol* ferry disaster."[12] The use of the word *chimmol* (sinking) was a decision made after an internal discussion.

The music video of this electronic pop song opens with a black telephone in dark room ringing twice. The ringing sounds like an alarm. The scene changes to a burning book with the song title in white capital letters. The song opens with buzzing, electronic noises over a ticking beat. We then see the five members in a warehouse, under a red light. The music video juxtaposes the members walking briskly—almost marching—to the beat, close-ups of their faces, and two red lights. Approximately forty-five seconds into the music video, we see Victoria perched on a ladder and in what looks the hull of a ship. We then see someone who appears to be trapped inside a building. The mood, created by lighting, scenery, and the performers' expressions, is austere and cold. Projected across the members of the group are short beams of light, resembling rippling water.

Approximately two minutes into the music video, there is a close-up of an exploding flower. When Luna sings, "Turn around just once / Look for the precious things," we see black-and-white images of the members, which in their lack of vibrancy and historical aesthetic might refer to the deceased.

Notably, the music video ends with the black telephone.

The first distress call from the *Sewol* came from a male student who used a telephone to call the national emergency number. "Save us! We're on a ship and I think it's sinking," the boy told the fire officer. Three minutes later, the crew called Jeju Harbor Affairs for help. From 8:55 to 9:37 a.m., Harbor Affairs at Jeju and at Jindo Island urged the crew to prepare the passengers for evacuation, but instead the crew instructed the passengers to stay where they were and wait for help. Survivors reported receiving repeated instructions over the loudspeaker to remain in their cabins. Most of the passengers heeded the instructions and died waiting for rescue.

Along with the images used in the video, the instrumental beat and sound merged with the short verses, in which the members' chants create a sense of urgency. Words such as *siljesanghwang* (real situation), *gyeong-go* (warning), *chimmol* (sinking), and *bisanggu* (emergency exit) might remind the listener of the sinking ferry.[13]

FTISLAND's "Pray"

FTISLAND is a boy band managed by FNC. Its members are Choi Jong Hoon, Lee Hong Gi, Lee Jae Jin, Choi Min Hwan, Song Seung Hyun. "Pray" was released in March 2015 as the title song of their fifth album, *I Will.* According to the band's YouTube page, the song is a prayer for truth in a world full of lies. Choi composed the melody, and the other four members cowrote the lyrics with him. "It is the track that all members are proud enough to say that it is the closest to the music style that FTISLAND pursued so far." More than a year after the song was released, on November 27, 2016, Lee Hong Gi posted on his Instagram account a photo of the *I Will* album cover. Under the photo he wrote, "Now I confess, this song is for you" and added "#SEWOL."

The black-and-white music video opens with an image of a large wooden cage and Lee Hong Gi trying to break out. The band is shown performing in a large room with glass walls. The black lining along the glass walls makes it look like the band is trapped. From time to time, we see the band performing from outside the room. Images of Lee trapped in the cage are juxtaposed against the band performing. The lyrics evoke themes of suspicion and obfuscation:

> The many lies whispered in another reality
> Truth disappears and [we are] trapped in darkness
> My cries growing smaller in the incompetent reality
> A meaningless thing in a world of lies
> See me now? See me now?
> I'm broken in my faith
> Oh, please God hear me?
> I can't do anything
> Oh, please God hear me?
> The world stopped
> Oh, please God hear me?
> The day we shout
> Oh, please God hear me?
> So we don't lose our way again
> I'll pray I'll pray I'll pray
> I'll pray for you

With these lines, the song references both the passengers' desperation and the many Koreans who mourned the victims and demanded that the Park administration explain the delay in rescuing the students, weaving together their pleas. There is water on the floor that splashes as the performers jump. Being trapped in water might symbolize the students' inability to escape. In addition, the explosive beat and Lee's powerful vocals creates a sense of desperation.

At this point, some people dressed in business suits but wearing clown makeup surround the glass room and watch the performance. The spectators smile gleefully, as if they are thoroughly enjoying watching the performance. Their smiles are deeply unsettling, especially in contrast to the band members' serious faces and Lee's disconsolate expression. The clownish spectators might represent the authorities who botched the rescue, journalists who sensationalized the tragedy, or right-wing politicians and Park's supporters who spread lies about the *Sewol.*

After the second verse, the music shatters the glass walls and the spectators are flung backward. The final image shows the glass room from afar, in a black fog. It looks as if the room is floating at sea.

Lee Seung-hwan's "Tragedy of the Era"

Lee Seung-hwan is one of Korea's best-known politically active musicians. To many Koreans, he is viewed as a "leftist celebrity" who maintains a critical gaze toward society and is not afraid of censorship. Thus, it is not surprising that he joined other K-pop performers who directly commented on the *Sewol* in their performances.

"Tragedy of the Era" is included in Lee's album *3+3*, released in October 2015. It was also featured in the soundtrack of the 2015 documentary film *Nappeun nara* (Cruel state), directed by Gim Jin-yeol, Yi Su-jeong, and Jeong Il-geon. The documentary explains how the victims' families fought the government from 2014 to 2015 to find the truth about the *Sewol*. It shows the commemorative classrooms, families marching to the National Assembly, and supporters signing petitions. The music video combines images from the documentary.

> The sky tilted that morning and friends cried
> They called their mom and dad and the adults shouted in a low voice
> Stay where you are
> Stay where you are

The repetition of "Stay where you are" is a reminder that the captain and crew of the *Sewol* were the first to abandon the ferry, after ordering the passengers to remain in place. Lee sings slowly, and his calm repetition of "Stay where you are" presents a stark contrast to the urgent moment when the ferry capsized.

At the end of the documentary film's music video, a caption appears in the lower right corner of the frame that references the *Sewol* Ferry Disaster Special Act ("Special Act") passed by the South Korean National Assembly on November 7, 2014, whose investigation was hindered by the government: "Do you remember the *Sewol* Special Act which was made possible because of 5.3 million citizens? It's time to create another miracle." These two sentences, which are not part of the song but are part of the documentary, express Lee's solidarity with the victims' families and urges the viewers to demand a thorough investigation by the government as an act of commemoration.

Kim Yoon Ah's "River"

Although "River" was on Kim Yoon Ah's album *The Pain of Others,* released on December 8, 2016, the song gained much attention two years later, when Kim performed it on the South Korean reality TV program *Begin Again.* In the episode that aired on March 30, 2018, Kim mentioned the *Sewol* before performing the song in Portugal: " 'Yes, we're from Korea. In Korea, a few years ago, many people lost their family members in a tragic accident. At that time, we couldn't do anything for them. The only thing I was able to do was making some songs, and the next song is one of them.' " The lyrics, which Kim's interview helped viewers better contextualize, are as follows:

> Your name has become a song
> flowing like a river in my heart
> If I keep walking along that river
> could I reach you?
> Could I see you someday?
> My longing for you has become a wind
> hovering endlessly in my heart
> As I call your name, the river flows
> to a place that can never return
> Who will hold your hand?
> Feelings of loneliness that I was left alone,
> my heart that was shattered into pieces,
> and memories I can't hold on to
> fill that river
> Your name, your voice,
> and the moments I held you
> scatter aimlessly in that river
> Your name has become a song
> flowing like a river in my heart
> If I throw myself into the river
> could I see you again?
> The river just keeps flowing away
> and disappears

The song, which starts slowly, climaxes with a sense of sorrow, which is conveyed through the wailing tone. The TV program that brought renewed attention to it juxtaposes close-up shots of Kim singing, bystanders stopping and listening attentively, and a bird's-eye view of the band performing near a riverbank in the evening.

Cheetah and Jang Seong-hwan's "Yellow Ocean"

"Yellow Ocean" became popular after the rappers Cheetah and Jang Seong-hwan performed it on *Hipobui minjok* (Tribe of hip hop) on December 27, 2016. Before Cheetah and Jang's performance, the audience was shown news clips of parents crying over their children who perished on the ferry. It also included a brief segment of Lucid Fall's "Still There, Still Here," a song that many interpret as an homage to the victims and their families. Previously, during a press conference held in December 2015 for the release of his seventh album, Lucid Fall declined to discuss the meaning of this song, asserting that their listeners should be free to interpret the song as they wished. Combined with its already evocative title, "Yellow Ocean," the lyrics reference imagery and feelings widely associated with the *Sewol,* conveying a sense of generational grief.

My friends
where could they be?
With drooping shoulders
would they be in the classroom?
Go back for me
to a warm home
On your way home
please look at the sky just once
Can you see me waving my hand?
Can you see me smiling?
I am wearing wings of eternity
and became a yellow butterfly
Before spring comes again
will you promise me one thing?
My friend,
don't fall apart

and live
The day the flowers bloomed
I was fading
but even if the flowers fade and disappear
I am still here
Can you see me smiling?
I am wearing wings of eternity
and became a yellow butterfly
Before spring comes again
will you promise me one thing?
My friend,
don't fall apart
and live

After the segment of Lucid Fall's song, Cheetah tearfully rapped about the people's sense of powerlessness and grief:

Back then, opening and closing my eyes and I even felt sorry about breathing that I clamped my mouth shut and put my hands together and prayed over and over
Obviously there was a truth and something to salvage
The truth is now surfacing little by little
The truth that lost its identity
They had no will and they watched and put on a show of lies
And many days passed since then but today we still remember
Because with the candles there are things we have to uncover
Those who would be beautiful around this time
The flowers that couldn't bloom as well as the hope
The unfortunate people and children who are still there without knowing the reason and what all this was for
I hope that place isn't as cold as those people's hearts
I hope those left behind heal as soon as possible
We're sorry we couldn't let go of you, who should have gone to a good place, with an easy heart
We won't forget
Sewol ferry that won't be forgotten in the passing time
Our light will beat their darkness
Yellow ribbons in the ocean

The truth will not sink
Yellow ribbons in the ocean
Ocean oh shine

Cheetah's rap reveals how the live coverage of the *Sewol* sinking traumatized Koreans, including K-pop stars of their generation. Wearing a school uniform and sitting at a student's desk, Jang opened the second verse by asking, "Is no one out there?" and reflected on the tragedy from the perspective of a high school student who could have been a classmate of the students who had died.

Is no one out there?
The cries that merely hit the walls
How frustrating it must have been
Just thinking of that time brings tears to my eyes
It's 2016, we must not forget
The big issue of the day, the reason I brought up this topic
But as the time passes, *Sewol* is forgotten
During a time where they should learn why did they have to suffer this?
Why did you not do anything during that time?
We cannot know, their hearts are colder than the ocean
Those who would have been our seniors remain as eighteen years old
The countless dead, missing, not only the students
And to the heroes that make us proud
I hope that you're at peace there
Spring is still cold, just like that day
What's it like there?
Sewol ferry that won't be forgotten in the passing time
Our light will beat their darkness
Yellow ribbons in the ocean
The truth will not sink
Yellow ribbons in the ocean
Ocean oh shine

The lyrics mention the *Sewol* with words and phrases such as *inyang* (salvage), *jinsil* (truth), *jinsang* (truth), *chotbul* (candle), *Sewol, Sewolho* (Sewol ferry), "yellow ribbons in the ocean," and "remember 4.16." In the final part of the song, the duo notes that the ferry was still at the bottom of the sea:

> The reason that my spring is still so cold
> The reason that falling petals are so sad
> Just like the waves near a tilted boat
> Even if time passes, don't forget, don't forget
> Petals wet from our tears, that's our spring
> The apologies from those without any remorse are our burden
> After that day, up in our faces is the longing with only a start, and no end in sight
> Remember 4.16
> Remember 4.16
> The tears fill my eyes, the date that's engraved in my heart
> April 16th, 2014

Reflecting journalists' accusations that the Park government delayed the ferry's recovery in order to "hide the truth," the rappers reply, "Our light will prevail over the dark forces. We raise candles to bring truths under the light. The truth will not be scuttled. The truth is now slowly floating to the surface." Asking for forgiveness, they promised that they will "remember April 16" and that the truth will eventually prevail.

Embodied performance acts underscored the messages of this song in real time. Both Cheetah and Jang performed onstage wearing yellow ribbons and yellow bracelets. They emphasized that the point was "not to make people sad, but to remind people not to forget," and that people should always "remember [this tragedy] in their hearts, instead of forgetting as time goes on." Cheetah could not hold back tears as she performed in front of the bereaved parents. She admitted that it was a song that she had wanted to write for a long time, but only if people would listen to it. "Before the performance, I, together with Jang, had visited Gwanghwamun Square to see the victims' family members putting on a choir show at an antipresident demonstration," Cheetah said. "I told them about my song and they approved and thanked me for the efforts. The song is not about reminding of the pain from two years ago. It's about not forgetting it." In addition, Cheetah promised to donate all profits from "Yellow Ocean" to *Sewol* nonprofits. The audience burst into tears, and the other contestants praised Cheetah and Jang for addressing this difficult topic.

SONGS AND MUSIC VIDEOS THAT REFER INDIRECTLY TO THE *SEWOL*

The Ark's "Light"

The members of The Ark, a girl group that has since disbanded, were Minju, Yuna, Yujin, Halla, and Jane. They released "Light" in April 2015. While the lyrics do not seem to have been inspired by the *Sewol,* the music video seems to depict it.

The music video opens with a mother and daughter sharing an umbrella. The actress Jo Min-su portrays the mother, and Halla portrays the daughter. They pass by a store, and the daughter's face lights up when she sees a purple backpack in the window. The daughter seems to want it, but the mother notes that the daughter already has a perfectly good orange one. The daughter walks away in a huff and the mother chases after her.

We then see the mother waking up, opening the refrigerator, and sipping banana milk. She takes another one and puts the straw in her daughter's mouth. She brushes her daughter's hair and kisses her forehead as the sleepy girl sips the banana milk. We then see the mother making *gimbap* and the daughter packing, presumably for a school trip. The daughter frets over what clothes to pack, and the mother fingers the frayed orange backpack. The two leave their home and walk arm in arm down the street. The forsythia hedges are in bloom, indicating that spring has arrived. As the mother and daughter part, the daughter uses two fingers to draw a smile on her face. The mother does likewise and smiles as she watches her daughter rush off. We then see the daughter and her classmates playing games on the bus. Meanwhile, the mother goes to her job in a restaurant. She makes a mistake and annoys a customer. As she tries to correct the mistake, she overhears a news report of a bus accident.

In the next scene, the mother is walking alone past a store. She drinks banana milk and makes *gimbap.* She puts on makeup and stares blankly at her reflection. She then packs for a trip. Taking out the carefully prepared food and a purple backpack, she puts it on what appears to be her daughter's grave. The grieving mother's face is juxtaposed with previous scenes of her and her daughter together. The lyrics, especially the following refrain, describe comforting loved ones:

Hold my hands when you need somebody
I'll be that somebody somebody
We're in this for life yeah
Look at me when you need shoulders to lean on
I'll be that somebody somebody
We're in this for life yeah

The story of students dying on a class trip—and the grief that remained for parents, as for the mother in the video—offered a parallel to the *Sewol* tragedy. Notably, while not specifically political, the video's empathic visuals and lyrics about ongoing shared support resonated with viewers who regarded the video as a tribute to the *Sewol.*

Red Velvet's "One of These Nights"

Red Velvet, is a girl group managed by SM Entertainment. Its members are Irene, Seulgi, Wendy, Joy, and Yeri. "One of These Nights" was released on March 17, 2016, exactly one month prior to the second anniversary of the *Sewol* and two lunar years after the sinking. While the lyrics express a general sense of longing, the images in the music video seem to make both implicit and explicit references to the disaster.

The music video begins with the members getting their hair done and putting on their makeup. They all look grim. A yellow butterfly is seen behind Yeri. Wendy walks past a message board that says "AIS 1516." (AIS is an abbreviation for Automatic Identification System, and the ferry set sail on April 15 and sank on April 16.) The interior of the set resembles a ship corridor more than it does a motel. Wendy stands still, and the entire frame changes into a keyhole of a door. Seulgi peers into the keyhole, then faces the camera and walks onto a balcony that is surrounded by water. Irene faces a mirror shaped like a porthole. She stays still, but Joy climbs the ladder and escapes. The image of Joy is interrupted by a cup of tea. Survivors of the *Sewol* stated that they realized that the ferry was in trouble when the soup in their bowls seemed to tilt. Seulgi and Wendy attempt to escape through a window, but it is too late for Wendy. Yeri is lying down in a boat. The room goes dark as Seulgi walks into the corridor. She has a chance to escape as the ship fills with water, but she accepts her imminent death and opens the door to heaven. "It's okay even if it's in a dream, let's meet again." Wendy crawls under a table, which many of the trapped passengers had done. The members of the group are surrounded by candles, honoring the dead, and Joy is wearing a yellow dress. Irene begins to drown. Yeri finally wakes up, but the boat has flooded and she is staring out at the sea. Yeri succumbs to the water. The porthole breaks open and floods with water, drowning Irene. Joy appears in black. Irene is on the ground, surrounded by blue walls. Furniture is floating above her. Someone walks down the hall as the lights go out one by one, which can symbolize either the power going out as the ferry sank and/or the lives lost in the disaster. The moon is behind.

While most of the lyrics seem politically neutral, many listeners seem to think that the line "Oh, I can't quickly forget because even when the pages of the calendar turn I'm still in the same place" refers to the commemorative classrooms, and perhaps more broadly to the way traumatic incidents can make time seem to stand still, or repeatedly return survivors to the time of the initial trauma. On the wall of each commemorative classroom hangs a calendar from April 2014. The words "class trip" are written across the dates from the 15th through the 18th. For these classrooms, time stopped on April 16, 2014. Until all bodies are recovered and a thorough investigation—one that reveals the cause of the sinking and why the students were left to die—is conducted, the students remain frozen on that day. The remnants' temporality refers to the many questions that remain to be answered and the current state of the investigation.

BTS's "Spring Day"

As one of the most popular boy bands in the world, BTS is under constant public scrutiny. Even when what they do seems completely innocent or innocuous, their intentions can be misconstrued or misinterpreted. For example, when BTS leader RM delivered an acceptance speech that mentioned in passing the shared "history of pain" between South Korea and the United States in connection with the Korean War, Chinese ultranationalists attacked BTS on social media. As idols are more susceptible to political scandals, it is understandable that they are less likely to admit whether or not a song is about the *Sewol*. However, we can infer that the BTS members and their song "Spring Day" might hold social consciousness about the *Sewol*. In 2021, *Kyunghyang Shinmun*, a Korean newspaper, reported that BTS had visited the *Sewol* victims' altar at the Gwanghwamun Square and offered their condolences to the families in 2014. They have also donated funds to *Sewol* nonprofits. It is therefore possible to conclude that although HYBE, BTS's management agency, has yet to clarify whether "Spring Day" is about the *Sewol,* BTS stands in solidarity with the families and expresses that solidarity in this work.

The music video opens with BTS member V standing alone at Iryeong train station. V steps off the platform and walks down to the tracks. Snow is falling. He kneels and puts his head on the track. Next we see the train moving. The song opens with the lyrics "I miss you." We then see Jungkook sitting alone in a train car, looking out the window. Many fans speculate that both V and Jungkook might symbolize people with survivor's guilt. We then see Jimin sitting alone on a beach, staring out at sea. His clothes are worn and he holds a pair of white sneakers. Jimin seems to represent the parents who waited for their children's bodies to be recovered. All three look somber.

We then see RM standing in a train car filled with abandoned clothes and suitcases, perhaps evoking the belongings of the student victims. As RM's rap solo contains the lyric "Snowpiercer," the song might refer to the film itself or to Curtis, the protagonist. Directed by Bong Joon-ho, *Snowpiercer* is a futuristic film set entirely inside a train. The film depicts how Curtis, a passenger in the tail car, stages a revolution to proceed to the head car to meet Wilford, the maker and head of the train. As RM marches forward, he might allude to Curtis's fight, confronting the issue of the *Sewol* ferry disaster.

RM exits the train and enters a building that looks like a motel. J-Hope and Suga are standing near the door. On top of the motel, a sign with the words "Omelas" blinks brightly. Omelas is a utopian city in Ursula Le Guin's novel *The Ones Who Walk Away from Omelas.* When RM enters the motel, he sees the other BTS members having a food fight. This could either refer to the student victims having fun on the school trip before the sinking or *Snowpiercer*'s Curtis facing a backlash during his revolution.

Next we see Jin standing in a stairwell, looking up into the camera, unable to move. Jin might symbolize the student victims for whom time has stopped (or perhaps for the fact that they were instructed not to move, to stay where they were). In a similar setting, Jungkook stands in front of a rusted merry-go-round, decorated, notably, with yellow ribbons, an image that makes the reader think about both missing children, lost youth, and the commemoration (and lapse of commemoration) of the disaster.

We then see the BTS members in the Omelas motel, brushing their teeth and doing laundry. There is a shot taken from inside the washing machine, which makes it seem like the viewer is looking at Jin through the porthole of a ship. There are stickers saying "Don't Forget" attached to the door of each washing machine. "Don't Forget" also refers to the *Sewol* in that the families' activism slogan is "We won't forget. We will remember."

Next we see the members sitting in a mountain of clothes that are nearly identical to the twenty-five-foot-tall mound of used clothing in Christian Boltanski's 2010 installation *No Man's Land.* As Boltanski's piece signifies objects that belonged to missing people, the mountain of clothes the BTS members are sitting on might refer to the *Sewol* victims whose bodies have never been recovered.

We see Jimin in front of the sea again, holding the shoes. The shoes might symbolize the victims and support the victims' families. As we saw earlier, in her intermedial performance *Empathy,* Korean artist Jayoung Chung reconstructed the *Sewol* mothers' shoes to carry an electrical current. As Chung defines empathy as "sharing one's pain and putting oneself in other's shoes," the act of physical contact becomes important in the performance. In this performance we note that it is Jimin, who also held shoes in a previous scene in the video in which he seemed to symbolize waiting parents, who is again highlighted, this time explicitly in front of the landscape where the *Sewol* victims perished.

Jungkook enters the Omelas hotel and walks past the laundry room. After that he is joined by the other members. Next, Jungkook finds other members sitting in the same train car. The members look less somber; some look out the window with a peaceful expression. Jimin is hugging his legs, and J-Hope comforts him as sunlight pours into the train car, creating a warm atmosphere.

Jimin steps out of the train with the other members. They march across a snowy field, toward a tree. Jimin holds the shoes, which are later hung on the tree. The act of hanging shoes on a tree is a way of memorializing a tragic death.

In this chapter I have focused on how popular music can serve as a memorial and as political commentary on social issues. Musicians who reveal that a song they released and performed is about the *Sewol* tend to commemorate the victims by drawing on the terminology used by the victims' families and *Sewol* activists. By contrast, musicians who are more equivocal tend to use imagery that can elicit associations with the *Sewol* and empathy for its victims and survivors. While the lyrics convey urgency and loss, the music videos remind listeners and viewers of the *Sewol.* Notably, in response to all these videos, fans themselves mobilized to explore and discuss connections they saw to the *Sewol,* providing the essential labor that has played a significant role in bringing attention to the *Sewol* and keeping it alive in the public memory.

In April 2020, I learned about the 416 Choir, a choir consisting of eighteen *Sewol* families (parents of both student victims and survivors) and approximately forty Korean citizens. The choir had published a collection of essays titled *Noraereul bulleoseo nega ondamyeon* (If you could come when I sing), and when I purchased the book, it also contained a CD with songs recorded by the choir. The book chronicles the choir's journey and includes short essays by the *Sewol* families. The families first sang in December 2014 after the *Sewol* Special Act was passed. They wanted to show their gratitude to the Korean people who supported them. In August 2015, they had their first performance as the 416 Choir at a memorial event commemorating the five hundredth day after the disaster.

When Bak Yo-seop, father of student victim Bak Si-chan, was asked to join the choir, he thought it was a crazy idea because there was much work to do to investigate the disaster, and he was not sure if he could sing at all in that situation.[14] However, he agreed to join the choir when a social worker told him that music can strengthen bonds between the victims' families and other Korean people. "I think music holds power. At first, I cried so much I could not sing. But as my heart grew stronger and stronger, I could sing. I would not say I overcame my sorrow—I would say my heart became stronger," Bak said in a radio interview.[15]

From 2015 to 2020, the choir had approximately 270 performances. The choir performed not only at *Sewol* events but also at the Wednesday demonstrations for the victims known as comfort women in front of the former Japanese embassy in Seoul, the Ssangyong Motors workers' strike in Pyongtaek and Mokdong, and also in North American cities—Los Angeles, San Francisco, New York, and Toronto. The choir performed children's songs, folk songs, and even popular K-pop songs.

On December 11, 2021, the 416 Choir had a concert at the S Theater of the Sejong Center for the Performing Arts, one of the largest arts and cultural venues in South Korea. Halfway through the performance, the lights turned the venue's background purple. A choir member stepped forward and said, "Mom misses you even though I look at your photo." She stepped back in her place. As the opening chords of BTS's "Spring Day" began, I heard sniffles. When the song started, another choir member narrated RM and Jungkook's opening verse, which was rewritten to reflect the families' sentiments:

> I miss you
> Saying this makes me miss you even more
> I miss you even though I look at your photo
> I hate us for missing you when we did not do anything
> But I miss you

Accompanied by live piano, the choir sang the rest of BTS's "Spring Day":

> I miss you I miss you
> I miss you I miss you
> How long do I have to wait
> How many nights do I have to pass
> To see you?
> To meet you?

CHAPTER 5

Performing Diasporic Healing

Sewol *Activism in Korean American Communities*

On May 11, 2014, a full-page advertisement appeared on the pages of the *New York Times.* At the top is an illustration of a sinking ship. Above the illustration is the headline "South Korea: The *Sewol* Ferry Has Sunk." The caption read, "More than three hundred lives were trapped in the ferry. Not one was rescued." The following takes up the lower half of the advertisement:

> BRING THE TRUTH TO LIGHT
>
> Why are Koreans outraged by President Park Geun-hye?
>
> *Incompetence and Negligence*
>
> The South Korean government lacked adequate emergency protocols and proper communication between agencies. They rejected outside help—from expert civilian divers and the US Navy—and gave rescue rights to a private company in which the government is a major shareholder. The bungled rescue efforts demonstrated the lack of leadership, incompetence, and negligence of the Park Administration.
>
> *Media Censorship and Manipulation*
>
> Criticism of President Park's handling of the ferry disaster is being silenced by government censorship of South Korea's mainstream media.

Online videos and commentaries exposing the truth behind the failed rescue operations have been deleted from the web.

The mainstream media has served as the government's mouthpiece by releasing disingenuous news stories that have misled public opinion. A video footage of President Park comforting a relative of a ferry victim was later found to have been staged for the mainstream media. In fact, the woman in the video had no connections to anyone aboard the ferry.

In order to prevent public discussion, members of President Park's party have introduced a bill that, if passed, would allow the authorities to fine or arrest anyone spreading rumors that may contain false information related to the ferry disaster.

Controlling the media. Manipulating public sentiment. Ignoring the public interest.

President Park's behavior is reverting the country back towards South Korea's authoritarian past. Koreans are outraged because they see democracy regressing.

We demand an immediate end to the South Korean government's control of the media, censorship of the truth, manipulation of public opinion, and suppression of the public's freedom of speech.

Join the conversation to help restore democracy and free speech in Korea. www.thetruthofsewolferry.com/truth

Organized by MissyUSA, an online community for Korean women residing in North America, this advertisement reflected the members' determination to hold the South Korean government accountable and stand in solidarity with the *Sewol* victims' families. By mentioning the government's "incompetence," "negligence," misrepresentations of the disaster, and the "outrage" of MissyUSA members, the advertisement delivers information that people who had not followed the disaster would not have known. The advertisement also performs collaborative public countermemory by calling out the government for the staged video footage of President Park Geun-hye and the fraud perpetrated by a woman pretending to be a family member of a *Sewol* victim.

MissyUSA's advertisement campaign in the *New York Times* was one of the many forms of activism performed by Koreans and Korean

Americans residing in North America, where I was living during the *Sewol*'s sinking, and beyond. Through their strategies of peaceful nonviolent activism to support the *Sewol* families and survivors in searching for the truth and achieving legal redress, these members of the Korean diaspora formed and strengthened community bonds. Furthermore, their continuous activism extended to interest in and activism for other current events in Korea and issues affecting Asian Americans. By examining various forms of *Sewol* activism by Koreans and Korean Americans in North American cities, this chapter focuses on how the communal consciousness shared in such communities in the aftermath of the *Sewol* ferry disaster enabled them to channel their helplessness, rage, and sorrow into collective action.

HOW KOREAN AMERICAN WOMEN ORGANIZED A TRANSBORDER MOVEMENT: MISSYUSA

Before the *Sewol* activism, there were many occasions on which Korean Americans took action to voice their concerns. In the 1980s, Korean Americans gathered in major North American cities to stand in solidarity with the Korean people protesting against the *yushin* dictatorship. The first North American protest to stand in solidarity with the Gwangju Uprisings of May 1980 took place on May 26, 1980, at Albany Park, Chicago, where six hundred Korean Americans attended.[1] Korean Americans' participation in community activism was not limited to current events on the Korean peninsula. The 1992 Los Angeles riots and the 1994 anti-immigration wave motivated Korean Americans to "transition from their role as complacent observer to participant and stakeholder."[2] Eun Sook Lee, founding board member of the Korean American Resource and Cultural Center of Chicago, discusses how Korean Americans' civic participation transformed Korean American communities and identities:

> From within their own diverse ranks, Korean Americans built a critical mass of politically engaged citizenry that organized around immigrant rights issues and succeeded in establishing a Korean American voice at the national level. The transformation of political agency within

> the Korean American community significantly impacted immigrant-related legislation, and furthermore, the political processes used by the Korean American community contributed to the development of new concepts on social change organizing that are relevant to the changing demographics and diversity of ethnic and immigrant communities in the American diaspora.[3]

More recently, the *Sewol* activism by Korean American women tapped into existing activist networks and protest repertoires. MissyUSA is an online community for Korean women residing in the United States. Although most members of this community are Korean or Korean American women, they are diverse in occupation and socioeconomic background. Originally it was not activist per se, but it has come to be a platform for organizing and performing activism. Jisue Lee and Ji Hei Kang have examined how MissyUSA's shared social consciousness helped build a collective identity in planning and participating in *Sewol* activism.[4] The community members actively engaged in collaborative activities from searching, curating, and managing information about the *Sewol* to streamlining group communication and mobilizing of resources for the *New York Times* advertisement. From May 1, 2014, to May 9, 2014, more than $160,000 was raised for the advertisement by four thousand members, far exceeding the original goal of $58,000. Lee and Kang argue that MissyUSA's Sewol activism serves as an example of how "loosely networked individuals can come together for a cause and transform an online community from a simple information ground into a powerful virtual organization, capable of implementing effective collective actions." Hyun Hee Kim views MissyUSA's collaborative activities as an example of "transborder civic engagement," transforming previously apolitical Korean and Korean American women into engaged citizens who demand government accountability.[5]

MissyUSA's second advertisement in the *New York Times* was published on August 14, 2014. At the top is an illustration of a capsized ship with strings around it. The strings are connected to a pair of large hands positioned above the ship, as if the ship is a marionette that someone else is manipulating. This might allude to the Park government's control of media coverage of the disaster and delaying the recovery of the sunken ferry. Under the illustration is the following text:

THE TRUTH SHALL NOT SINK

Losing a loved one to a deadly accident would be anyone's worst nightmare. For hundreds of Korean people, this nightmare has yet to come to an end.

Victims' Families on Hunger Strike

Since April, the families of the victims have been requesting a thorough investigation by the Korean government to find the true cause of the accident and help prevent a similar disaster from happening again. Their cries are falling on deaf ears as President Park Geun-hye and her party continue to ignore their plea. Rather than offering support and condolences for the families to mourn in peace, members of the ruling party manipulated public sentiment by spreading false rumors. The undercover police illegally surveilled the families and riot police violently blocked their peaceful rallies. While the mainstream media remains a broken whistleblower for the public, the families are now on a month-long hunger strike, sleeping on the streets near the National Assembly building in their efforts to find the truth.

Corruption, Negligence, and Deregulation

The illegally remodeled and overloaded ferry was a product of governmental corruption and corporate greed bred by deregulation of safety laws. When coupled with the government's lack of a central emergency response coordinator and President Park's absence for seven hours after the accident, it was a perfect recipe for a tragic catastrophe. Yet, only a few low-ranking government employees were arrested along with workers of the shipping company following a superficial investigation.

A Special Legislation to Bring Change

The sinking of the *Sewol* is not just an accident. It is a man-made disaster caused by greed, corruption and incompetence of the government. The only way to prevent history from repeating itself is to find the truth. The victims' families have proposed the *Sewol* Ferry Act to set up an independent committee with subpoena and prosecutorial powers. It will be the only way for South Korea to restore the grounds for a safe and democratic nation where liberty and justice prevail.

Join the victims' families in their fight for truth and justice by signing an online petition supporting the *Sewol* Ferry Act. www.sewoltruth.com

The second and third advertisements provide an update on the aftermath of the disaster, stress the need for a thorough investigation, and support the enactment of the *Sewol* Special Act. The third *New York Times* advertisement was published on September 24, 2014, under the heading "The Collapse of Truth and Justice in South Korea?" On the right side of the advertisement is a photo of President Park Geun-hye standing and staring straight ahead. On the left side of the advertisement is the following text:

Harsh Reality for the Grieving Families

Five months have passed since the *Sewol* ferry disaster, but many questions remain unanswered. Instead of offering an apology and explanation for failing to take effective executive actions in the critical hours after the ferry accident, South Korean President Park Geun-hye has condemned those who asked questions about her whereabouts during the time of the accident. President Park has also ordered the local public prosecutor to track anyone making negative comments on the internet about her. The ferry victims' families were placed under illegal surveillance with no legitimate reason and the government manipulated public sentiment by releasing false information about the families to the media to instigate reports that painted the families in negative light.

Unbalanced Scale of Justice

It has recently come to light that during the 2012 presidential campaign season in South Korea, the Korean National Intelligence Service was deeply involved in swaying public opinion in favor of now-President Park by using social media to praise Ms. Park and smear her rival candidates. Since then, the Central District Court has convicted the former intelligence chief of violating a law that prohibited the agency from engaging in domestic politics but dismissed charges against him of violating Korean election law, sparing the president from a possibly serious political stigma.

Broken Promise and Unheard Voices

> In order to console the public amidst the scandals surrounding both the ferry accident and the 2012 election, as well as to help her party in upcoming local elections, President Park had promised to support a special law that would give investigation and prosecutorial rights to an independent committee to probe the numerous issues circling around the ferry disaster. Only five months later, President Park has flipped her stance and dismissed the legislation, despite hundreds of legal scholars and lawyers in South Korea have indicated that President Park's argument against the special law is flawed and confirmed that the special law does not violate Korea's constitution. Over five million people have raised their voices in support of the ferry victims' families and the special law by signing a petition and participating in peaceful rallies. Such public efforts are being continually ignored by President Park and the ruling party.
>
> We demand an enactment of the special law to find truth and justice for the *Sewol* victims and their families.
>
> We demand an immediate end to the disruption of democratic values in South Korea.

MissyUSA's three advertisements drew considerable attention not only in the diaspora but also in Korea. Having ordered a thorough investigation of so-called misinformation and rumors about the *Sewol* ferry disaster, the Blue House responded directly to MissyUSA's campaign.[6] Kim Ki-chun, chief of the Presidential Secretariat, said, "By posting an advertisement criticizing the Korean government, [MissyUSA has] undermined Korea's status," and announced that he would "respond strongly." The Blue House sought legal recourse, such as applying defamation to "Haeoreumi," the organizer of MissyUSA. In October 2014, the conservative Blue Union filed a complaint with the Seoul Central District Prosecutor's Office for defamation and other charges against MissyUSA. Blue Union then submitted a petition to the Ministry of Justice to deny them entry to Korea and requested that the US Federal Bureau of Investigation, the Homeland Security Administration, and the Internal Revenue Service investigate MissyUSA's fundraising efforts. The Blue House had never before taken this kind of legal action against an online community. From this example one can see how the Park administration tried to control and censor online communities, which is precisely what MissyUSA had accused it of doing.

In addition to online activism and its newspaper campaign, MissyUSA extended their activities to participation in demonstrations in North America.[7] In Los Angeles, home to the largest Korean American community in the United States, more than four hundred people attended the in-person demonstrations in May 2014. Other North American cities with a prominent Korean diasporic community, such as Atlanta, Boston, Houston, New York, Philadelphia, Pittsburgh, and San Diego, also held in-person demonstrations. At these gatherings, organizers collected signatures for a petition to enact the *Sewol* Special Act that would authorize a thorough investigation. Many Korean Americans found like-minded residents to bond with at these events and began to form *Sewol* activist groups in their communities. The MissyUSA demonstrations became a breeding ground for a new chapter of Korean American activism, producing tens if not hundreds of *Sewol* support communities.

REDEFINING KOREAN AMERICAN COMMUNITY: SESAMO

After the sinking of the *Sewol* ferry, many North American cities with large Korean American populations founded *Sewol* Sesamo nonprofit organizations. The name Sesamo refers to the Korean word for people who stand in solidarity with the *Sewol* families. These organizations encouraged Korean Americans to support the *Sewol* families by leading demonstrations at Korean malls and supermarkets, raising money, and hosting film screenings and meetings with *Sewol* families. Through their activism, the members of Sesamo bond through shared communal consciousness and reconfigure their identities as diasporic Koreans living in the United States. In the next section I introduce three Korean American Sesamo communities and their activities.

Getting Wet in the Rain Together: Houston's Hambi

Gu Bo-gyeong (Bokyoung Koo), who immigrated to the United States in 2012, is a Korean American living in Houston. During our interview conducted over Zoom on May 31, 2022, she shared her experience of how her participation in *Sewol* activism brought her to find Hambi, Houston's Korean American Sesamo community. Gu said that she cannot forget the two Danwon High School students she saw on the news: Su-bin, who banged on the ferry windows, trying to escape, and Cha-yeong, who gave his life vest to his friends and swam from the ferry without one. She asked herself, What if they were my children? What would I do?

On May 11, 2014, Gu attended one of the first nationwide protests, organized by MissyUSA, at the Houston Galleria. It was her first foray into *Sewol* activism. This was also when she met other Korean Americans who also wanted to support the victims' families. A few months later, Gu and other Korean Americans residing in Houston formed a Sesamo community that they named Jageun Sori (Small Sound), with Gu as its vice president. One of the group's first accomplishments was collecting one thousand local signatures in support of the *Sewol* Special Act and forwarding them to the Gwanghwamun Square in Korea. In 2015, Jageun Sori invited the mothers of student victims Yun-min and Jae-wuk to Houston to meet their group. Inviting *Sewol* families to the United States to converse in person with Korean Americans became one of the most important activities of many Sesamo communities because it allowed the bereaved families to tell their stories directly to the Koreans of the diaspora.

Gu's activism was also embedded in her daily life. In 2016 and 2018, Gu read the biographies of the *Sewol* students for one hundred days while making 108 bows. In Korean Buddhism, 108 bows is a reflective practice, and by completing these, Gu was making a wish for the victims to rest in peace. In addition, Gu marks the birthday of each of the student victims with a post on Houston Hambi's Facebook page as an act of remembrance.

In December 2016, Gu founded Sewolho Hambi, which was later registered as a nonprofit in March 2021. Hambi, which is short for *Hamkke matneun bi* (Getting wet in the rain together), signifies solidarity with the *Sewol* families and other supporters. Spearheaded by Gu, Hambi engaged in many activities to support the *Sewol* families. In 2019, Hambi welcomed the mothers of student victims Geon-wu and Jun-yeong. In 2022, Hambi invited and met with the father of Ae-jin, a *Sewol* survivor. In addition to meetings with *Sewol* parents, they hold regular demonstrations in front of Korean supermarkets and raise money for the *Sewol* families by selling homemade Korean goods. Because most of Hambi's activities are carried out with Korean American families and close friends in Houston, Gu said that networking with *Sewol* activists from other North American cities is very important in expanding their work. Although Gu was reluctant to introduce herself as an activist, she smiled proudly when announcing that Hambi now has branches in Dallas, San Antonio, Austin, Los Angeles, Austria, Norway, and Saudi Arabia.

Extending Activism from Sewol *to Woori: Philadelphia Sesamo*

On July 28, 2022, I conducted a Zoom interview with six members of Philadelphia Sesamo: Gwon O-dal (Odal Kwon), Gim Yeong-geun (Young Kim), Gim Tae-hyeong (Taehyoung Kim), Yi Jong-guk (Chong-kuk Lee), Mel Lee, and Suna Lee. When I first contacted them for an interview, I noticed that, unlike other Sesamo communities, Philadelphia Sesamo did not have a member serving as the head representative. Instead, the group has a horizontal leadership structure in which the members make decisions together, based on their discussions as a community.

According to Yi Jong-guk, Philadelphia Sesamo began right after the disaster, when Mel Lee organized the city's first protest in alliance with MissyUSA's nationwide protests. After that, Yi organized a Philadelphia gathering in May and another in June 2014. They advertised the gathering in the local Korean American newspaper and held Wednesday evening meetings at the food court of a local mall.

When I asked the members if they already had engaged in any activism related to current events in Korean before the *Sewol,* Mel Lee, who grew up in Gwangju, the city known for democratic uprisings in the 1970s and 1980s, said she had always been interested in Korean current events and even attended the 2008 US beef protests in Seoul before she immigrated to the United States. Yi, who immigrated to the United States in the 1980s, reminisced how five thousand Korean Americans gathered in New York to protest and stand in solidarity with the Korean people during the June Uprisings in 1980. By contrast, Gwon O-dal commented that he had not participated in any protests before the *Sewol,* although he always kept up with the news. But when he saw the advertisement for meeting with the victims' families in the fall of 2014, he started attending the Sesamo meetings. Like Gwon, while many Korean Americans had taken an interest in Korean events before the *Sewol,* they might not have done anything about them. But after the *Sewol,* the people decided that they could no longer be silent. This shows that the *Sewol,* the most galvanizing incident in contemporary Korean history, motivated citizens in the diaspora to take action.

During the past eight years of Philadelphia Sesamo activities, the number of members has slowly declined from 40–50 people to 20–30 people. Although some of the interest in the *Sewol* seems to have faded, Philadelphia Sesamo continues to meet every other Wednesday. Even during the pandemic, they met over Zoom to discuss future plans. Although the members have faced a backlash and arguments with conservative Korean Americans, they are steadfast in continuing their work because, according to Suna Lee, they want to. "Nobody forces us to do anything. We just voluntarily find something to do about this tragedy," she said.

In addition, its flat leadership structure makes Philadelphia Sesamo unique; veteran and new activists work together. "The veteran activists are old and experienced, but they don't take lead; rather, they support younger activists to do so," commented Gwon. "We are just doing what we are supposed to do as members of society," Yi said, and the other members nodded in agreement. Gwon added, "There are conservative Korean Americans and many who oppose our ideas but I think we managed to change their views as well."

Philadelphia Sesamo's activities are not limited to supporting *Sewol* families; they also founded the Woori Center (led by Yi Jong-guk and Mel Lee), extending their activism to broader issues that affect Asian Americans. Mel Lee noted,

> At the 2017 Seoul Forum, I asked Mr. Yu Gyeong-geun [Ye-eun's father], "What would you like the overseas communities to do?" and he answered, "Please do your best so that an incident like the *Sewol* does not happen in your community. Please pay attention to the issues in your community and do your best in making a safer and more just society." I cannot forget that. The Woori Center that Chong-kuk Lee and I run is an extension of the Sesamo activities. The center strives for social and racial justice, advocates for systemic change, and provides education and arts programs for local residents. Previously all Korean diasporic communities were formed around religious gatherings such as churches, but with Sesamo, communities can form without being dependent on churches. Living overseas can be very lonely, but via Sesamo activities,

> one can feel connected. Sesamo has become a family and community brought together by the *Sewol* victims.

The movement to support the *Sewol* families gradually extended the members' interests and activities to other issues in the Asian American community.

Standing in Solidarity Until the End: San Francisco's One Heart for Justice

San Francisco's One Heart for Justice started when Gim Nak-gyeong (Shawn Nak Kyung Kim), a Korean American who immigrated to the United States when she was in middle school, posted on the MissyUSA forum asking if there would be a protest in San Jose. The first protest in San Jose, which occurred on May 18, 2014, led to two and then to three. The participants were all strangers at first but quickly became friends who wanted to support the *Sewol* families. In 2014, Gim Nak-gyeong founded One Heart for Justice with approximately one hundred members, and the group was registered as a nonprofit in 2019. One of its most active members is Gim Mi-suk (Misuk Nam), who resides near Berkeley but makes the two-hour drive to attend.

The main goal of One Heart for Justice is to publicize the *Sewol,* to support the victims' families morally and financially to the end. And the end, for One Heart, is when the families feel that full transparency and accountability has been achieved. Their main activities are fundraising, picketing, and handing out yellow ribbons at Korean supermarkets in San Jose and San Francisco Union Square. They even organized a flash mob at the Golden Gate Bridge. All of their gatherings require permission from the local police and take place under their protection. One of their most significant activities was the construction of the *Sewol* bench at Palo Alto Mitchell Park with the funds from the 4.16 Foundation.

Elizabeth W. Son's idea of memorials as scriptive things that invite "collective engagement in the ethical work of remembering histories of violence" is useful in thinking of how the *Sewol* bench represents the will to remember the disaster despite the passing of time and other Korean Americans who hold different political ideas.[8] Gim Nak-gyeong and Gim Mi-suk recounted how conservative older Koreans would curse at them, call them "commies," and even disrupt their protests by making noise from across the street.

One Heart for Justice is deeply committed to remembering the *Sewol* through cultural events. They regularly hold film screenings and concerts that commemorate the disaster. Since 2021, they have organized an annual art contest for young Korean American students, who submit works that commemorate or deliver information about the *Sewol.* Drawings and video essays created by elementary school, middle school, and high school students are exhibited on their website.[9] Many of these works include yellow ribbons and express solidarity by portraying the holding of hands and with writings such as "I miss you" and "remember."

UCLA KOREAN CULTURE NIGHT'S SEWOL: *A PASSING OF TIME* (2017)

The Korean Culture Night (KCN) is one of the biggest undergraduate student productions at UCLA and the largest Korean student art production in the United States. The KCN takes place each April and shares Korean culture with the local community. The KCN's 2017 production featured a multimedia performance titled Sewol: *A Passing of Time.* The performance tells the stories of seven Korean high school students. Each student has a struggle—with family and/or school—and hopes to attend college. The students' everyday lives seem peaceful until some of them board the *Sewol.* This student production, which was both entertaining and reflective, interweaves b-boy dance, fan dance, modern dance, and *pungmul*—a traditional Korean percussive music and dance genre—between the scenes.

Through an email interview in March 2020 with Diane Na Yeon Kim, the director of the performance, I was able to discuss and understand the production process of Sewol: *A Passing of Time.* In particular, our interview shed light on what the disaster meant for a Korean American undergraduate as well as on the role that performance played in coming to terms with it. When I asked about her reasons for staging the *Sewol* ferry disaster, she said,

> I was able to connect with it more because I see them [the student victims] as my peers. I still see them as friends that had dreams and aspirations and hopes that were not able to be fulfilled. Seeing those friends

> not being remembered or overlooked was something I couldn't stand, and that moved me to want to do something about it.
>
> I see it as a tragedy that cannot be talked about enough, and I saw it as my duty as someone who identifies as Korean American to share this story with my community in a way that they could relate to as well. It's an incident that could have happened to any one of us, and that's what I tried to portray in our production and hopefully translated to our Korean American community as well.

A year prior to the production, when deciding whether or not to stage it, Kim had an argument with the show's producers, who worried that local sponsors might not support the production. As late as 2016, Koreans and Korean Americans were still finding it difficult to have political discussions about the *Sewol.* As most first-generation Korean Americans residing in Koreatown, Los Angeles, identify as conservative or very conservative, many of them were politically aligned with the Park administration.[10] And as the KCN depends on local sponsorships from Korean American businesses in Los Angeles, Kim and the show's producers worried that they would not receive enough funding. Fortunately, KCN was able to receive sponsorship from local Korean American businesses.

In 2016, Kim's mother had joined San Francisco's One Heart for Justice, which supported the victims' families, and had met some of the mothers, who were demonstrating in front of Gwanghwamun Square. Through her own mother, Kim was able to contact the mother of one of the *Sewol* victims. After a phone conversation, Kim felt determined that this was a story that KCN needed to tell. With the permission of the mothers and honoring their request to depict the students as they had been—just regular high school students with normal dreams and daily lives—Kim began to write the script in June 2016.

For Kim, the most challenging part about writing the script was staying true to the story while convincing the audience that they were not much different from the students who had died. Kim read articles, listened to interviews of the victims' families, and viewed news coverage in order to amass as many facts as she could and understand the event as much as possible. Kim knew that she needed a factual but engaging depiction of the event. She decided to focus on the students' daily problems and struggles, such as with family, relationships, or school, to show the audience that what happened to them could have happened to anyone—to someone we know, or even ourselves.

Once a draft of the script was completed, KCN did a reading in November 2016 and started practicing every Monday and Wednesday night for two hours. After a full retreat with all cast and staff in late March, they rehearsed almost daily until the production on April 13, 2017. When directing the performance, Kim tried to educate the cast on the significance of the incident. They viewed a documentary about the disaster and delved into the students' lives. In order to get the cast to draw from sorrow, she had them watch YouTube clips of the victims' grieving families. Kim also urged the cast to relive their own experiences of loss and of injustice.

The climax of the performance is in the middle of act 2. After the students have boarded the ferry and begun their trip, there is a loud bang and the lights flicker. The students become alarmed. Over the loudspeaker, a crew member tells them to stay where they are: "Don't move, and stay still." The scared students huddle together. Then the stage goes dark and the projection shows footage from the student victims' cell phones where the ferry is tilted and water is entering. Next we see news footage that makes the false claim that all students have been rescued, followed by clips of the families' anguish when they realize that their children have drowned. Although the footage is painful to watch, Kim "really wanted to show the audience the reality of what was lost, which we will never be able to fully empathize with or show properly." She also believes that "it was necessary to show them the true reality of what they [victims and families] went through and to remind the audience that although this was being shown through a production, actual lives were lost in the incident and those repercussions affected real people." By creating spaces of memory and mourning for young Korean Americans, Sewol*: A Passing of Time* represents KCN's desire to commemorate the disaster and find redress.

PERFORMING COLLECTIVE QUOTIDIAN RESISTANCE: RELAY FASTING FOR *SEWOL*

Relay Fasting for *Sewol* is short for "Relay fasting for enactment of the *Sewol* Special Act that the *Sewol* victims' families are demanding." A post on their Facebook page on August 22, 2014, reads,

100 days after the disaster, there was no glimpse of the truth, and the families of the victims including Gim Yeong-o (father of student victim Gim Ye-eun) went into hunger strike demanding the Special Act and a thorough investigation. Gim's fasting neared 40 days, but the ruling party and the President's office did not show their efforts to reveal the truth from the families' point of view; rather rumors that the families want compensation were spread, and the ruling party and the President's office tried to pass a special law without the authority to investigate and indict.

The victims were told to stay put while the ferry was sinking, and the families and nation are now being told to stay put for trying to enact the *Sewol* Special Act. Heavy-hearted Koreans residing abroad, signed the 10 million petition campaign, and started the "Relay Fasting for *Sewol*" on August 18, 2014, in solidarity with the families. After a few days of relay fasting, Gim, who reached the fortieth day of his fasting, was hospitalized and the People's Committee for the *Sewol* Ferry Disaster organized a hunger strike in support the *Sewol* families calling attention to the *Sewol* Special Act.

We, Koreans residing abroad, in solidarity with the PCSD will continue Gim's 40-day fasting via our relay fasting campaign until the *Sewol* Special Act is legislated. The families with great sadness of losing loved ones are trying to find the truth and to prevent any similar disasters happening in the future. We will support you from where we are, although we would like to be with you in Gwanghwamun Square. We will be at your side. We will not stay put.

We only want to find out why those children died. Enact the *Sewol* Special Act with the authority to subpoena information and prosecute to carry out a thorough investigation and punish those responsible. Also, introduce measures to prevent any similar disasters from happening in the future to build a safe country together.

These are our demands. The only way to forget the *Sewol* is find out why the *Sewol* ferry sank, why the passengers were not rescued, and to punish those responsible, so that this tragedy is never repeated. After the discussion, the families of the victims decided to reject the bill agreed by Saenuri and the opposition New Politics Alliance for Democracy. Instead they demanded an inquiry panel to be established with judicial powers.

Just as the Pope, who held the hands of the families when President Park did not and said that "one cannot be neutral about human pain," we will not stay silent but come closer to the families. We

> will push for a proper *Sewol* Special Act to be legislated with all our efforts together. We will be with you until the end. We will not forget and we will act.

Although the *Sewol* Special Act passed many years ago, the group's members continue to fast as a means of commemorating the disaster and supporting the families. The participants are diasporic Koreans living in North America, Europe, and Asia. In addition to posting about relay fasting, they comment on the progress of the investigation, politics, and social issues. They complain about the situation and criticize the Moon government for not being more proactive.

These collective quotidian acts can be examined in light of James C. Scott's idea of everyday resistance. While Scott contrasts everyday and collective resistance, he recognizes that both are necessary for the political struggle because they complement each other.[11] Scott reminds us that "events to which the state, the ruling classes, and the intelligentsia accord most attention" are what become defined as resistance, and historians "have missed most acts of resistance throughout history by paying attention to formal organization and public demonstrations."[12] Although these relay fasts do not receive attention from government organizations or the media, they are intentional acts of everyday resistance that manifest within a broader sociopolitical context.

In addition, there is power in performing something repeatedly over time. Many members fast regularly. For example, Bak Jun, who lives in Toronto, fasts every Friday. This kind of nonviolent, peaceful action that continues over time is the embodiment of resilient resistance. In Susan Leigh Foster's article "Choreographies of Protest," the notion of "choreography" enables one to perceive social construction through which decision-making is negotiated within a cultural and historical field.[13] Foster argues for the physicality that constructs both individual agency and sociality through her examination of three instances of protest. She analyzes how each protest incorporated tactics of nonviolent direct action for which bodies rehearsed specific procedures of noncooperation. In relation to Foster's idea of choreography, I view the participants' fasting as a signifying practice in that the act of fasting is a form of physical preparation and theorizing that advances *Sewol* activism.

BRINGING DIASPORIC ACTIVISM TO SEOUL: SUBWAY ADVERTISEMENT (2022)

416 Global Networks is an online network of Koreans living outside Korea who support *Sewol* activities and the victims' families. In March 2022, the group requested to place a subway advertisement on lines 3 and 4 in Seoul's subway stations. The advertisement shows a drawing of eighteen female students wearing yellow shirts and posing as if for a class picture. Behind them is the red lighthouse at Paengmok Port with a yellow ribbon painted on it. Next to the drawing are the words "How are you? We still want to know why they were not rescued. Revealing the truth is the job of those alive." The advertisement was meant for the upcoming eighth anniversary of the *Sewol* ferry disaster, mourning the victims and urging the Korean government to take action. Even in diasporic communities, people were well aware of the Moon administration's neglect and had picketed and protested the government's inaction.

The Seoul Transportation Corporation (STC) rejected the advertisement, however, claiming that its "expression of political principles, claims and policies could interfere with the political neutrality of the Seoul Transportation Corporation." The STC explained its decision after deliberating on "opinion advertising" with nine outside committee members, including the chairman of the Advertising Review Committee. Opinion advertisements are those "in which individuals and organizations state their opinions on important issues and issues that have not yet reached social consensus."

According to the public corporation's advertising review committee, seven out of nine members opposed the advertisement because it had a political purpose. Committee member A argued that it is necessary "to look at whether there is no room for misunderstanding [the *Sewol* ferry disaster] as a means for social issue making and political activities. It is also undeniable that the *Sewol* has become a political issue in the course of activities of overseas Koreans. It is also necessary to review whether it focuses only on activities related to specific organizations and certain political parties."

Committee member B stated that "most of the [written] expressions are classified as political advertisements that express political principles, arguments, and policies according to deliberation standards. If you reduce political opinions and change them to memorial contents for the deceased, you can post them." Committee member C said that "considering the wording and the progress after the accident, it is not just a memorial, but a purpose of criticism based on a certain political position." Committee member D said that "the *Sewol* ferry incident shocked and saddened the entire nation, but there are matters that could interfere with the political neutrality of the STC." The other two members opposed the advertisement, seeing it as "an issue that may cause social controversy and civil complaints" and "a case where social consensus is not reached due to conflicting opinions."

Another committee member even expressed opposition based on personal satisfaction with the investigation, an opinion that had nothing to do with the Seoul Transportation Corporation's advertising review checklist. "The *Sewol* ferry disaster has already been sufficiently clarified through the court and the investigation committee, so further truth-seeking behavior is an act that only increases social costs," he said. "In particular, it is not in line with Seoul subway advertisements operated by Seoul citizens."

Surprised by this unexpected response, 416 Global Networks asked the Seoul Transportation Corporation to clarify what it meant by its decision. 416 Global Networks also submitted a statement and filed a petition with the National Human Rights Commission (NHRC) to object to the STC's decision. "No one in any administration should see the *Sewol* ferry memorial politically," a member of 416 Global Networks said. "It is regrettable that our society has become a society that could not produce even five simple sentences to commemorate the disaster. All nine members of the advertising review committee said that it was political and that it was not allowed."

When this story was reported in the press and in social media, Korean citizens were shocked that a government institution had rejected the advertisement. Judith Butler reminds us that mourning is political, and indeed, in this case the act of mourning student victims who had perished on a ferry was ruled political by an official body. This shows how during the past eight years, the act of mourning the *Sewol,* which was once considered expression of personal grief and not a political act, is no longer so simple. Instead, mourning the *Sewol* has become a political statement associated with jockeying between political parties. Because Korea's two major political parties had used the *Sewol* to spread hate speech and/or form alliances, it became difficult to stand for the original intention of mourning the victims without activating an array of other partisan issues.

The NHRC also recommended that the STC's decision was a violation of freedom of expression, but the STC rejected this finding. The NHRC argued that "the advertisement does not directly express political principles, claims, and policies such as a specific politician's name, appearance, or political party" and should be interpreted strictly. Representative Jang Hye-young of the Justice Party said, "Eight years after the *Sewol* ferry disaster, the tasks of finding the truth, punishing the person in charge, and preventing recurrence are still unresolved. In this situation, the reality that public institutions, which should realize public values, ignore the voices of citizens demanding truth, paradoxically show the need for truth-finding."

As we have seen in this chapter, from organizing newspaper and subway advertisement campaigns, engaging with the local community in leading demonstrations at Korean malls and supermarkets, raising money, hosting and meeting with *Sewol* families, and creating stage productions, to engaging with acts of everyday resistance repeatedly over time, various forms of activism have been performed by Koreans and Korean Americans residing in North America and beyond. Such activism not only supports the *Sewol* families and survivors in searching for the truth and achieving legal redress, in part by bringing additional Korean and international pressure to bear on authorities, but also helps the members of the Korean diaspora bond with other members of the community. Moreover, by taking an interest in other current events in Korea and issues affecting Asian Americans, these members reconfigure their identities as diasporic Koreans.

With activism around the *Sewol* in these diasporic communities, a few key trends can be seen. First, online networking and social media have been important as ways to bring people together around specific issues, which in the cases described above were also followed by on-the-street appearances and actions. Second, spaces and resources outside Korea have been used to push against domestic policies of media suppression and the criminalization of protest. Third, there are important ways that *Sewol* activism has provided a voice for a younger generation of Koreans in the United States and Korean Americans (as well as for diasporic Koreans living elsewhere) to challenge long-standing norms of Korean community politics that until recently have tended to skew more conservatively.

Epilogue

Beyond the Sewol

On the evening of October 29, 2022, a crowd crush took place during Halloween festivities in the Itaewon district of Seoul, South Korea, resulting in the deaths of more than 150 people. Immediately after the disaster, the Korean people began to question the systemic causes and failures that had caused this tragedy and discovered that no crowd control measures had been in place. Nearly a decade after the sinking of the *Sewol* ferry, the Korean people learned that the local authorities are still not making public safety a priority. The similarities between the *Sewol* ferry disaster and Itaewon crowd crush are unmistakable: Both disasters were preventable, public safety was not protected, rescue efforts were bungled, the South Korean government mishandled the aftermath of the disasters, and the families of the victims are being harassed and demonized.

As Itaewon planned to celebrate its first Halloween without COVID-19 restrictions, the streets were expected to be full of people attending the festivities. On the evening of October 29, more than 130,000 people gathered in the Itaewon district. However, the Seoul Metropolitan Government Security Division had ignored the request from the local police station to add extra backup in preparation for the crowd.[1] Only 11 of the 137 police officers in Itaewon were on duty when the first emergency call for help came in at 6:34 p.m., several hours before the crowd crush. More calls came in over the next three hours, but the police failed to respond promptly.[2] Because of understaffing, the police did not arrive at the scene until 10:39 p.m.; by then it was too late.[3]

In addition to the disregard for public safety and the botched rescue, the South Korean government failed to extend sincere condolences and offer redress for survivors and families of the victims. The government tried to evade responsibility and minimize the magnitude of the crowd crush by warning government officials to use the terms "accident" and "deceased" instead of "disaster" and "victims."[4]

When the families of the victims tried to locate their children's bodies, they were not given this information promptly. Several families testified that they had to visit several hospitals before finally finding the bodies.[5] When families requested to be put in touch with families of other victims, the government declined to share their contact information, citing privacy issues. According to these families, some government officials admitted that they had been ordered not to share families' contact information.[6] The families thus had to resort to other means, such as waiting at memorials or requesting help from nonprofit organizations that were helping the families. It seems that the South Korean government wanted to prevent the families from meeting to discuss what had happened. Moreover, some relatives claimed that even while officials denied them access to valuable information, the government repeatedly phoned and surveilled them.

As of this writing (April 2024), President Yoon Suk-yeol and higher officials have declined to issue a sincere apology and have even made insensitive remarks about the victims and their families.[7] Prime Minister Han Duck-soo was documented joking in a way that seemed to minimize the government's accountability while discussing the crowd crush during a press conference. Right-wing politicians and their supporters began blaming the victims for celebrating Halloween in the first place. And again, as after the *Sewol,* public figures disparaged the families looking for answers. Gim Mi-na, a member of the Changwon City Council, posted on her social media account that the victims' families are "selling their children." People Power Party's Representative Gwon Seong-dong said, in response to the formation of the Itaewon Family Council, "You should not go the same way as the *Sewol.*" Such comments had corrosive effects on those who were already suffering. One teenager who survived the crowd crush took his own life after reading malicious comments blaming the victims.[8]

A week after the crowd crush, I visited the site to pay my condolences. Adjacent to the narrow and steep alleys and right outside Exit 1 of Itaewon subway station, I saw a pile of chrysanthemums, notes, photos, and trinkets. A crowd of people was gathered, praying, and adding commemorative items to the pile that was already covering most of the sidewalk.

A few days before December 16, 2022, the *49-jae* (the forty-ninth day after the disaster), a public altar with photos of the victims was set up near Noksapyeong subway station. People were able to visit and pay their condolences. As I stood in front of the altar holding a single chrysanthemum, I was at a loss for words. Staring back at me were four long rows of photos in black frames. Most of those pictured were women in their twenties. Although the news had reported that the majority of victims were young women, I had not realized how young they were and how vulnerable they now seemed. There was already a long line of people in front of me waiting to pay their respects. As the line crept forward, I was able to look at the face in each photo. Many of the photos had snacks or heat packs attached next to them, representing the wishes from loved ones that these objects would ease the victims' journeys to the afterlife.

Families of other disaster victims also reached out to mourn the Itaewon disaster and stand in solidarity with the families. Gim Jeong-hae, mother of *Sewol* victim An Ju-hyeon, criticized the South Korean government saying, "What we hoped for was a safe society that would allow children to live with peace of mind, but nothing has changed even after eight years have passed."[9] Jang Hun, father of *Sewol* victim Jang Jun-hyeong and head of 4.16 Safe Society Institute, denounced the chronic disregard for safety in South Korean society.[10]

The *Sewol* ferry disaster inevitably comes to mind as South Korea struggles to understand why more than 150 people—mostly in their twenties—died in an Itaewon alley on October 29, 2022. What lessons, if any, has society learned? What practical improvements in public safety have been implemented? There has been much conflict between political parties of the left and right, and, to most South Koreans, the biggest problem arising from the *Sewol* ferry disaster has been the ensuing political strife. Investigations of such disasters, generally led by the national legislature, politicians, and social media, tend to demonize specific groups, assign blame, and foment anger to obtain political advantage rather than revealing the root cause of social problems and investing in solutions. The resulting polarization then itself becomes a primary issue, making accountability activists susceptible to blame and attack, exhausting the public, and leading to patterns of cover-up rather than closure.

The *Sewol* ferry disaster, South Korea's worst maritime disaster in recent history, resulted from many factors, including the government's dereliction of its duty to protect the public. To some, the incident reflected a larger problem in Korean society: A small but privileged minority can break the law with impunity, while the law-abiding majority is left unprotected. Greed was another likely cause of the sinking of the *Sewol*; the ferry's operator allegedly overloaded the ship with heavy freight to save money, making it less stable and prone to capsizing. The contrast between those who lived and those who died was accentuated by the civilian divers and others who risked their lives to save the people on the ferry.

A key point of this book's research is that traumatic experiences can be channeled into action for social change and that performance can play a key role in facilitating this process. This kind of activism can transform Koreans' collective sadness into agential states of collective mobilization. Undeniably, there have been times when South Korea needed to mourn; the country's rapid modernization came at a cost. Respect for human rights and empathy for socially disenfranchised groups were either treated as secondary issues or willfully trampled on under the pretext of economic advancement. There have been several periods of national mourning: 32 people perished in the Seongsu Bridge collapse of 1994; and a year later in 1995, 502 people died in the Sampoong Department Store collapse. The death of 304 people on the *Sewol* in 2014, mostly innocent teenagers, led to collective political resistance to Korea's conservative government. Park Geun-hye's administration collapsed three years later when she was impeached, making way for the Moon Jae-in administration. However, the Moon administration and his party, the Democratic Party of Korea, were eager to exploit the opportunity for political gain by eliciting empathy over the tragedy. To many South Koreans who had hoped for better governance, the Democratic Party's incompetence was even more disappointing than that of the previous government. Both the Democratic Party and the People Power Party have failed to effect a decisive and revolutionary change in the public safety system.

This is precisely why this book is titled *Beyond the* Sewol rather than *After the* Sewol—because the *Sewol* has not yet ended. Rather, the disaster has continued into the aftermath of the sinking—the systemic failures of the ferry, the botched rescue operation, the way the Park administration tried to play down its own culpability and interfered with the SIC's investigation, the surveillance of the victims' families and supporters, the Moon administration's incompetence, and then yet another preventable tragedy have culminated in a decade-long disaster whose impacts continue to unfold.

However, by identifying and analyzing a multimedia collection of performative works commemorating the *Sewol,* this book reveals the ways that activists and artists have mobilized and, through performative strategies, have transformed the *Sewol* from an unresolved national trauma into a catalyst for the creation of a safer, fairer, and more compassionate society. By illuminating a genre-spanning corpus of works that has unfolded (and continues to unfold) over the past ten years and analyzing its contents and contexts, this study also contributes to the making of the counter-memory archive. This counter-memory archive not only allows us to see and remember what happened with the ferry but also helps us understand the linkages between different disasters and kinds of injustice, such as the ways the *Sewol* connects to the Itaewon crowd crush.

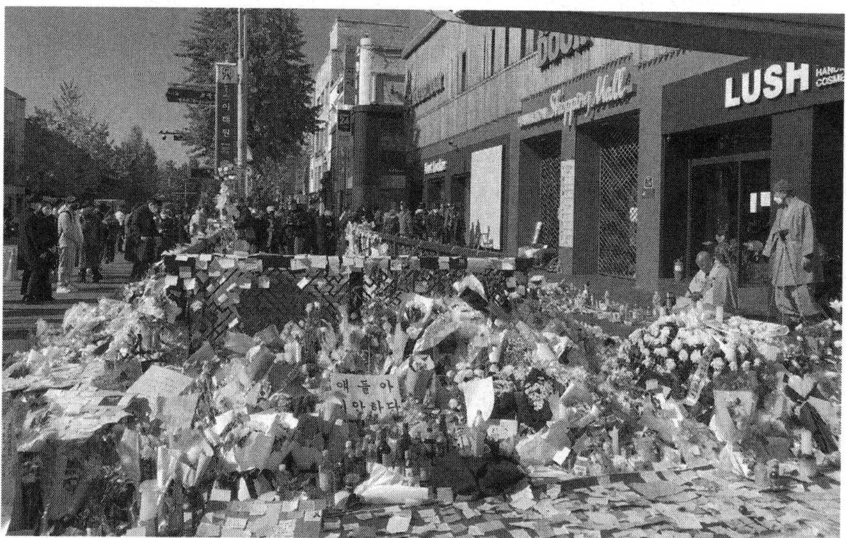

FIGURE 6.1. Adjacent to the narrow and steep alleys and right outside Exit 1 of Itaewon subway station, I saw a pile of chrysanthemums, notes, photos, and trinkets. A crowd of people was gathered, praying, placing flowers, notes, and photos on top of the pile that was already covering most of the sidewalk. Photo by Areum Jeong.

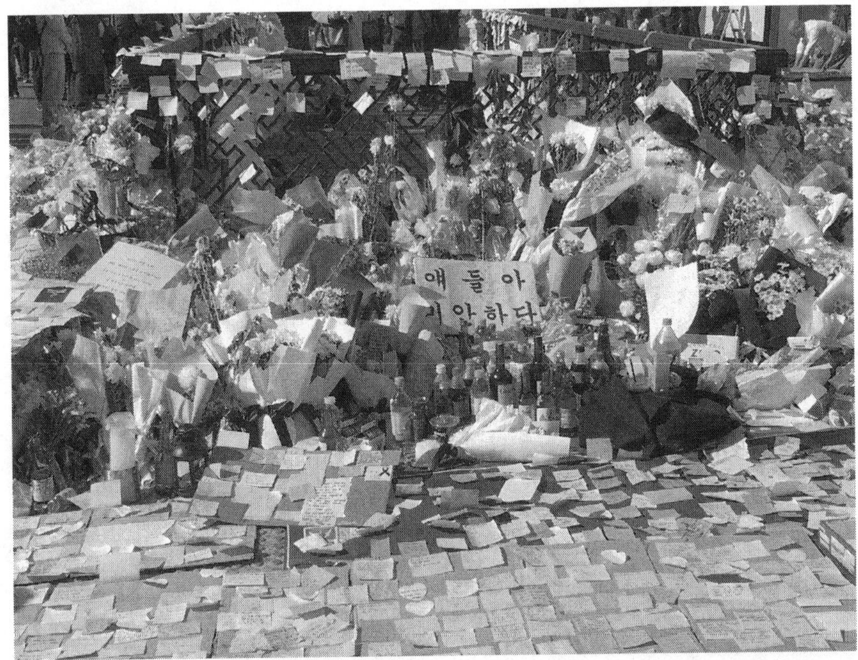

FIGURE 6.2. Acts of commemoration in Itaewon. Photo by Areum Jeong.

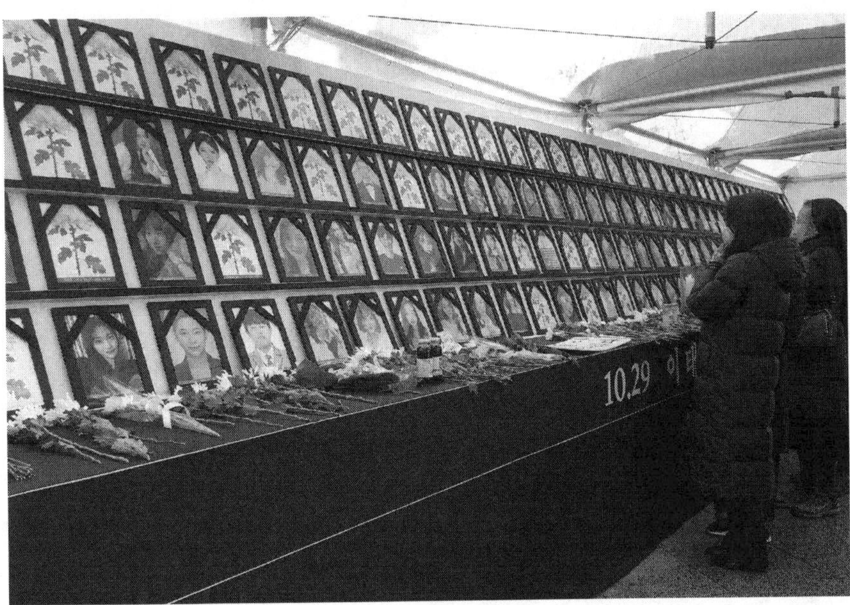

FIGURE 6.3. December 16, 2022, was *49-jae*, the forty-ninth day after the disaster. A public altar was set up near Noksapyeong subway station. People were able to visit and pay their respects. Photo by Areum Jeong.

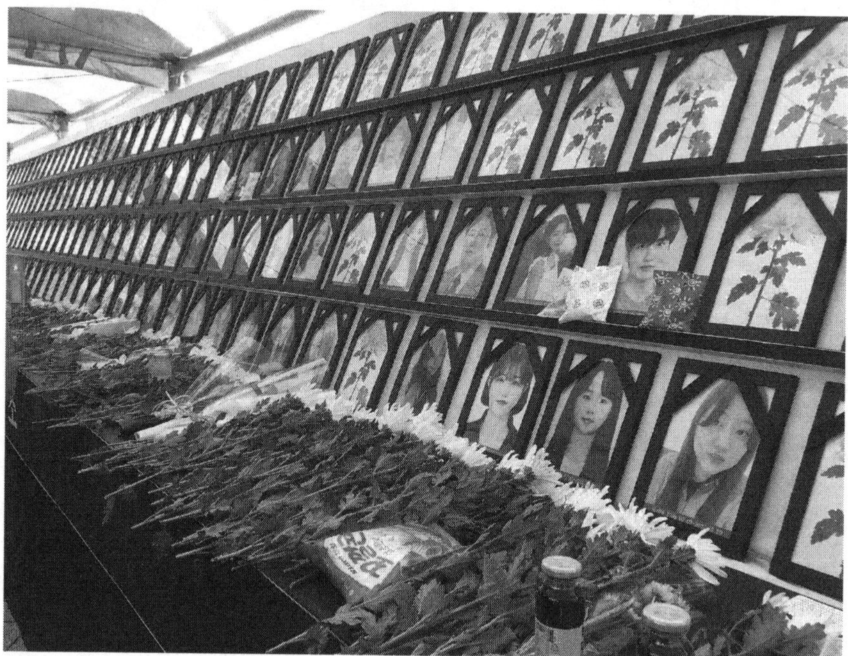

FIGURE 6.4. Many of the photos had snacks or heat packs attached next to them, representing the wishes from loved ones that these objects would ease the victims' journeys to the afterlife. Photo by Areum Jeong.

Performance is a uniquely subversive means of calling out self-serving government acts of authority, and viewing such performances elicits affect that can be conducive to forging a caring and bonded community. Performance keeps participants from remaining stuck in a single place or identity (which is important for moving though trauma), and elicits remembering, linking it to redressive demands, reconfiguring what it means to witness, commemorate, and memorialize.

My work illuminates specific performative strategies that Korean activists and artists have utilized to commemorate the *Sewol*, and it analyzes what has made them effective and transformative. These strategies include intense collaboration with survivors and victims' families, and centering their goals and ethics of consent to promote witnessing rather than spectacle. These works have wedded acts of remembering this tragedy and each of its victims to the political work of demanding government transparency, accountability, justice, and redress, with the ultimate goal of creating a safer, fairer, and more caring Korean nation and society.

These contributions help me theorize performance's political workings in a general way but also in a way that is specific to South Korea post-*Sewol*. That analysis also spotlights the role of art and culture in the unfolding of a new chapter of activism in South Korea.

NOTES

INTRODUCTION

1. Gwon Yeong-bin, *Meonameon sewolho: Sewolho teukjowiwa hamkkehan sigan* (*Sewol* far away: The time with the *Sewol* Special Investigation Committee) (Seongnam: Pyeolchim Press, 2017), 21.
2. Hyeon So-eun, "'Jeongyura idae ipsi haksabiri' choesunsil, hangsosimseodo jingyeok 3nyeon" ("Jeong Yu-ra's Ewha University entrance scandal," Choe Sun-sil, sentenced to 3 years in prison), *Hankyoreh,* November 14, 2017, http://www.hani.co.kr/arti/society/society_general/818911.html.
3. Jeong Yu-gyeong, "'Nunmul geulsseong' mun daetongnyeong, sewolho yujokdeurege "'neujeotjiman sagwadeurinda'" ("Tears in his eyes," President Moon delivers "belated apologies" to *Sewol* families), *Hankyoreh,* August 16, 2017, http://www.hani.co.kr/arti/politics/politics_general/807043.html.
4. Yu Han-tae, "Munjaein teukbyeolseongmyeong, 'daetongnyeong seuseuro bakkyeoya'" (Moon Jae-in's special statement, "The president herself must change"), *Sisa News,* May 20, 2014, http://sisa-news.com/news/article.html?no=60670.
5. Namhee Lee, "The Undongkwon as a Counterpublic Sphere," in *The Making of Minjung: Democracy and the Politics of Representation in South Korea* (Ithaca, NY: Cornell University Press, 2009), 148.
6. Jiyeon Kang, "The Birth of the Internet Youth Protest: The 2002 Candlelight Vigils," in *Igniting the Internet: Youth and Activism in Postauthoritarian South Korea* (Honolulu: University of Hawai'i Press, 2016), 82–83.
7. Jin-Wook Shin, "Changing Patterns of South Korean Social Movements, 1960s–2010s: Testimony, Firebombs, Lawsuit and Candlelight," in *Civil Society and the State in Democratic East Asia: Between Entanglement and Contention in Post High Growth,* ed. David Chiavacci, Simona Grano, and Julia Obinger (Amsterdam: Amsterdam University Press, 2020), 239–268.

8. Shin, "Changing Patterns of South Korean Social Movements, 1960s–2010s," 261.
9. Gim Bang-ok, "Geomyeol, hogeun sayukdoeneun yeongeuk" (Theatre that is censored or bred), in *Sewolho ihuui hangukyeongeuk: Beullaengniseuteueseo beullaektenteukkaji* (Korean theatre after the *Sewol*: From blacklist to Black Tent), ed. Korean Theatre Critics Association (Seoul: Yeongeukkwa Ingan Press, 2017), 54.
10. Yang Geun-ae, *"Ihu"ui yeongeuk, dallajin segye* (Theatre "after," changed world) (Seoul: Yeongeukgwa Ingan Press, 2020), 5.
11. Jeong So-ang, "Sewolho gujo silpae, haegyeongui geojinmareul balkhyeoya handa" (Failure to rescue *Sewol* ferry must reveal coast guard's lies), *Ohmynews,* October 14, 2014, http://www.ohmynews.com/NWS_ Web/view/at_pg.aspx?cntn_cd=A0002043104.
12. Gwon, *Meonameon sewolho,* 23.
13. In South Korea, right-leaning politicians dominated politics after the Korean War until 1998, when Kim Dae-jung, a left-leaning politician, became president. Right-leaning political parties are rooted in pro-Japanese and pro-American forces, and tend to be conservative in dealing with North Korea. Left-leaning political parties tend to advocate for improved relations with North Korea and support greater human rights.
14. Gang Na-ru, "Jasik ireun sewolho yujogeun eotteoke jongbugi doeeonna" (How did *Sewol* families become *jongbuk*), *KBS News,* May 6, 2019, https://mn.kbs.co.kr/news/view.do?ncd=4194889.
15. Gwon, *Meonameon sewolho,* 21.
16. Gwon, *Meonameon sewolho,* 48–49.
17. Gwon, *Meonameon sewolho,* 49.
18. Gwon, *Meonameon sewolho,* 63.
19. Gwon, *Meonameon sewolho,* 77–78.
20. Gwon, *Meonameon sewolho,* 9.
21. Gwon, *Meonameon sewolho,* 156–159.
22. Gwon, *Meonameon sewolho,* 19–20.
23. Gim Min-ju, "Joyunseon, daibingbel tiket maesue akpyeong jisikkaji . . ." (Jo Yun-seon bought up all tickets for The Truth Shall Not Sink with *Sewol* and even ordered negative reviews . . .), *Kookje Shinmun,* February 1, 2017, http://www.kookje.co.kr/news2011/asp/newsbody.asp?code=0100&key=20170201.99002002810.
24. Gim Min-ju, "Joyunseon, daibingbel tiket maesue akpyeong jisikkaji . . ."
25. Yi Su-jin, "Sewolho eommadeurui ballyeongi, geuraedo nunmuri naneun kkadageun" (Reasons for tears despite *Sewol* mothers' mediocre acting),

Ohmynews, January 27, 2017, http://star.ohmynews.com/NWS_ Web/OhmyStar/at_pg.aspx?CNTN_CD=A0002283695.

26. Yu Gyeong-geun, "Tto dasi gukoeboncheong apimnida" (I am in front of the National Assembly Headquarters again), Facebook, December 6, 2020, https://www.facebook.com/gyounggeun.yoo/posts/3845745208817731.
27. Jeon Gwang-jun, "Sewolho yujokdeuri 3nyeonmane dasi kkeonaen 'nalgeun chimnang'" (The "old sleeping bag" the *Sewol* families took out after 3 years), *Hankyoreh,* December 6, 2020, http://www.hani.co.kr/arti/society/society_general/973005.html.
28. Hong Yong-deok, "'Napgoldang baekjihwa' yadang gongyage sewolho huisaengja yugajok 'seongeoe agyong malla'" (Opposition party promises to wipe out the ossuary and the victims' families of the *Sewol* ferry tell them not to abuse it in the elections), *Hankyoreh,* June 5, 2018, https://www.hani.co.kr/arti/area/area_general/847806.html.
29. Gim Won-jin, "Ttae doemyeon chajaoneun bulcheonggaek 'sewolho hyeomopyoheyon,' nuga eonje peotteurina" ("*Sewol* ferry hate speech," who spreads it and when), *Kyunghyang Shinmun,* April 11, 2020, https://www.khan.co.kr/national/national-general/article/202004111119011.
30. Diana Taylor, *The Archive and the Repertoire: Performing Cultural Memory in the Americas* (Durham, NC: Duke University Press, 2003), 2.
31. Joseph Roach, *Cities of the Dead: Circum-Atlantic Performance* (New York: Columbia University Press, 1996), 4.
32. Richard Schechner, *Performance Studies: An Introduction* (New York: Routledge, 2006), 30.
33. J. L. Austin, *How to Do Things with Words* (Cambridge, MA: Harvard University Press, 1962), 6.
34. Judith Butler, "Rethinking Vulnerability and Resistance," in *Vulnerability in Resistance,* ed. Judith Butler, Zeynep Gambetti, and Leticia Sabsay (Durham, NC: Duke University Press, 2016), 13.
35. Butler, "Rethinking Vulnerability and Resistance," 25.
36. Sara Ahmed, "Happy Objects," in *The Affect Theory Reader,* ed. Melissa Gregg and Gregory J. Seigworth (Durham, NC: Duke University Press, 2010), 29–51.
37. Marita Sturken, *Tangled Memories: The Vietnam War, the AIDS Epidemic, and the Politics of Remembering* (Berkeley: University of California Press, 1997), 3.
38. Sturken, *Tangled Memories,* 9.
39. Sturken, *Tangled Memories,* 10.
40. Marita Sturken, *Tourists of History: Memory, Kitsch, and Consumerism from*

Oklahoma City to Ground Zero (Durham, NC: Duke University Press, 2007), 3.

41. Susan Stewart, *On Longing: Narratives of the Miniature, the Gigantic, the Souvenir, the Collection* (Durham, NC: Duke University Press, 1992), 135.
42. J. Halberstam, *In a Queer Time and Place: Transgender Bodies, Subcultural Lives* (New York: New York University Press, 2005), 1.
43. Halberstam, *In a Queer Time and Place,* 1.
44. Dori Laub, "Bearing Witness, or the Vicissitudes of Listening," in *Testimony: Crises of Witnessing in Literature, Psychoanalysis, and History,* ed. Shoshana Felman and Dori Laub (New York: Routledge, 1992), 57–74, 57.
45. Caroline Wake, "The Accident and the Account: Towards a Taxonomy of Spectatorial Witness in Theatre and Performance Studies," in *Visions and Revisions: Performance, Memory, Trauma,* ed. Bryoni Trezise and Caroline Wake (Copenhagen: Museum Tusculanum Press, 2013), 33–56.
46. Wake, "The Accident and the Account," 43.
47. Dominick LaCapra, *Writing History, Writing Trauma* (Baltimore, MD: Johns Hopkins University Press, 2001), 180.
48. LaCapra, *Writing History, Writing Trauma,* 102.
49. Augusto Boal, *Games for Actors and Non-Actors* (London: Routledge, 1992), xxvi.
50. Marcela A. Fuentes, "Zooming In and Out: Tactical Media Performance in Transnational Contexts," in *Performance, Politics, and Activism,* ed. John Rouse and Peter Lichtenfels (London: Palgrave Macmillan, 2013), 32–33.
51. Fuentes, "Zooming In and Out," 32.
52. Chungmoo Choi, "The Discourse of Decolonization and Popular Memory: South Korea," *Positions: Asia Critique* 1, no. 1 (1993): 77–102; Chungmoo Choi, "Transnational Capitalism, National Imaginary, and the Protest Theater in South Korea," *boundary 2* 22, no. 1 (1995): 235–261; Namhee Lee, "Between Indeterminacy and Radical Critique: Madang-guk, Ritual, and Protest," *Positions: East Asia Cultures Critique* 11, no. 3 (2003): 555–584.
53. Kang, *Igniting the Internet.*
54. Elizabeth W. Son, *Embodied Reckonings: "Comfort Women," Performance, and Transpacific Redress* (Ann Arbor: University of Michigan Press, 2018).
55. Son, *Embodied Reckonings,* 19.
56. Son, *Embodied Reckonings,* 21.
57. In her research on comfort women activism in South Korea and the diaspora, Son analyzes how a bronze statue of a girl evokes survivors' fight for justice and how the materiality of the statue elicits embodied engagements and performance of care. See Son, *Embodied Reckonings,* 154.

58. Son, *Embodied Reckonings,* 158.
59. Nan Kim explains how the color yellow came to define activism and dissident identity in South Korea, tracing how yellow objects circulated in "layered metaphorical assemblages that constituted new forms of public memory and new practices of political mobilization." She proposes that we think of yellow ribbons as "the things that acted as visual and material synecdoche for interrelated historical narratives," and she argues that the yellow ribbons provided a "public sign of remembrance and sympathy as well as an emblem of dissent among those who had defied the repression under Park." See Nan Kim, "The Color of Dissent and a Vital Politics of Fragility in South Korea," *Journal of Asian Studies* 77, no. 4 (2018): 971–990. Hong Kal examines how Korean artist Hong Sung-dam represents the *Sewol* in his art and analyzes how his paintings translate affect, triggering an empathic response that moves viewers. See Hong Kal, "The Art of Witnessing: The *Sewol* Ferry Disaster in Hong Sung-dam's Paintings," *Korean Studies* 43 (2019): 96–119.
60. Dwight Conquergood, "Rethinking Ethnography: Towards a Critical Cultural Politics," *Communication Monographs* 58, no. 2 (1991): 179–194; D. Soyini Madison, *Acts of Activism: Human Rights as Radical Performance* (Cambridge: Cambridge University Press, 2010).

CHAPTER 1. REDRESSIVE THEATRE: THE *SEWOL* MOTHERS ON THE STAGE

1. Hyeon Jung Lee and Yesung Lee, "Gender Differences in Parental Grief: The Case of the Bereaved Families of the *Sewol* Ferry Disaster," *Family and Culture* 30, no. 3 (2018): 1–41.
2. Judith Butler, *Gender Trouble: Feminism and the Subversion of Identity* (New York: Routledge, 1990), 25.
3. Desintha Asriani, "Being Mother: Comparative Study of the Contested Motherhood Between South Korea and Indonesia," *International Journal of Management, Entrepreneurship, Social Science and Humanities* 1, no. 1 (2017): 15–23, 15.
4. Haejoang Cho, "Living with Conflicting Subjectivities: Mother, Motherly Wife, and Sexy Woman in the Transition from Colonial-Modern to Postmodern Korea," in *Under Construction: The Gendering of Modernity, Class, and Consumption in the Republic of Korea,* ed. Laurel Kendall (Honolulu: University of Hawai'i Press, 2002), 167–168.

5. Cho, "Living with Conflicting Subjectivities," 189.
6. Nancy Abelmann, "Women's Class Mobility and Identities in South Korea: A Gendered, Transnational, Narrative Approach," *Journal of Asian Studies* 56, no. 2 (1997): 400.
7. Myung-hye Kim, "Late Industrialization and Women's Work in Urban South Korea: An Ethnographic Study of Upper-Middle-Class Families," *City and Society* 6, no. 2 (1992): 169.
8. Jeong-Lim Nam, "Gender Politics in the Korean Transition to Democracy," *Korean Studies* 24 (2000): 94–112.
9. Rho Young-Sook, "The Study on the Formation of the May Mothers House" (MA thesis, Chonnam National University, 2015), 28.
10. Jiyeon Kang, "Internet Activism Transforming Street Politics: The 2008 'Mad Cow' Candlelight Festivals and New Democratic Sensibilities," in *Igniting the Internet,* 113.
11. Jeon Jiyeol et al., "A Grounded Theory Study of the Grieving Processes of Bereaved Parents After the *Sewol* Ferry Disaster," *Korean Journal of Counseling and Psychotherapy* 31, no. 1 (2019): 1–48.
12. Nam Ji-su, "New Documentary Theatre: Across the Boundary Between the Real and the Fiction" (PhD diss., Dongguk University, 2015), 2–8.
13. Bak Yu-rim, "A Thesis on the Director Kim Jae-Yeop's Theatre from the Perspective of New Documentary Theatre" (MA thesis, Dongguk University, 2019), 2.
14. Gim Bang-ok, "Chotbulsiwiwa salmui yeongeukhwa" (Candlelight protests and dramatization of life), in *Sewolho ihuui hangukyeongeuk: Beullaengniseuteueseo beullaektenteukkaji* (Korean theatre after the *Sewol*: From blacklist to Black Tent), ed. Korean Theatre Critics Association (Seoul: Yeongeukkwa Ingan Press, 2017), 358.
15. Yang, *"Ihu"ui yeongeuk, dallajin segye,* 20–21.
16. Seong Ji-su, "Sewolho yeongeugeui mosaek—changjakja, gwangaek, gongganui jaeguseongeul jungsimeuro" (Contemplating Sewol theatre—focusing on the creators, audiences, and space) (PhD diss., Seoul National University, 2017), 10.
17. Diana Taylor, "Making a Spectacle: The Mothers of the Plaza de Mayo," *Journal of the Motherhood Initiative for Research and Community Involvement* 3, no. 2 (2001): 97–109.
18. Taylor, "Making a Spectacle," 106.
19. Jinah Kim, "The Insurgency of Mourning: *Sewol* Across the Transpacific," *Amerasia Journal* 46, no. 1 (2000): 84–100, 87–88.
20. Interview with author, Seoul, Korea, August 12, 2020.

21. Dominick LaCapra, "Trauma, History, Memory, Identity: What Remains?," *History and Theory* 55 (2016): 375–400.
22. Gim Geum-yeong, "Sewolho eommadeul, mudaeolla pangpang utgigo naeryeowa peongpeong ureotda" (*Sewol* mothers laughed onstage and cried backstage), *CNB Journal,* February 3, 2017, http://weekly.cnbnews.com/news/article.html?no=121141.
23. Gim Geum-yeong, "Sewolho eommadeul, mudaeolla pangpang utgigo naeryeowa peongpeong ureotda."
24. Gim Geum-yeong, "Sewolho eommadeul, mudaeolla pangpang utgigo naeryeowa peongpeong ureotda."
25. Yu Ji-yeong, "Sewolho eommaga beullaektenteueseo komidi yeongeugeul haetda" (*Sewol* mothers performed comedy at Black Tent), *Ohmynews,* January 25, 2017, http://star.ohmynews.com/NWS_Web/OhmyStar/at_pg.aspx?CNTN_CD=A0002283198.
26. Gim Se-wun, "Gimtaeheyon, sewolho eommadeureun sejelyeonieyo" (Gim Tae-hyeon, *Sewol* mothers are the best actors), *Voice of the People,* July 4, 2017, http://www.vop.co.kr/A00001175304.html.
27. Gim Se-wun, "Gimtaeheyon, sewolho eommadeureun sejelyeonieyo."
28. Areum Jeong, "Beyond the *Sewol*: Performing Acts of Activism in South Korea," *Performance Research* 24, no. 5 (2019): 33–43.
29. Jae Kyoung Kim, "2017 Black Tent Theatre Project in Gwanghwamun Square: Staging Tragic Memory Building Solidarity Through Public Theatre," *Asian Theatre Journal* 36, no. 1 (2019): 138.
30. Chae Yun-tae, "Gwanghwamun Sewolhocheonmak 18il cheolgeo . . . gieok anjeon jeonsigonggan joseong" (Gwanghwamun *Sewol* tent to be demolished on the 18th . . . exhibition on memory and safety to be created), *Hankyoreh,* March 14, 2019, http://www.hani.co.kr/arti/area/area_general/885925.html.
31. Seon Dam-eun, "50nyeon munojo samseongjeonja hangungnochong sanha nojo seollipanda" (Labor union to be established in Samsung Electronics in 50 years), *Hankyoreh,* November 2, 2019, http://www.hani.co.kr/arti/society/labor/915470.html.
32. Mun Ho-seung et al., *4.16* Sewol *Ferry Disaster Report* (Seoul: Special Investigation Committee for the Humidifier Disinfectant Case and the 4.16 *Sewol* Ferry Disaster, 2022).
33. Young-Hoon Ko, "416sewolhochamsapihaeja geongang mit saenghwalsiltaejosa gyeolgwa balpyo" (A study on the *Sewol* victims' health and living conditions), Beyond Trauma Symposium, Seoul, December 3, 2018; Park Ji-Young, "416sewolhochamsapihaeja jiljeokyeongu gyeolgwa balpyo" (A

qualitative study on the victims' families of the *Sewol* ferry tragedy), Beyond Trauma Symposium, Seoul, December 3, 2018.

34. *KBS Special*, April 19, 2018, http://program.kbs.co.kr/1tv/culture/kspecial/pc.
35. "Nebeonjjae bom, gajokgeukdan noran ribon" (The fourth spring, family theatre troupe Yellow Ribbon), *EBS*, April 17, 2018, https://www.ebs.co.kr/tv/show?prodId=126851&lectId=10870219.
36. Gim Mi-ji, "4.16 gajokgeukdan noranribon janggijarang" (4.16 family theatre troupe Yellow Ribbon *Talent Show*), *Korean Theatre*, August 2019, 14–17.
37. Son Ui-yeon, "Aideul kkum geuryeoyo . . . 4.16 gajokgeukdan noranribon" (Staging the children's dreams . . . 4.16 family theatre troupe Yellow Ribbon), *Edaily*, April 16, 2019, https://www.edaily.co.kr/news/read?newsId=01315286622456776&mediaCodeNo=257.
38. Gim Mi-ji, "4.16 gajokgeukdan noranribon janggijarang," 17.
39. Laub, "Bearing Witness, or the Vicissitudes of Listening," 67.
40. Laub, "Bearing Witness, or the Vicissitudes of Listening," 69.
41. Gim Mi-ji, "4.16 gajokgeukdan noranribon janggijarang," 17.
42. Son, "Aideul kkum geuryeoyo."
43. N. Kim, "The Color of Dissent," 986.
44. N. Kim, "The Color of Dissent," 984.
45. Nan Kim, "Candlelight and the Yellow Ribbon: Catalyzing Re-Democratization in South Korea," *Asia-Pacific Journal: Japan Focus* 15, no. 14 (2017): 1–17, 12 https://apjjf.org/2017/14/Kim.html.
46. Gim Jeong-hyo, "Sewolhowa itaewonui yeondae . . . itaewonchamsa teukbyeolbeop jejeong chokgu" (Solidarity between the Sewol ferry and Itaewon . . . Call for the enactment of a special law on the Itaewon disaster), *Hankyoreh*, June 28, 2023, https://www.hani.co.kr/arti/society/society_general/1097883.html.
47. Walter Benjamin, "Theses on the Philosophy of History," in *Illuminations*, ed. Hannah Arendt (New York: Schocken Books, 1969), 253–264, 261.

CHAPTER 2. MEMORIALIZING THROUGH PERFORMANCE: SITE-SPECIFIC PERFORMANCES WITH OBJECTS IN ANSAN AND PAENGMOK PORT

1. See Rick Dolphijn and Iris van der Tuin, " 'Matter Feels, Converses, Suffers, Desires, Yearns and Remembers': Interview with Karen Barad," in *New Materialism: Interviews and Cartographies*, ed. Dolphijn and

van der Tuin (Ann Arbor: Open Humanities Press, 2012), 59, http://dx.doi.org/10.3998/ohp.11515701.0001.001.

2. Jane Bennett, *Vibrant Matter: A Political Ecology of Things* (Durham, NC: Duke University Press, 2010), 9.
3. Ahmed, "Happy Objects," 33.
4. Sturken, *Tangled Memories,* 3.
5. Sturken, *Tangled Memories,* 2.
6. Sturken, *Tangled Memories,* 9.
7. Sturken, *Tangled Memories,* 10.
8. Sturken, *Tourists of History,* 3.
9. Stewart, *On Longing,* 135.
10. Halberstam, *In a Queer Time and Place,* 1.
11. Halberstam, *In a Queer Time and Place,* 1.
12. Son, *Embodied Reckonings,* 154, 158.
13. N. Kim, "The Color of Dissent," 971.
14. N. Kim, "The Color of Dissent," 984, and "Candlelight and the Yellow Ribbon," 12.
15. Kal, "The Art of Witnessing."
16. Yang, *"Ihu"ui yeongeuk, dallajin segye.*
17. Seong, "Sewolho yeongeugeui mosaek—changjakja, gwangaek, gongganui jaeguseongeul jungsimeuro."
18. Gu Jae-won, "Gungnae yuil damunhwa teukgu . . . Munhwa dayangseongi dosi gyeongjaengnyeok" (Korea's only multicultural special zone . . . Multiculturalism is the city's strength), *Kyeonggi Ilbo,* April 17, 2019, https://www.kyeonggi.com/article/201904171056497.
19. Gim Ji-hye, "Sewolho chumogongwoneul dulleossan galdeunggwa jaengjeomdeul" (Dilemmas and issues surrounding the *Sewol* memorial park), *Kyunghyang Shinmun,* April 16, 2018, http://h2.khan.co.kr/201804161555011?fbclid=IwAR2j76vdpSj0pqVNPARB8aIcF0kOuwW3g9CVZs66zGjrZZZ8rVBU1h8T5hI.
20. "The Children's Room," *Ohmynews,* http://www.ohmynews.com/NWS_Web/Event/pageflow/remember0416.aspx.
21. Judith Butler, *Precarious Life: The Powers of Mourning and Violence* (London: Verso, 2004).
22. Susan Sontag, *Regarding the Pain of Others* (New York: Picador, 2003), 26.
23. Stephenie Young, "The Forensic Imagination: Evidence, Photography, and the Post-Yugoslav Document," paper presented at the American Comparative Literature Association annual meeting, Boston, MA, March 18, 2016.
24. Gyeong Tae-yeong, "Sewolho chumogyosil haebeobeun eomna?" (No solution

for the *Sewol* commemorative classrooms?), *Kyunghyang Shinmun,* February 18, 2016, http://h2.khan.co.kr/201602171657421.

25. Gyeong, "Sewolho chumogyosil haebeobeun eomna?"
26. Gyeong, "Sewolho chumogyosil haebeobeun eomna?"
27. Chaim Noy, "Embodying Ideologies in Tourism: A Commemorative Visitor Book in Israel as a Site of Authenticity," in *Authenticity in Culture, Self, and Society,* ed. J. Patrick Williams (New York: Peter Lang, 2009), 219–240, 219.
28. Noy, "Embodying Ideologies in Tourism," 222, 223.
29. Scott Gabriel Knowles, "Why Disaster Investigations Fail," public lecture at 2017 *Sewol* Academy, Seoul, Korea, August 4, 2017.
30. Victor Turner, "The Center out There: Pilgrim's Goal," *History of Religions* 12, no. 3 (1973): 191–230, 191.
31. Turner, "The Center out There," 192.
32. *Ansansunryegil,* https://obanii.wixsite.com/daum131/blank-2.
33. *Camino de Ansan* Facebook page, https://www.facebook.com/camino.ansan/.
34. Mun Ho-seung et al., *4.16* Sewol *Ferry Disaster Report,* 147.
35. Mun Ho-seung et al., *4.16* Sewol *Ferry Disaster Report,* 156.
36. Mun Ho-seung et al., *4.16* Sewol *Ferry Disaster Report,* 156.
37. Mun Ho-seung et al., *4.16* Sewol *Ferry Disaster Report,* 157.
38. Mun Ho-seung et al., *4.16* Sewol *Ferry Disaster Report,* 157.
39. Mun Ho-seung et al., *4.16* Sewol *Ferry Disaster Report,* 159.
40. Mun Ho-seung et al., *4.16* Sewol *Ferry Disaster Report,* 169.
41. Mun Ho-seung et al., *4.16* Sewol *Ferry Disaster Report,* 170.
42. An Gwan-ok, "'Sesangeseo gajang seulpeun hanggu' paengmokhang... sewolho chamsa heunjeok sarajina" ("The saddest port in the world," Paengmok Port... Will the *Sewol* ferry disaster remnants disappear), *Hankyoreh,* January 10, 2019, http://www.hani.co.kr/arti/area/area_general/877751.html.
43. N. Kim, "The Color of Dissent," 971.
44. Valet Parking, *The Blanket Project,* http://www.blanket416.net.
45. "Laundry Day," *The Blanket Project,* http://www.blanket416.net.
46. Sturken, *Tangled Memories,* 10.
47. Sturken, *Tangled Memories,* 184, 185.
48. Henri Lefebvre, *The Production of Space,* trans. Donald Nicholson-Smith (Oxford: Blackwell, 1991), 170.
49. Lefebvre, *The Production of Space,* 177.
50. Lefebvre, *The Production of Space,* 195.
51. Pierre Nora, "Between Memory and History: Les Lieux de Memoire," *Representations* 26 (1989): 22.

52. Gim Jeong-hun and Bae Myeong-jae, "[Sewolho gajok 'huimangbeoseu' donghaenggi] jinsireun chimmolhaji anchiman teukbyeolbeop eopsineun ichimnida" ([*Sewol* family "hope bus" journal] The truth does not sink but will be forgotten without the Special Law), *Kyunghyang Shinmun,* July 2, 2014, http://news.khan.co.kr/kh_news/khan_art_view.html?art_id=201407022136555.
53. Gwon Yeong-bin, *Meonameon sewolho: Sewolho teukjowiwa hamkkehan sigan* (*Sewol* far away: The time with the *Sewol* Special Investigation Committee) (Seongnam: Pyeolchim Press, 2017), 23.
54. Gwon, *Meonameon sewolho,* 19.
55. Gwon, *Meonameon sewolho,* 21.
56. Gang Jae-gu, "21ilgan 3100km dallin jinsilbeoseu, 10man gungmincheongwon ikkeureonaen sewolho eomma" (*Sewol* mother gathers hundred thousand signatures for national consensus after 21 days and 3,100 km on the Truth Bus), *Hankyoreh,* November 2, 2020, http://www.hani.co.kr/arti/society/society_general/968122.html.
57. Bak Su-ji, "Hwanggyoan, sewolho 7sigan daetongnyeongjijeonggirongmulro 'bongin'" (Hwang Gyo-an seals *Sewol* 7 hours as presidential records), *Hankyoreh,* May 3, 2017, http://www.hani.co.kr/arti/politics/politics_general/793361.html.
58. Gang Jae-gu, "21ilgan 3100km dallin jinsilbeoseu."
59. Gang Jae-gu, "21ilgan 3100km dallin jinsilbeoseu."
60. Sturken, *Tangled Memories,* 184.
61. Choe Sang-Hun, "South Korea to Pardon Ex-President Park Geun-hye, Imprisoned for Corruption," *New York Times,* December 23, 2021, https://www.nytimes.com/2021/12/23/world/asia/south-korea-park-geun-hye-pardon.html.

CHAPTER 3. REIMAGINING JUSTICE: THE *SEWOL* IN SOUTH KOREAN THEATRE AND PERFORMANCE

1. Gwon, *Meonameon sewolho.*
2. Constitutional Court 2016Hun-Na1, March 10, 2017, https://isearch.ccourt.go.kr/view.do.
3. Joshua Takano Chambers-Letson, "A Race So Different: Staging Racial Exception in Ping Chong's *Chinoiserie,*" *MELUS: Multi-Ethnic Literature of the U.S.* 36, no. 4 (2011): 115–139, 118.

4. Son, *Embodied Reckonings.*
5. Son, *Embodied Reckonings,* 66.
6. Gim Mi-do, "Beullaengniseuteu, yesulhaengdong, geurigo chotbulhyeokmyeong!" (Blacklist, arts activism, and candlelight revolution!), public presentation, Seoul Foundation for Arts and Culture, Cultural Policy Committee, Policy Forum #2, Seoul, Korea, September 15, 2017.
7. Kal, "The Art of Witnessing."
8. Gim Mi-do, "Beullaengniseuteu, yesulhaengdong, geurigo chotbulhyeokmyeong!"
9. Gim Min-ju, "Joyunseon, daibingbel tiket maesue akpyeong jisikkaji . . ."
10. Gim Mi-do, "Beullaengniseuteu, yesulhaengdong, geurigo chotbulhyeokmyeong!"
11. Gu Gyo-hyeong, "Sewolho ihu jipoe jayudo garaanjatda" (Freedom of assembly under attack after *Sewol*), *Kyunghang Shinmun,* September 3, 2015, http://news.khan.co.kr/kh_news/khan_art_view.html?art_id=201509030705055.
12. Gang Byeong-jin and Yi Yun-seop, "2wol 24il, gwanghwamune natanan yuryeongdeul" (The ghosts that appeared at Gwanghwamun on Feb. 24), *HuffPost Korea,* February 25, 2016, https://www.huffingtonpost.kr/2016/02/25/story_n_9313630.html.
13. Kee-Yoon Nahm, "Daring to See Red: Theater Company Gorae's Red Poem," *Theatre Times,* January 18, 2017, https://thetheatretimes.com/daring-see-red-theater-company-goraes-red-poem/.
14. Yi Hae-seong, "Bullaektenteu yeondaegi" (Black Tent journey), in *Sewolho ihuui hangukyeongeuk: Beullaengniseuteueseo beullaektenteukkaji* (Korean theatre after the *Sewol*: From blacklist to Black Tent), ed. Korean Theatre Critics Association (Seoul: Yeongeukkwa Ingan Press, 2017), 412.
15. Translated by the Korea Legislation Research Institute, https://elaw.klri.re.kr/eng_service/lawView.do?hseq=1&lang=ENG.
16. Translated by the Korea Legislation Research Institute, https://elaw.klri.re.kr/eng_service/lawView.do?hseq=1&lang=ENG.
17. Jayoung Chung, Q&A at the Asia Culture Center, July 29, 2018.
18. Namsanyesulsenteo (Namsan Arts Center), http://www.nsac.or.kr/Home/ArtsCenter/Intro.aspx.
19. Bak Sang-hyeon, Q&A at the Namsan Arts Center, May 19, 2019.
20. Yi Jae-ho, "Sewolho chamsa mangeon ilsamneun moksadeul, dangjang hoegaehara" (Pastors that speak ill of the *Sewol* ferry disaster must repent), *Gidokgyo Han-gook Shinmun,* June 3, 2014, http://www.cknews.co.kr/news/articleView.html?idxno=3742.

21. Yi Hwa-jin, "Gukgahante beoryeojin sewolho mingan jamsusadeul" (Civilian divers abandoned by the nation), *KBS News,* April 22, 2019, https://news.kbs.co.kr/news/view.do?ncd=4184965.
22. Yi Jin-hui, "Mingan jamsusaro sewolho yujok dowatjiman . . . joein numyeong sidallida ityeojyeo" (Civilian divers helped *Sewol* families . . . but framed and forgotten), *Hankook Ilbo,* April 14, 2018, https://www.hankookilbo.com/News/Read/201804140937770206.
23. Gim Bang-ok, "Sewolhoui jaehyeoneun ganeunghanga" (Is it possible to represent the *Sewol*?), *Yeon-geukin,* June 13, 2019, http://webzine.e-stc.or.kr/01_guide/actreview_view.asp?SearchKey=&SearchValue=&rd=&flag=READ&Idx=1339.
24. 4.16 Act, *Joneomgwa anjeone gwanhan 4.16 ingwonseoneon dodbogi* (An examination of the 4.16 human rights manifesto on dignity and safety) (Seoul: Joyongshin Press, 2016), 9–10.
25. The Seoul City government demolished the *Sewol* memorial hall in July 2021.

CHAPTER 4. SINGING FOR A SPRING DAY: THE *SEWOL* IN K-POP

1. Park Yoon-kyung, "Learning About the *Sewol* Through BTS," *Hankyoreh,* April 26, 2020, https://english.hani.co.kr/arti/english_edition/e_national/942009; Italian ARMY [Angela Pulvirenti], "What You Still Don't Know About BTS 'Spring Day,'" YouTube video, 17:04, https://www.youtube.com/watch?v=FrT4a_Fw6pE&t=4s.
2. Park Yoon-kyung, "Learning About the *Sewol* Through BTS."
3. Youkyung Lee, "How Sparks at S. Korean Women's School Led to Anti-Park Fire," *AP News,* March 14, 2017, https://apnews.com/article/f26782acb46246a0835ecfc412ed7db1.
4. Hyeon So-eun, "'Jeongyura idae ipsi haksabiri' choesunsil, hangsosimseodo jingyeok 3nyeon" ("Jeong Yu-ra's Ewha University entrance scandal," Choe Sun-sil, sentenced to 3 years in prison), *Hankyoreh,* November 14, 2017, http://www.hani.co.kr/arti/society/society_general/818911.html.
5. Hyekyung Woo et al., "Public Trauma After the *Sewol* Ferry Disaster: The Role of Social Media in Understanding the Public Mood," *International Journal of Environmental Research and Public Health* 12 (2015): 10974–10983.
6. N. Kim, "Candlelight and the Yellow Ribbon," 8.
7. Han Haejoang Cho, "National Subjects, Citizens and Refugees: Thoughts on the Politics of Survival, Violence and Mourning Following the *Sewol* Ferry

Disaster in South Korea," in *New Worlds from Below: Informal Life Politics and Grassroots Action in Twenty-First Century Northeast Asia,* ed. Tessa Morris-Suzuki and Eun Jeong Soh (Canberra: Australian National University Press, 2017), 180.

8. Korea Foundation, "2023 Analysis of Global Hallyu Status," April 5, 2024, https://www.kf.or.kr/archives/ebook/ebook_view.do?p_cidx=4041&p_cfidx=128941.
9. Emery Schubert, "Musical Identity and Individual Differences in Empathy," in *Handbook of Musical Identities,* ed. Raymond MacDonald, David J. Hargreaves, and Dorothy Miell (Oxford: Oxford University Press, 2017), 322–342, 333.
10. Patrik N. Juslin and Daniel Vastfjall, "Emotional Responses to Music: The Need to Consider Underlying Mechanisms," *Behavioral and Brain Sciences* 31 (2008): 559–621.
11. Hauke Egermann and Stephen McAdams, "Empathy and Emotional Contagion as a Link Between Recognized and Felt Emotions in Music Listening," *Music Perception: An Interdisciplinary Journal* 31, no. 2 (2013): 139–156.
12. Baek Yeong-hui, "Sewolho 2jugi, aidolbuteo indibaendeukkaji 'gayogye sok sewolho'" (The second anniversary of the *Sewol,* from idols to indie bands "*Sewol* in pop music"), *Etnews,* April 11, 2016, https://m.etnews.com/20160411000334?obj=Tzo4OiJzdGRDbGFzcyI6Mjp7czo3OiJyZWZlcmVyIjtOO3M6NzoiZm9yd2FyZCI7czoxMzoid2ViIHRvIG1vYmlsZSI7fQ%3D%3D.
13. I translated all lyrics in this study from Korean to English. Here are the complete lyrics for "Red Light": "Ay wait a minute / Follow the rules of the jungle / The weak will get eaten / They just push me forward yeah / Push me forward nah / You'll get stepped on if you lose focus / Ay ay jt's a Red Light Light / This is a real situation / Don't even know what's wrong / Ay ay it's a Red Light Light / Listen to the person who's warning you / Red Light / Breathe for a moment / Eh oh eh oh / This isn't a war / Open your eyes wide / You're about to crash, stop the speeding / Be the witness of change / In front of the rough caterpillar that is pushing / When everyone is sinking in front of that / It turns on Red Light / The clear Red Light / Turns on by itself Red Light / Boy your excuses of trying your best / Are just filled with doubts to me / True love might just be / A very slow wave (a very slow wave) / Ay ay it's a Red Light Light / Let's look for the special emergency exit / filled with light in each other / Ay ay think about it, what was it / That made us stop / Red light / Turn around just once / Eh oh eh oh / Look for the precious things / Open your eyes wide / You're about to crash, stop the

speeding / Be the witness of change / In front of the rough caterpillar that is pushing / When everyone is sinking in front of that / It turns on Red Light / The clear Red Light / Turns on by itself Red Light / It turns on Red Light / Two Red Light / In front of the hot sun and you is the Red Light / A miracle is coming / Although it took so long / We're waiting for and wanting the green light / Stop the speeding / This is a real situation, listen to the voice / Open your eyes wide / Yeah, look at the world before you / They push you forward / About to crash, you're being pushed / Caterpillar, that's madness / It turns on Red Light / The clear Red Light / Turns on by itself Red Light / It turns on Red Light / Two Red Light / In front of the hot sun and you is the Red Light."

14. CBS Sisa Jaki staff, "Hapchangdani doen sewolho gajokdeul" (*Sewol* families become a choir), *Nocut News,* April 16, 2020, https://www.nocutnews.co.kr/news/5329579.
15. CBS Sisa Jaki staff, "Hapchangdani doen sewolho gajokdeul."

CHAPTER 5. PERFORMING DIASPORIC HEALING: *SEWOL* ACTIVISM IN KOREAN AMERICAN COMMUNITIES

1. "1980nyeon 5wol 26il sikagoseo yeolleotda" (Took place on May 26, 1980, in Chicago), *Korea Times,* March 29, 2016, http://www.koreatimes.com/article/20160328/978603.
2. Eun Sook Lee, "The Political Awakening of Korean Americans," in *Koreans in the Windy City: 100 Years of Korean Americans in the Chicago Area,* ed. Hyock Chun, Kwang Chung Kim, and Shin Kim (New Haven: East Rock Institute for the Centennial Publication Committee of Chicago, 2005), 337.
3. Eun Sook Lee, "The Political Awakening of Korean Americans."
4. Jisue Lee and Ji Hei Kang, "Crying Mothers Mobilise for a Collective Action: Collaborative Information Behaviour in an Online Community," *Information Research* 23, no. 2 (2018): 792, http://InformationR.net/ir/23-2/paper792.html.
5. Hyun Hee Kim, "Transborder Civic Engagement and Identity Politics: Korean American Women's Campaign for the *Sewol* Ferry Disaster," *Journal of Multicultural Society* 13, no. 2 (2020): 107–142, http://journal.kci.go.kr/sims/archive/articleView?artiId=ART002596869.
6. Mun Ho-seung et al., *4.16* Sewol *Ferry Disaster Report,* 195–196.
7. Park Hyun, "Korean-Americans Protest the *Sewol* Tragedy Across the US,"

Hankyoreh, May 20, 2014, https://english.hani.co.kr/arti/english_edition/e_national/637996.html.

8. Son, *Embodied Reckonings,* 149.
9. See their online *Sewol* contest exhibition: https://1heart4justice.org/gallery-2/.
10. Erin Rode, "Increasing Numbers of Korean Americans Are Identifying as Democrats," *USC Annenberg Media,* April 28, 2018, http://www.uscannenbergmedia.com/2018/04/28/increasing-numbers-of-korean-americans-are-identifying-as-democrats/.
11. James C. Scott, *Weapons of the Weak: Everyday Forms of Peasant Resistance* (New Haven, CT: Yale University Press, 1985), 33.
12. James C. Scott, "Everyday Forms of Resistance," in *Everyday Forms of Peasant Resistance,* ed. F. D. Colburn (New York: Routledge, 1989), 29; Francis Wade, "Most Resistance Does Not Speak Its Name: An Interview with James C. Scott," *Los Angeles Review of Books,* January 22, 2018, https://lareviewofbooks.org/article/most-resistance-does-not-speak-its-name-an-interview-with-james-c-scott/.
13. Susan Leigh Foster, "Choreographies of Protest," *Theatre Journal* 55, no. 3 (2003): 395–412.

EPILOGUE: BEYOND THE *SEWOL*

1. Mun Sang-hyeon, "Itaewon chamsa geunal gyeongchareun eodireul bogo isseonna" (Itaewon tragedy, where were the police looking at that day?), *Sisain,* November 16, 2022, https://www.sisain.co.kr/news/articleView.html?idxno=48980.
2. Jonathan Head and Tessa Wong, "Itaewon Crush: First Emergency Call Came Hours Before Crush," *BBC,* November 1, 2022, https://www.bbc.com/news/world-asia-63467204.
3. Michelle Ye Hee Lee et al., "Crucial Lapses Led to Tragically Delayed Rescue in a Seoul Alley," *Washington Post,* November 16, 2022, https://www.washingtonpost.com/investigations/2022/11/16/seoul-crowd-crush-itaewon-victims.
4. "Itaewon 'chamsa' 'huisaengja' daesin 'sago' 'samangja'ra bureuraneun jeongbu" (The government that orders to say "accident" and "deceased" instead of Itaewon "tragedy" and "victims"), *Hankyoreh,* November 1, 2022, https://www.hani.co.kr/arti/opinion/editorial/1065288.html.
5. Yi Chang-hun, "Uri ttal eodiseo channayo . . . Sinsokan sisin bunsane aekkeulleun yujokdeul" (Where can I find my daughter . . . Bereaved families grieve

at the speedy dispersal of the bodies), *JoongAng Ilbo,* October 30, 2022, https://www.joongang.co.kr/article/25113361#home.

6. Baek Dam, "Chamsa yujokdeul jeungeon 'dareun gajokdeulgwa sotong wonhaetjiman jeongbuga muksal'" (Bereaved families testify they wanted communication with other families but the government ignored them), *Nocut News,* November 27, 2022, https://www.nocutnews.co.kr/news/5855563.
7. No Ji-min, "Itaewon chamsa handal, yugajok sagwayogue dabeomneun daetongnyeong" (A month after the Itaewon tragedy, president silent at families' demand for apology), *Media Today,* November 29, 2022, http://www.mediatoday.co.kr/news/articleView.html?idxno=307192.
8. Gim Ye-rim, "Itaewon chamsa 2cha gahae mangmal . . . saengjonja joechaekgam kiwo" (Itaewon disaster secondary abuse . . . raises survivor guilt), *Yonhap News,* December 15, 2022, https://www.yonhapnewstv.co.kr/news/MYH20221215013800641.
9. Yi Jun-seok, "Dongbyeongsangnyeon sewolho yugajokdeuri itaewone ttuiun pyeonji" (The letter *Sewol* families sent to Itaewon), *Nocut News,* November 2, 2022, https://www.nocutnews.co.kr/news/5842510.
10. Choe Yeong-gwon, "Sewolho yujogi barabon itaewon chamsa" (The Itaewon disaster from the perspective of the *Sewol* families), *Seoul Shinmun,* November 9, 2022, https://www.seoul.co.kr/news/newsView.php?id=20221109500201.

BIBLIOGRAPHY

ONLINE MATERIAL

"1980nyeon 5wol 26il sikagoseo yeolleotda" (Took place on May 26, 1980, in Chicago). *Korea Times,* March 29, 2016. http://www.koreatimes.com/article/20160328/978603.

An Gwan-ok. "'Sesangeseo gajang seulpeun hanggu' paengmokhang... Sewolho chamsa heunjeok sarajina" ("The saddest port in the world," Paengmok Port... Will the *Sewol* ferry disaster remnants disappear). *Hankyoreh,* January 10, 2019. http://www.hani.co.kr/arti/area/area_general/877751.html.

Ansansunryegil. https://obanii.wixsite.com/daum131/blank-2.

Baek Dam. "Chamsa yujokdeul jeungeon 'dareun gajokdeulgwa sotong wonhaetjiman jeongbuga muksal'" (Bereaved families testify they wanted communication with other families but the government ignored them). *Nocut News,* November 27, 2022. https://www.nocutnews.co.kr/news/5855563.

Baek Yeong-hui. "Sewolho 2jugi, aidolbuteo indibaendeukkaji 'gayogye sok sewolho'" (The second anniversary of the *Sewol,* from idols to indie bands "*Sewol* in pop music"). *Etnews,* April 11, 2016. https://m.etnews.com/20160411000334?obj=Tzo4OiJzdGRDbGFzcyI6Mjp7czo3OiJyZWZlcmVyIjtOO3M6NzoiZm9yd2FyZCI7czoxMzoid2ViIHRvIG1vYmlsZSI7fQ%3D%3D.

Bak Su-ji. "Hwanggyoan, sewolho 7sigan daetongnyeongjijeonggirongmulro 'bongin'" (Hwang Gyo-an seals *Sewol* 7 hours as presidential records). *Hankyoreh,* May 3, 2017. http://www.hani.co.kr/arti/politics/politics_general/793361.html.

"Camino de Ansan." Facebook. https://www.facebook.com/camino.ansan/.

CBS Sisa Jaki Staff. "Hapchangdani doen sewolho gajokdeul" (*Sewol* families become a choir). *Nocut News,* April 16, 2020. https://www.nocutnews.co.kr/news/5329579.

Chae Yun-tae. "Gwanghwamun Sewolhocheonmak 18il cheolgeo . . . gieok anjeon jeonsigonggan joseong" (Gwanghwamun *Sewol* tent to be demolished on the 18th . . . exhibition on memory and safety to be created). *Hankyoreh,* March 14, 2019. http://www.hani.co.kr/arti/area/area_general/885925.html.

"The Children's Room." *Ohmynews.* http://www.ohmynews.com/NWS_Web/Event/pageflow/remember0416.aspx.

Choe Sang-Hun. "South Korea to Pardon Ex-President Park Geun-hye, Imprisoned for Corruption." *New York Times,* December 23, 2021. https://www.nytimes.com/2021/12/23/world/asia/south-korea-park-geun-hye-pardon.html.

Choe Yeong-gwon. "Sewolho yujogi barabon itaewon chamsa" (The Itaewon disaster from the perspective of the *Sewol* families). *Seoul Shinmun,* November 9, 2022. https://www.seoul.co.kr/news/newsView.php?id=20221109500201.

Gang Byeong-jin and Yi Yun-seop. "2wol 24il, gwanghwamune natanan yuryeongdeul" (The ghosts that appeared at Gwanghwamun on Feb. 24). *HuffPost Korea,* February 25, 2016. https://www.huffingtonpost.kr/2016/02/25/story_n_9313630.html.

Gang Jae-gu. "21ilgan 3100km dallin jinsilbeoseu, 10man gungmincheongwon ikkeureonaen sewolho eomma" (*Sewol* mother gathers hundred thousand signatures for national consensus after 21 days and 3,100 km on the Truth Bus). *Hankyoreh,* November 2, 2020. http://www.hani.co.kr/arti/society/society_general/968122.html.

Gang Na-ru. "Jasik ireun sewolho yujogeun eotteoke jongbugi doeeonna" (How did *Sewol* families become *jongbuk*). *KBS News,* May 6, 2019. https:// mn.kbs.co.kr/news/view.do?ncd=4194889.

Gim Bang-ok. "Sewolhoui jaehyeoneun ganeunghanga" (Is it possible to represent the *Sewol*?). *Yeon-geukin,* June 13, 2019. http://webzine.e-stc.or.kr/01_guide/actreview_view.asp?SearchKey=&SearchValue=&rd=&flag=READ&Idx=1339.

Gim Geum-yeong. "Sewolho eommadeul, mudaeolla pangpang utgigo naeryeowa peongpeong ureotda" (*Sewol* mothers laughed onstage and cried backstage). *CNB Journal,* February 3, 2017. http://weekly.cnbnews.com/news/article.html?no=121141.

Gim Jeong-hun and Bae Myeong-jae. "[Sewolho gajok 'huimangbeoseu' donghaenggi] jinsireun chimmolhaji anchiman teukbyeolbeop eopsineun ichimnida" ([*Sewol* family "hope bus" journal] The truth does not sink but will be forgotten without the Special Law). *Kyunghyang Shinmun,* July 2, 2014. http://news.khan.co.kr/kh_news/khan_art_view.html?art_id=201407022136555.

Gim Jeong-hyo. "Sewolhowa itaewonui yeondae...itaewonchamsa teukbyeolbeop jejeong chokgu" (Solidarity between the *Sewol* ferry and Itaewon...Call for the enactment of a special law on the Itaewon disaster). *Hankyoreh,* June 28, 2023. https://www.hani.co.kr/arti/society/society_general/1097883.html.

Gim Ji-hye. "Sewolho chumogongwoneul dulleossan galdeunggwa jaengjeomdeul" (Dilemmas and issues surrounding the *Sewol* memorial park). *Kyunghyang Shinmun,* April 16, 2018. http://h2.khan.co.kr/201804161555011?fbclid=IwAR2j76vdpSj0pqVNPARB8aIcF0kOuwW3g9CVZs66zGjrZZZ8rVBU1h8T5hI.

Gim Min-ju. "Joyunseon, daibingbel tiket maesue akpyeong jisikkaji..." (Jo Yun-seon, bought up all tickets for *The Truth Shall Not Sink with* Sewol and even ordered negative reviews...). *Kookje Shinmun,* February 1, 2017. http://www.kookje.co.kr/news2011/asp/newsbody.asp?code=0100&key=20170201.99002002810.

Gim Se-wun. "Gimtaeheyon, sewolho eommadeureun sejelyeonieyo" (Gim Taehyeon, *Sewol* mothers are the best actors). *Voice of the People,* July 4, 2017. http://www.vop.co.kr/A00001175304.html.

Gim Won-jin. "Ttae doemyeon chajaoneun bulcheonggaek 'sewolho hyeomopyoheyon,' nuga eonje peotteurina" ("*Sewol* ferry hate speech," who spreads it and when). *Kyunghyang Shinmun,* April 11, 2020. https://www.khan.co.kr/national/national-general/article/202004111119011.

Gim Ye-rim. "Itaewon chamsa 2cha gahae mangmal...saengjonja joechaekgam kiwo" (Itaewon disaster secondary abuse...raises survivor guilt). *Yonhap News,* December 15, 2022. https://www.yonhapnewstv.co.kr/news/MYH20221215013800641.

Gu Gyo-hyeong. "Sewolho ihu jipoe jayudo garaanjatda" (Freedom of assembly under attack after *Sewol*). *Kyunghang Shinmun,* September 3, 2015. http://news.khan.co.kr/kh_news/khan_art_view.html?art_id=201509030705055.

Gu Jae-won. "Gungnae yuil damunhwa teukgu...Munhwa dayangseongi dosi gyeongjaengnyeok" (Korea's only multicultural special zone...Multiculturalism is the city's strength). *Kyeonggi Ilbo,* April 17, 2019. https://www.kyeonggi.com/article/201904171056497.

Gyeong Tae-yeong. "Sewolho chumogyosil haebeobeun eomna?" (No solution for the *Sewol* commemorative classrooms?). *Kyunghyang Shinmun,* February 18, 2016. http://h2.khan.co.kr/201602171657421.

Head, Jonathan, and Tessa Wong. "Itaewon Crush: First Emergency Call Came Hours Before Crush." *BBC,* November 1, 2022. https://www.bbc.com/news/world-asia-63467204.

Hong Yong-deok. "'Napgoldang baekjihwa' yadang gongyage sewolho huisaengja yugajok 'seongeoe agyong malla'" (Opposition party promises to wipe out the ossuary and the victims' families of the *Sewol* ferry tell them not to abuse it in the elections). *Hankyoreh,* June 5, 2018. https://www.hani.co.kr/arti/area/area_general/847806.html.

Hyeon So-eun. "'Jeongyura idae ipsi haksabiri' choesunsil, hangsosimseodo jingyeok 3nyeon" ("Jeong Yu-ra's Ewha University entrance scandal," Choe Sun-sil, sentenced to 3 years in prison). *Hankyoreh,* November 14, 2017. http://www.hani.co.kr/arti/society/society_general/818911.html.

"Itaewon 'chamsa' 'huisaengja' daesin 'sago' 'samangja'ra bureuraneun jeongbu" (The government that orders to say "accident" and "deceased" instead of Itaewon "tragedy" and "victims"). *Hankyoreh,* November 1, 2022. https://www.hani.co.kr/arti/opinion/editorial/1065288.html.

Jeon Gwang-jun. "Sewolho yujokdeuri 3nyeonmane dasi kkeonaen 'nalgeun chimnang'" (The "old sleeping bag" the *Sewol* families took out after 3 years). *Hankyoreh,* December 6, 2020. http://www.hani.co.kr/arti/society/society_general/973005.html.

Jeong So-ang. "Sewolho gujo silpae, haegyeongui geojinmareul balkhyeoya handa" (Failure to rescue *Sewol* ferry must reveal coast guard's lies). *Ohmynews,* October 14, 2014. http://www.ohmynews.com/NWS_ Web/view/at_pg.aspx?cntn_cd=A0002043104.

Jeong Yu-gyeong. "'Nunmul geulsseong' mun daetongnyeong, sewolho yujokdeurege 'neujeotjiman sagwadeurinda'" ("Tears in his eyes," President Moon delivers "belated apologies" to *Sewol* families). *Hankyoreh,* August 16, 2017. http://www.hani.co.kr/arti/politics/politics_general/807043.html.

KBS Special. April 19, 2018. http://program.kbs.co.kr/1tv/culture/kspecial/pc.

Korea Foundation. "2023 Analysis of Global Hallyu Status." April 5, 2024. https://www.kf.or.kr/archives/ebook/ebook_view.do?p_cidx=4041&p_cfidx=128941.

"Laundry Day." *The Blanket Project.* http://www.blanket416.net.

Lee, Michelle Ye Hee, Meg Kelly, Atthar Mirza, Grace Moon, Min Joo Kim, and Stefanie Le. "Crucial Lapses Led to Tragically Delayed Rescue in a Seoul Alley." *Washington Post,* November 16, 2022. https://www.washingtonpost.com/investigations/2022/11/16/seoul-crowd-crush-itaewon-victims.

Lee, Youkyung. "How Sparks at S. Korean Women's School Led to Anti-Park Fire." *AP News,* March 14, 2017. https://apnews.com/article/f26782acb46246a0835ecfc412ed7db1.

Mun Sang-hyeon. "Itaewon chamsa geunal gyeongchareun eodireul bogo isseonna" (Itaewon tragedy, where were the police looking that day?). *Sisain,* November 16, 2022. https://www.sisain.co.kr/news/articleView.html?idxno=48980.

Nahm, Kee-Yoon. "Daring to See Red: Theater Company Gorae's Red Poem."

Theatre Times, January 18, 2017. https://thetheatretimes.com/daring-see-red-theater-company-goraes-red-poem/.

Namsanyesulsenteo (Namsan Arts Center). http://www.nsac.or.kr/Home/ArtsCenter/Intro.aspx.

"Nebeonjjae bom, gajokgeukdan noran ribon" (The fourth spring, family theatre troupe Yellow Ribbon). *EBS,* April 17, 2018. www.ebs.co.kr/tv/show?prodId=126851&lectId=10870219.

No Ji-min. "Itaewon chamsa handal, yugajok sagwayogue dabeomneun daetongnyeong" (A month after the Itaewon tragedy, president silent at families' demand for apology). *Media Today,* November 29, 2022. http://www.mediatoday.co.kr/news/articleView.html?idxno=307192.

Park Hyun. "Korean-Americans Protest the *Sewol* Tragedy Across the US." *Hankyoreh,* May 20, 2014. https://english.hani.co.kr/arti/english_edition/e_national/637996.html.

Park Yoon-kyung. "Learning About the *Sewol* Through BTS." *Hankyoreh,* April 26, 2020. https://english.hani.co.kr/arti/english_edition/e_national/942009.

Rode, Erin. "Increasing Numbers of Korean Americans Are Identifying as Democrats." *USC Annenberg Media,* April 28, 2018. http://www.uscannenbergmedia.com/2018/04/28/increasing-numbers-of-korean-americans-are-identifying-as-democrats/.

Seon Dam-eun. "50nyeon munojo samseongjeonja hangungnochong sanha nojo seollipanda" (Labor union to be established in Samsung Electronics in 50 years). *Hankyoreh,* November 2, 2019. http://www.hani.co.kr/arti/society/labor/915470.html.

Son Ui-yeon. "Aideul kkum geuryeoyo . . . 4.16 gajokgeukdan noranribon" (Staging the children's dreams . . . 4.16 family theatre troupe Yellow Ribbon). *Edaily,* April 16, 2019. https://www.edaily.co.kr/news/read?newsId=01315286622456776&mediaCodeNo=257.

Valet Parking. *The Blanket Project.* http://www.blanket416.net.

Wade, Francis. "Most Resistance Does Not Speak Its Name: An Interview with James C. Scott." *Los Angeles Review of Books,* January 22, 2018. https://lareviewofbooks.org/article/most-resistance-does-not-speak-its-name-an-interview-with-james-c-scott/.

Yi Chang-hun. "Uri ttal eodiseo channayo . . . Sinsokan sisin bunsane aekkeulleun yujokdeul" (Where can I find my daughter . . . Bereaved families grieve at the speedy dispersal of the bodies). *JoongAng Ilbo,* October 30, 2022. https://www.joongang.co.kr/article/25113361#home.

Yi Hwa-jin. "Gukgahante beoryeojin sewolho mingan jamsusadeul" (Civilian divers abandoned by the nation). *KBS News,* April 22, 2019. https://news.kbs.co.kr/news/view.do?ncd=4184965.

Yi Jae-ho. "Sewolho chamsa mangeon ilsamneun moksadeul, dangjang hoegaehara" (Pastors who speak ill of the *Sewol* ferry disaster must repent). *Gidokgyo Han-gook Shinmun,* June 3, 2014. http://www.cknews.co.kr/news/articleView.html?idxno=3742.

Yi Jin-hui. "Mingan jamsusaro sewolho yujok dowatjiman . . . joein numyeong sidallida ityeojyeo" (Civilian divers helped *Sewol* families . . . but framed and forgotten). *Hankook Ilbo,* April 14, 2018. https://www.hankookilbo.com/News/Read/201804140937770206.

Yi Jun-seok. "Dongbyeongsangnyeon sewolho yugajokdeuri itaewone ttuiun pyeonji" (The letter *Sewol* families sent to Itaewon). *Nocut News,* November 2, 2022. https://www.nocutnews.co.kr/news/5842510.

Yi Su-jin. "Sewolho eommadeurui ballyeongi, geuraedo nunmuri naneun kkadageun" (Reasons for tears despite *Sewol* mothers' mediocre acting). *Ohmynews,* January 27, 2017. http://star.ohmynews.com/NWS_ Web/OhmyStar/at_pg.aspx?CNTN_CD=A0002283695.

Yu Gyeong-geun. "Tto dasi gukoeboncheong apimnida" (I am in front of the National Assembly Headquarters again). Facebook, December 6, 2020. https://www.facebook.com/gyounggeun.yoo/posts/3845745208817731.

Yu Ji-yeong. "Sewolho eommaga beullaektenteueseo komidi yeongeugeul haetda" (*Sewol* mothers performed comedy at Black Tent). *Ohmynews,* January 25, 2017. http://star.ohmynews.com/NWS_Web/OhmyStar/at_pg.aspx?CNTN_CD=A0002283198.

PRINT MATERIAL

4.16 Act. *Joneomgwa anjeone gwanhan 4.16 ingwonseoneon dodbogi* (An examination of the 4.16 human rights manifesto on dignity and safety). Seoul: Joyongshin Press, 2016.

Abelmann, Nancy. "Women's Class Mobility and Identities in South Korea: A Gendered, Transnational, Narrative Approach." *Journal of Asian Studies* 56, no. 2 (1997): 398–420.

Ahmed, Sara. "Happy Objects." In *The Affect Theory Reader,* edited by Melissa Gregg and Gregory J. Seigworth, 29–51. Durham, NC: Duke University Press, 2010.

Asriani, Desintha. "Being Mother: Comparative Study of the Contested Motherhood Between South Korea and Indonesia." *International Journal of Management, Entrepreneurship, Social Science and Humanities* 1, no. 1 (2017): 15–23.

Austin, J. L. *How to Do Things with Words.* Cambridge, MA: Harvard University Press, 1962.

Bak Yu-rim. "A Thesis on the Director Kim Jae-Yeop's Theatre from the Perspective of New Documentary Theatre." MA thesis, Dongguk University, 2019.

Benjamin, Walter. "Theses on the Philosophy of History." In *Illuminations*, edited by Hannah Arendt, 253–264. New York: Schocken Books, 1969.

Bennett, Jane. *Vibrant Matter: A Political Ecology of Things*. Durham, NC: Duke University Press, 2010.

Boal, Augusto. *Games for Actors and Non-Actors*. London: Routledge, 1992.

Butler, Judith. *Gender Trouble: Feminism and the Subversion of Identity*. New York: Routledge, 1990.

Butler, Judith. *Precarious Life: The Powers of Mourning and Violence*. London: Verso, 2004.

Butler, Judith. "Rethinking Vulnerability and Resistance." In *Vulnerability in Resistance*, edited by Judith Butler, Zeynep Gambetti, and Leticia Sabsay, 12–27. Durham, NC: Duke University Press, 2016.

Chambers-Letson, Joshua Takano. "A Race So Different: Staging Racial Exception in Ping Chong's *Chinoiserie*." *MELUS: Multi-Ethnic Literature of the U.S.* 36, no. 4 (2011): 115–139.

Cho, Haejoang. "Living with Conflicting Subjectivities: Mother, Motherly Wife, and Sexy Woman in the Transition from Colonial-Modern to Postmodern Korea." In *Under Construction: The Gendering of Modernity, Class, and Consumption in the Republic of Korea*, edited by Laurel Kendall, 165–195. Honolulu: University of Hawai'i Press, 2002.

Cho, Han Haejoang. "National Subjects, Citizens and Refugees: Thoughts on the Politics of Survival, Violence and Mourning Following the *Sewol* Ferry Disaster in South Korea." In *New Worlds from Below: Informal Life Politics and Grassroots Action in Twenty-First Century Northeast Asia*, edited by Tessa Morris-Suzuki and Eun Jeong Soh, 167–196. Canberra: Australian National University Press, 2017.

Choi, Chungmoo. "The Discourse of Decolonization and Popular Memory: South Korea." *Positions: Asia Critique* 1, no. 1 (1993): 77–102.

Choi, Chungmoo. "Transnational Capitalism, National Imaginary, and the Protest Theater in South Korea." *boundary 2* 22, no. 1 (1995): 235–261.

Conquergood, Dwight. "Rethinking Ethnography: Towards a Critical Cultural Politics." *Communication Monographs* 58, no. 2 (1991): 179–194.

Dolphijn, Rick, and Iris van der Tuin. "'Matter Feels, Converses, Suffers, Desires, Yearns and Remembers': Interview with Karen Barad." In *New Materialism: Interviews and Cartographies*, edited by Rick Dolphijn and Iris van der Tuin. Ann Arbor: Open Humanities Press, 2012. http://dx.doi.org/10.3998/ohp.11515701.0001.001.

Egermann, Hauke, and Stephen McAdams. "Empathy and Emotional Contagion as a Link Between Recognized and Felt Emotions in Music Listening." *Music Perception: An Interdisciplinary Journal* 31, no. 2 (2013): 139–156.

Foster, Susan Leigh. "Choreographies of Protest." *Theatre Journal* 55, no. 3 (2003): 395–412.

Fuentes, Marcela A. "Zooming In and Out: Tactical Media Performance in Transnational Contexts." In *Performance, Politics, and Activism,* edited by John Rouse and Peter Lichtenfels, 32–55. London: Palgrave Macmillan, 2013.

Gim Bang-ok. "Chotbulsiwiwa salmui yeongeukhwa" (Candlelight protests and dramatization of life). In *Sewolho ihuui hangukyeongeuk: Beullaengniseuteueseo beullaektenteukkaji* (Korean theatre after the *Sewol*: From blacklist to Black Tent), edited by Korean Theatre Critics Association, 345–362. Seoul: Yeongeukkwa Ingan Press, 2017.

Gim Bang-ok. "Geomyeol, hogeun sayukdoeneun yeongeuk" (Theatre that is censored or bred). In *Sewolho ihuui hangukyeongeuk: Beullaengniseuteueseo beullaektenteukkaji* (Korean theatre after the *Sewol*: From blacklist to Black Tent), edited by Korean Theatre Critics Association, 51–66. Seoul: Yeongeukkwa Ingan Press, 2017.

Gim Mi-do. "Beullaengniseuteu, yesulhaengdong, geurigo chotbulhyeokmyeong!" (Blacklist, arts activism, and candlelight revolution!). Public presentation at Seoul Foundation for Arts and Culture, Cultural Policy Committee, Policy Forum #2, Seoul, September 15, 2017.

Gim Mi-ji. "4.16 gajokgeukdan noranribon janggijarang" (4.16 family theatre troupe Yellow Ribbon *Talent Show*). *Korean Theatre,* August 2019, 14–17.

Gwon Yeong-bin. *Meonameon sewolho: Sewolho teukjowiwa hamkkehan sigan* (*Sewol* far away: The time with the *Sewol* Special Investigation Committee). Seongnam: Pyeolchim Press, 2017.

Halberstam, J. *In a Queer Time and Place: Transgender Bodies, Subcultural Lives.* New York: New York University Press, 2005.

Jeon Jiyeol et al. "A Grounded Theory Study of the Grieving Processes of Bereaved Parents After the *Sewol* Ferry Disaster." *Korean Journal of Counseling and Psychotherapy* 31, no. 1 (2019): 1–48.

Jeong, Areum. "Beyond the *Sewol*: Performing Acts of Activism in South Korea." *Performance Research* 24, no. 5 (2019): 33–43. https://doi.org/10.1080/13528165.2019.1671715.

Jeong, Areum. "From Witnessing to Redress: Objects, Remnants, and Wreckage After the *Sewol*." *Theatre Journal* 75, no. 2 (2023): 167–186. https://doi.org/10.1353/tj.2023.a908733.

Jeong, Areum. "Performing Memory and Testimony After a National Disaster: The *Sewol* Mothers in *Talking About Her* (2016), *VEGA* (2016), and *His and Her Closet* (2016)." *Studies in Theatre and Performance Online* (2023). https://doi.org/10.1080/14682761.2023.2230625.

Jeong, Areum. "Representing the Unrepresentable in South Korean Activist Performances." *New Theatre Quarterly* 36, no. 4 (2020): 292–305. https://doi.org/10.1017/S0266464X20000640.

Juslin, Patrik N., and Daniel Vastfjall. "Emotional Responses to Music: The Need to Consider Underlying Mechanisms." *Behavioral and Brain Sciences* 31 (2008): 559–621.

Kal, Hong. "The Art of Witnessing: The *Sewol* Ferry Disaster in Hong Sung-dam's Paintings." *Korean Studies* 43 (2019): 96–119.

Kang, Jiyeon. *Igniting the Internet: Youth and Activism in Postauthoritarian South Korea.* Honolulu: University of Hawai'i Press, 2016.

Kim, Hyun Hee. "Transborder Civic Engagement and Identity Politics: Korean American Women's Campaign for the *Sewol* Ferry Disaster." *Journal of Multicultural Society* 13, no. 2 (2020): 107–142. http://journal.kci.go.kr/sims/archive/articleView?artiId=ART002596869.

Kim, Jae Kyoung. "2017 Black Tent Theatre Project in Gwanghwamun Square: Staging Tragic Memory and Building Solidarity Through Public Theatre." *Asian Theatre Journal* 36, no. 1 (2019): 122–143.

Kim, Jinah. "The Insurgency of Mourning: *Sewol* Across the Transpacific." *Amerasia Journal* 46, no. 1 (2000): 84–100.

Kim, Myung-hye. "Late Industrialization and Women's Work in Urban South Korea: An Ethnographic Study of Upper-Middle-Class Families." *City and Society* 6, no. 2 (1992): 156–173.

Kim, Nan. "Candlelight and the Yellow Ribbon: Catalyzing Re-Democratization in South Korea." *Asia-Pacific Journal: Japan Focus* 15, no. 14 (2017): 1–17. https://apjjf.org/2017/14/Kim.html.

Kim, Nan. "The Color of Dissent and a Vital Politics of Fragility in South Korea." *Journal of Asian Studies* 77, no. 4 (2018): 971–990.

Knowles, Scott Gabriel. "Why Disaster Investigations Fail." Public lecture at 2017 *Sewol* Academy, Seoul, August 4, 2017.

Ko Young-Hoon. "416sewolhochamsapihaeja geongang mit saenghwalsiltaejosa gyeolgwa balpyo" (A study on the *Sewol* victims' health and living conditions). Beyond Trauma Symposium, Seoul, December 3, 2018.

Korean Theatre Critics Association, ed. *Sewolho ihuui hangukyeongeuk: Beullaengniseuteueseo beullaektenteukkaji* (Korean theatre after the *Sewol*: From blacklist to Black Tent). Seoul: Yeongeukkwa Ingan Press, 2017.

LaCapra, Dominick. "Trauma, History, Memory, Identity: What Remains?" *History and Theory* 55 (2016): 375–400.

LaCapra, Dominick. *Writing History, Writing Trauma.* Baltimore, MD: Johns Hopkins University Press, 2001.

Laub, Dori. "Bearing Witness, or the Vicissitudes of Listening." In *Testimony: Crises of Witnessing in Literature, Psychoanalysis, and History,* edited by Shoshana Felman and Dori Laub, 57–74. New York: Routledge, 1992.

Lee, Eun Sook. "The Political Awakening of Korean Americans." In *Koreans in the Windy City: 100 Years of Korean Americans in the Chicago Area,* edited by Hyock Chun, Kwang Chung Kim, and Shin Kim, 337–350. New Haven, CT: East Rock Institute for the Centennial Publication Committee of Chicago, 2005.

Lee, Hyeon Jung, and Yesung Lee. "Gender Differences in Parental Grief: The Case of the Bereaved Families of the *Sewol* Ferry Disaster." *Family and Culture* 30, no. 3 (2018): 1–41.

Lee, Jisue, and Ji Hei Kang. "Crying Mothers Mobilise for a Collective Action: Collaborative Information Behaviour in an Online Community." *Information Research* 23, no. 2 (2018): 792. http://InformationR.net/ir/23-2/paper792.html.

Lee, Namhee. "Between Indeterminacy and Radical Critique: Madang-guk, Ritual, and Protest." *Positions: East Asia Cultures Critique* 11, no. 3 (2003): 555–584.

Lee, Namhee. *The Making of Minjung: Democracy and the Politics of Representation in South Korea.* Ithaca, NY: Cornell University Press, 2009.

Lefebvre, Henri. *The Production of Space.* Translated by Donald Nicholson-Smith. Oxford: Blackwell, 1991.

Madison, D. Soyini. *Acts of Activism: Human Rights as Radical Performance.* Cambridge: Cambridge University Press, 2010.

Mun Ho-seung et al. *4.16* Sewol *Ferry Disaster Report.* Seoul: Special Investigation Committee for the Humidifier Disinfectant Case and the 4.16 *Sewol* Ferry Disaster, 2022.

Nam, Jeong-Lim. "Gender Politics in the Korean Transition to Democracy." *Korean Studies* 24 (2000): 94–112.

Nam Ji-su. "New Documentary Theatre: Across the Boundary Between the Real and the Fiction." PhD diss., Dongguk University, 2015.

Nora, Pierre. "Between Memory and History: Les Lieux de Memoire." *Representations* 26 (1989): 7–24.

Noy, Chaim. "Embodying Ideologies in Tourism: A Commemorative Visitor Book in Israel as a Site of Authenticity." In *Authenticity in Culture, Self, and Society,* edited by J. Patrick Williams, 219–240. New York: Peter Lang, 2009.

Park Ji-Young. "416sewolhochamsapihaeja jiljeokyeongu gyeolgwa balpyo" (A qualitative study on the victims' families of the *Sewol* ferry tragedy). Beyond Trauma Symposium, Seoul, December 3, 2018.

Rho Young-Sook. "The Study on the Formation of the May Mothers House." MA thesis, Chonnam National University, 2015.

Roach, Joseph. *Cities of the Dead: Circum-Atlantic Performance.* New York: Columbia University Press, 1996.

Schechner, Richard. *Performance Studies: An Introduction.* New York: Routledge, 2006.

Schubert, Emery. "Musical Identity and Individual Differences in Empathy." In *Handbook of Musical Identities,* edited by Raymond MacDonald, David J. Hargreaves, and Dorothy Miell, 332–344. Oxford: Oxford University Press, 2017.

Scott, James C. "Everyday Forms of Resistance." In *Everyday Forms of Peasant Resistance,* edited by F. D. Colburn, 3–33. New York: Routledge, 1989.

Scott, James C. *Weapons of the Weak: Everyday Forms of Peasant Resistance.* New Haven, CT: Yale University Press, 1985.

Seong Ji-su. "Sewolho yeongeugeui mosaek—changjakja, gwangaek, gongganui jaeguseongeul jungsimeuro" (Contemplating *Sewol* theatre—focusing on the creators, audiences, and space). PhD diss., Seoul National University, 2017.

Shin, Jin-Wook. "Changing Patterns of South Korean Social Movements, 1960s–2010s: Testimony, Firebombs, Lawsuit and Candlelight." In *Civil Society and the State in Democratic East Asia: Between Entanglement and Contention in Post High Growth,* edited by David Chiavacci, Simona Grano, and Julia Obinger, 239–268. Amsterdam: Amsterdam University Press, 2020.

Son, Elizabeth W. *Embodied Reckonings: "Comfort Women," Performance, and Transpacific Redress.* Ann Arbor: University of Michigan Press, 2018.

Sontag, Susan. *Regarding the Pain of Others.* New York: Picador, 2003.

Stewart, Susan. *On Longing: Narratives of the Miniature, the Gigantic, the Souvenir, the Collection.* Durham, NC: Duke University Press, 1992.

Sturken, Marita. *Tangled Memories: The Vietnam War, the AIDS Epidemic, and the Politics of Remembering.* Berkeley: University of California Press, 1997.

Sturken, Marita. *Tourists of History: Memory, Kitsch, and Consumerism from Oklahoma City to Ground Zero.* Durham, NC: Duke University Press, 2007.

Taylor, Diana. *The Archive and the Repertoire: Performing Cultural Memory in the Americas.* Durham, NC: Duke University Press, 2003.

Taylor, Diana. "Making a Spectacle: The Mothers of the Plaza de Mayo." *Journal of the Motherhood Initiative for Research and Community Involvement* 3, no. 2 (2001): 97–109.

Turner, Victor. "The Center out There: Pilgrim's Goal." *History of Religions* 12, no. 3 (1973): 191–230.

Wake, Caroline. "The Accident and the Account: Towards a Taxonomy of Spectatorial Witness in Theatre and Performance Studies." In *Visions and Revisions:*

Performance, Memory, Trauma, edited by Bryoni Trezise and Caroline Wake, 33–56. Copenhagen: Museum Tusculanum Press, 2013.

Woo, Hyekyung, et al. "Public Trauma After the *Sewol* Ferry Disaster: The Role of Social Media in Understanding the Public Mood." *International Journal of Environmental Research and Public Health* 12 (2015): 10974–10983.

Yang Geun-ae. *"Ihu"ui yeongeuk, dallajin segye* (Theatre "after," changed world). Seoul: Yeongeukgwa Ingan Press, 2020.

Yi Hae-seong. "Bullaektenteu yeondaegi" (Black Tent journey). In *Sewolho ihuui hangukyeongeuk: Beullaengniseuteueseo beullaektenteukkaji* (Korean theatre after the *Sewol*: From blacklist to Black Tent), edited by Korean Theatre Critics Association, 407–413. Seoul: Yeongeukkwa Ingan Press, 2017.

Young, Stephenie. "The Forensic Imagination: Evidence, Photography, and the Post-Yugoslav Document." Paper presented at the American Comparative Literature Association annual meeting. Boston, MA, March 18, 2016.

INDEX

Page numbers in **boldface** type indicate illustrations.

ABOUT THE AUTHOR

Areum Jeong is an interdisciplinary scholar and educator of Korean and Korean diasporic cinema, literature, popular culture, theatre, and performance. She is currently an assistant professor of Korean studies at Arizona State University. She holds a PhD in Theater and Performance Studies from the University of California, Los Angeles.

HAWAI'I STUDIES ON KOREA

WAYNE PATTERSON
The Ilse: First-Generation Korean Immigrants, 1903–1973

LINDA S. LEWIS
Laying Claim to the Memory of May: A Look Back at the 1980 Kwangju Uprising

MICHAEL FINCH
Min Yŏng-gwan: A Political Biography

MICHAEL J. SETH
Education Fever: Society, Politics, and the Pursuit of Schooling in South Korea

CHAN E. PARK
Voices from the Straw Mat: Toward an Ethnography of Korean Story Singing

ANDREI N. LANKOV
Crisis in North Korea: The Failure of De-Stalinization, 1956

HAHN MOON-SUK
And So Flows History

TIMOTHY R. TANGHERLINI AND SALLIE YEA, EDITORS
Sitings: Critical Approaches to Korean Geography

ALEXANDER VOVIN
Koreo-Japonica: A Re-evaluation of a Common Genetic Origin

YUNG-HEE KIM
Questioning Minds: Short Stories of Modern Korean Women Writers

TATIANA GABROUSSENKO
Soldiers on the Cultural Front: Developments in the Early History of North Korean Literature and Literary Policy

KYUNG-AE PARK, EDITOR
Non-Traditional Security Issues in North Korea

CHARLOTTE HORLYCK AND MICHAEL J. PETTID, EDITORS
Death, Mourning, and the Afterlife in Korea: Critical Aspects of Death from Ancient to Contemporary Times

CARL F. YOUNG
Eastern Learning and the Heavenly Way: The Tonghak and Ch'ŏndogyo Movements and the Twilight of Korean Independence

DON BAKER, WITH FRANKLIN RAUSCH
Catholics and Anti-Catholicism in Chosŏn Korea

SONJA M. KIM
Imperatives of Care: Women and Medicine in Colonial Korea

YEAN-JU LEE
Divorce in South Korea: Doing Gender and the Dynamics of Relationship Breakdown

SANGPIL JIN
Surviving Imperial Intrigues: Korea's Struggle for Neutrality amid Empires, 1882–1907

ANDREW DAVID JACKSON, CODRUȚA SÎNTIONEAN, REMCO BREUKER, AND CEDARBOUGH SAEJI, EDITORS
Invented Traditions in North and South Korea

YOONKYUNG LEE
Between the Streets and the Assembly: Social Movements, Political Parties, and Democracy in Korea

OLGA FEDORENKO
Flower of Capitalism: South Korean Advertising at a Crossroads

VLADIMIR TIKHONOV
The Red Decades: Communism as Movement and Culture in Korea, 1919–1945

SHINYOUNG KWON

Moral Authoritarianism: Neighborhood Associations in the Three Koreas, 1931–1972

AREUM JEONG

Beyond the *Sewol*: Activist Theatre and Performance in South Korea and the Diaspora